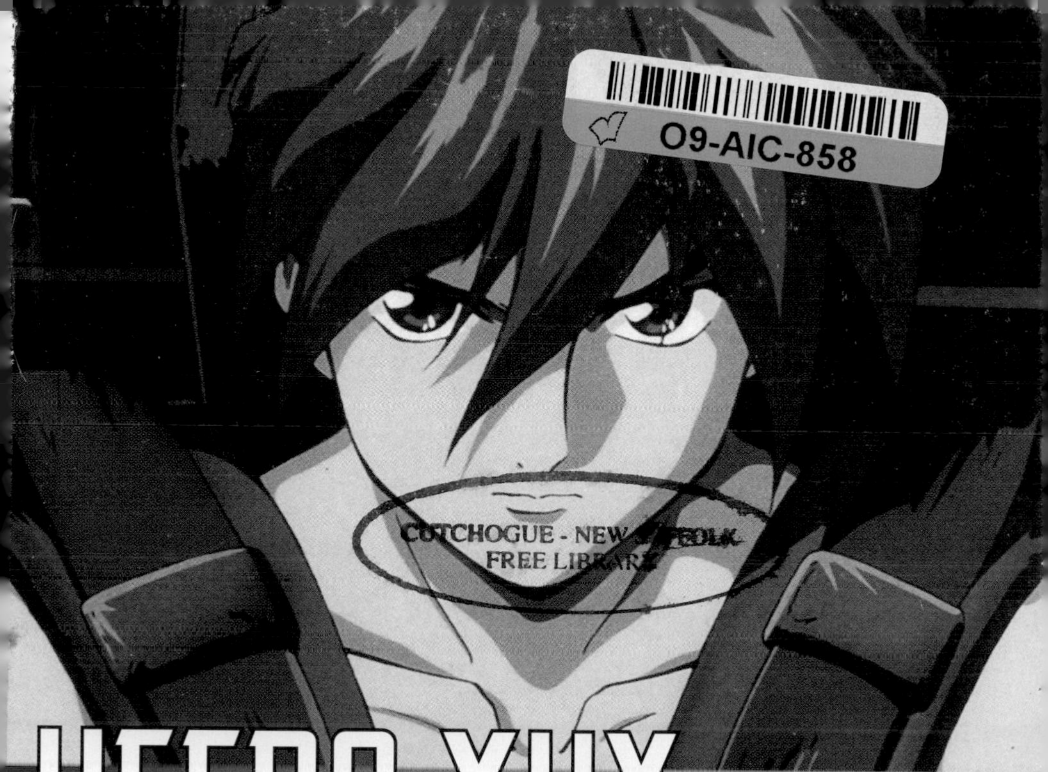

HEERO YUY

ヒイロ・ユイ

PREVIOUS ACTIVITIES:

In the year AC 195, this young man was sent to Earth as the pilot of the Wing Gundam. He was given the codename Heero Yuy in honor of the martyred leader of the space colonies. After many battles, he played a vital role in ending the conflict between Earth and the space colonies.

CURRENT STATUS:

In AC 196, now that his fighting skills are no longer needed, Heero is leading a quiet and inconspicuous life. However, he retains ownership of the powerful Wing Gundam Zero, and uses his computer hacking talents to keep an eye out for crises that require his intervention.

DUO MAXWELL

デュオ・マックスウェル

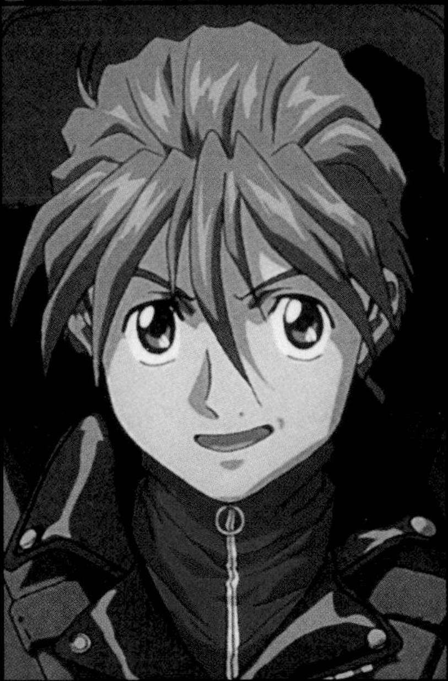

PREVIOUS ACTIVITIES:

Duo, a member of the scavenger organization called the Sweeper Group, was sent to Earth as pilot of the Gundam Deathscythe. During the struggle against OZ, he became friends with the enigmatic Heero Yuy and made the acquaintance of a pretty young soldier named Hilde.

CURRENT STATUS:

With the war over, Duo has returned to his previous trade as a salvage dealer. He's frequently seen in Hilde's company, but he still checks in on his fellow Gundam pilots from time to time.

QUATRE RABERBA WINNER

カトル・ラバーバ・ウィナー

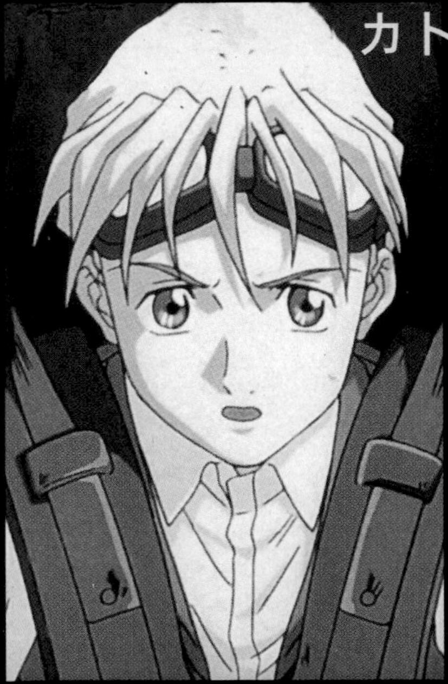

PREVIOUS ACTIVITIES:

The only son of the wealthy Winner family, Quatre journeyed to Earth as the pilot of the Gundam Sandrock. The death of his father was a devastating shock to this sensitive young man, but he recovered and went on to become the confident leader of the five Gundam pilots.

CURRENT STATUS:

With the help of his 29 sisters, Quatre has taken charge of his father's space colony-construction empire. He's now busy rebuilding the damage caused by the war—and, thanks to his prominent social status, he also plays a role in the political development of the space colonies.

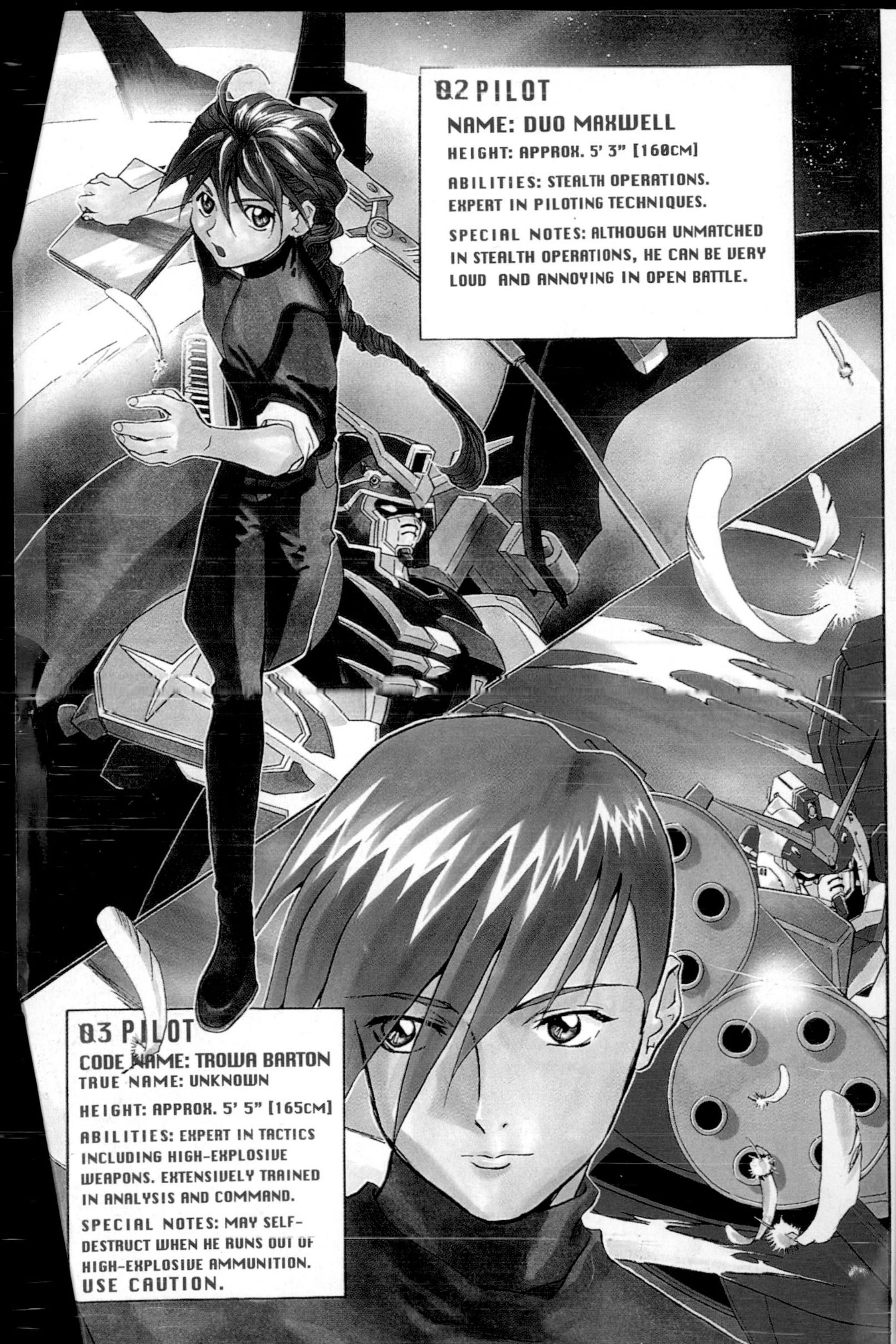
02 PILOT
NAME: DUO MAXWELL
HEIGHT: APPROX. 5' 3" [160CM]
ABILITIES: STEALTH OPERATIONS. EXPERT IN PILOTING TECHNIQUES.
SPECIAL NOTES: ALTHOUGH UNMATCHED IN STEALTH OPERATIONS, HE CAN BE VERY LOUD AND ANNOYING IN OPEN BATTLE.
03 PILOT
CODE NAME: TROWA BARTON
TRUE NAME: UNKNOWN
HEIGHT: APPROX. 5' 5" [165CM]
ABILITIES: EXPERT IN TACTICS INCLUDING HIGH-EXPLOSIVE WEAPONS. EXTENSIVELY TRAINED IN ANALYSIS AND COMMAND.
SPECIAL NOTES: MAY SELF-DESTRUCT WHEN HE RUNS OUT OF HIGH-EXPLOSIVE AMMUNITION. USE CAUTION.

TROWA BARTON

トロワ・バートン

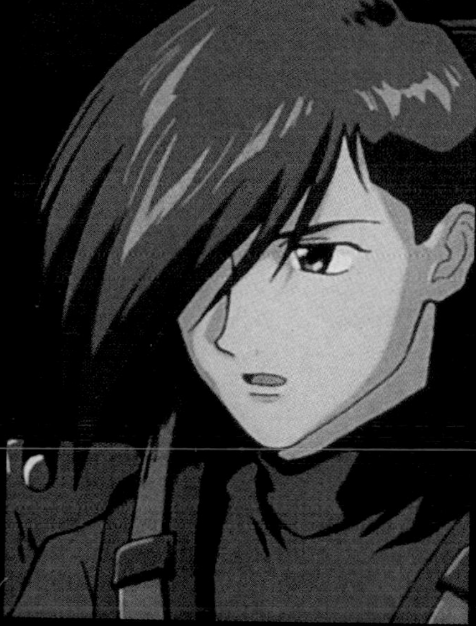

PREVIOUS ACTIVITIES:

This mysterious young man was sent to Earth as the pilot of the Gundam Heavyarms. Throughout the war between Earth and the space colonies, his background and true identity remained unknown. Still, he proved a loyal and trustworthy comrade to the other Gundam pilots.

CURRENT STATUS:

Trowa continues performing as a circus clown, now as a genuine vocation rather than as a cover for his military operations. His circus troupe serves as a foster family of sorts, with acrobat Catherine Bloom as a surrogate sister.

CHANG WUFEI

張　五飛

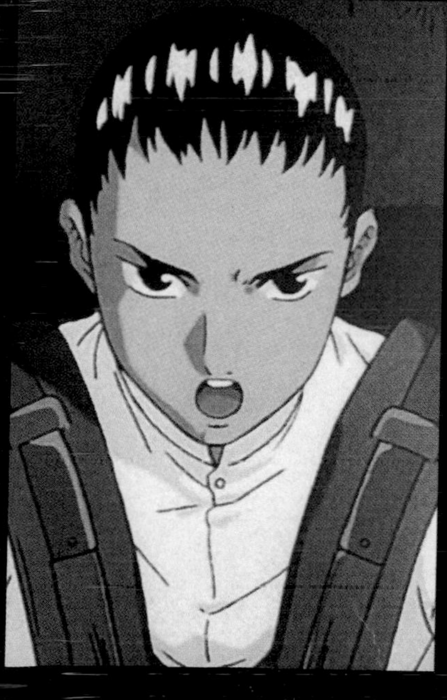

PREVIOUS ACTIVITIES:

Wufei was sent to Earth as the pilot of the Shenlong Gundam. He served as an emissary of the Long clan, a legendary line of Chinese warriors. However, his home colony was destroyed during the wars of AC 195, leaving Wufei as perhaps the last survivor of his line.

CURRENT STATUS:

Wufei's current activities are unknown, and he has little interaction with the other Gundam pilots. Having lost his home and family, he is left with only his martial skills, his burning sense of justice, and a great deal of unresolved anger. . . .

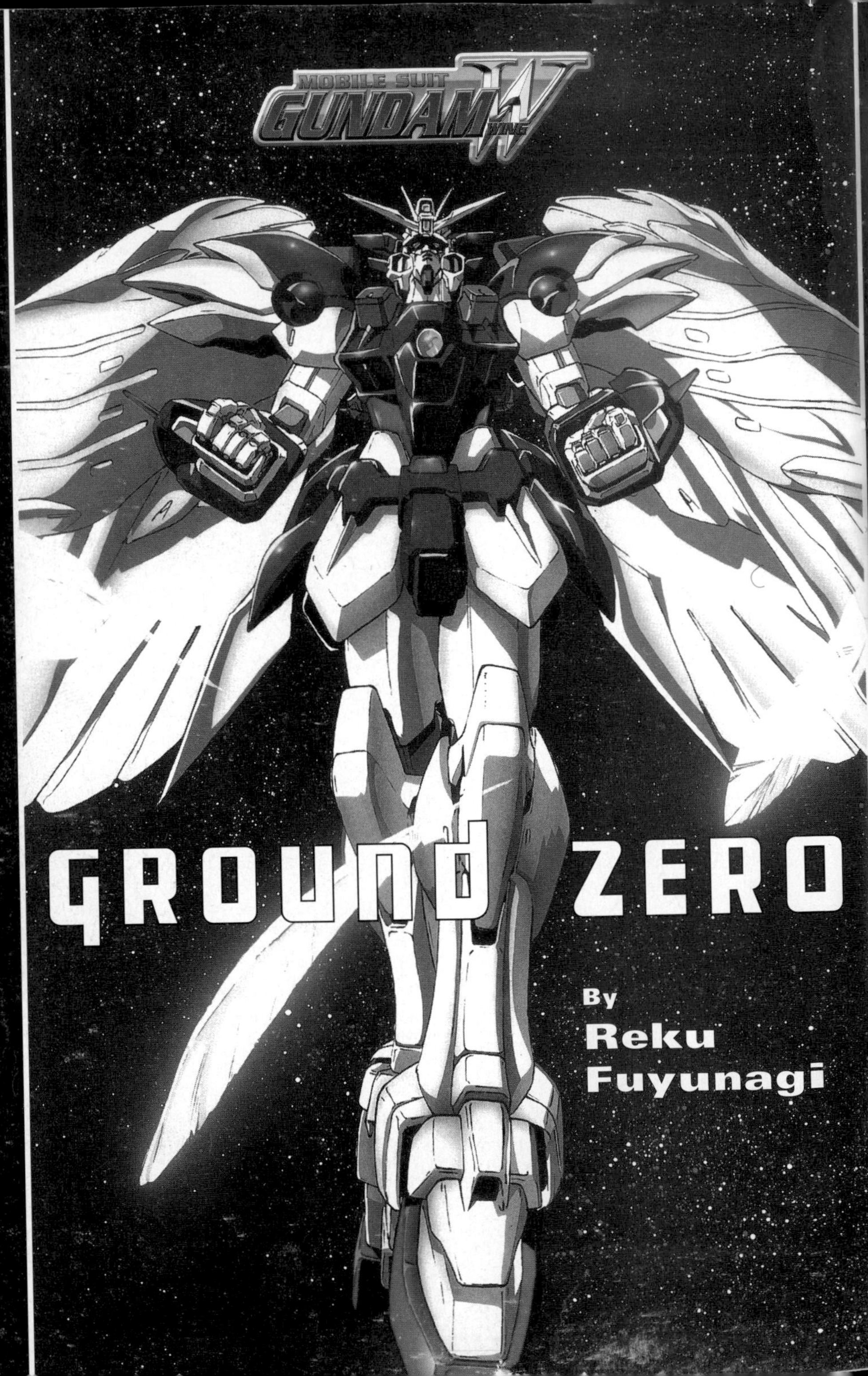
MOBILE SUIT GUNDAM WING
GROUND ZERO
By
Reku
Fuyunagi

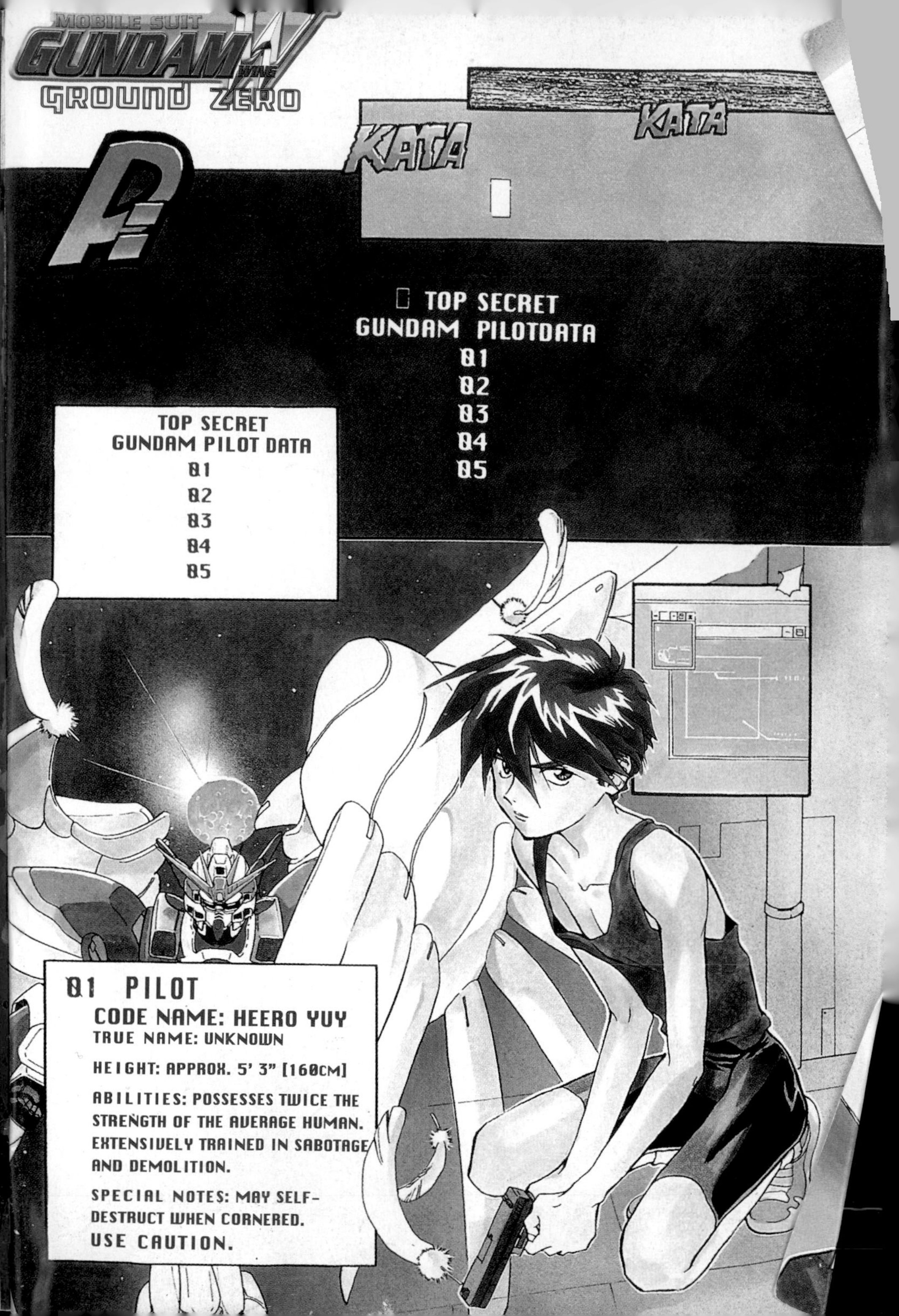
MOBILE SUIT GUNDAM WING
GROUND ZERO
KATA
KATA
TOP SECRET
GUNDAM PILOTDATA
01
02
03
04
05
TOP SECRET
GUNDAM PILOT DATA
01
02
03
04
05
01 PILOT
CODE NAME: HEERO YUY
TRUE NAME: UNKNOWN
HEIGHT: APPROX. 5' 3" [160CM]
ABILITIES: POSSESSES TWICE THE STRENGTH OF THE AVERAGE HUMAN. EXTENSIVELY TRAINED IN SABOTAGE AND DEMOLITION.
SPECIAL NOTES: MAY SELF-DESTRUCT WHEN CORNERED.
USE CAUTION.

TROWA BARTON

トロワ・バートン

PREVIOUS ACTIVITIES:

This mysterious young man was sent to Earth as the pilot of the Gundam Heavyarms. Throughout the war between Earth and the space colonies, his background and true identity remained unknown. Still, he proved a loyal and trustworthy comrade to the other Gundam pilots.

CURRENT STATUS:

Trowa continues performing as a circus clown, now as a genuine vocation rather than as a cover for his military operations. His circus troupe serves as a foster family of sorts, with acrobat Catherine Bloom as a surrogate sister.

CHANG WUFEI

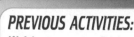

張　五飛

PREVIOUS ACTIVITIES:

Wufei was sent to Earth as the pilot of the Shenlong Gundam. He served as an emissary of the Long clan, a legendary line of Chinese warriors. However, his home colony was destroyed during the wars of AC 195, leaving Wufei as perhaps the last survivor of his line.

CURRENT STATUS:

Wufei's current activities are unknown, and he has little interaction with the other Gundam pilots. Having lost his home and family, he is left with only his martial skills, his burning sense of justice, and a great deal of unresolved anger....

MOBILE SUIT GUNDAM WING

GROUND ZERO

By
Reku
Fuyunagi

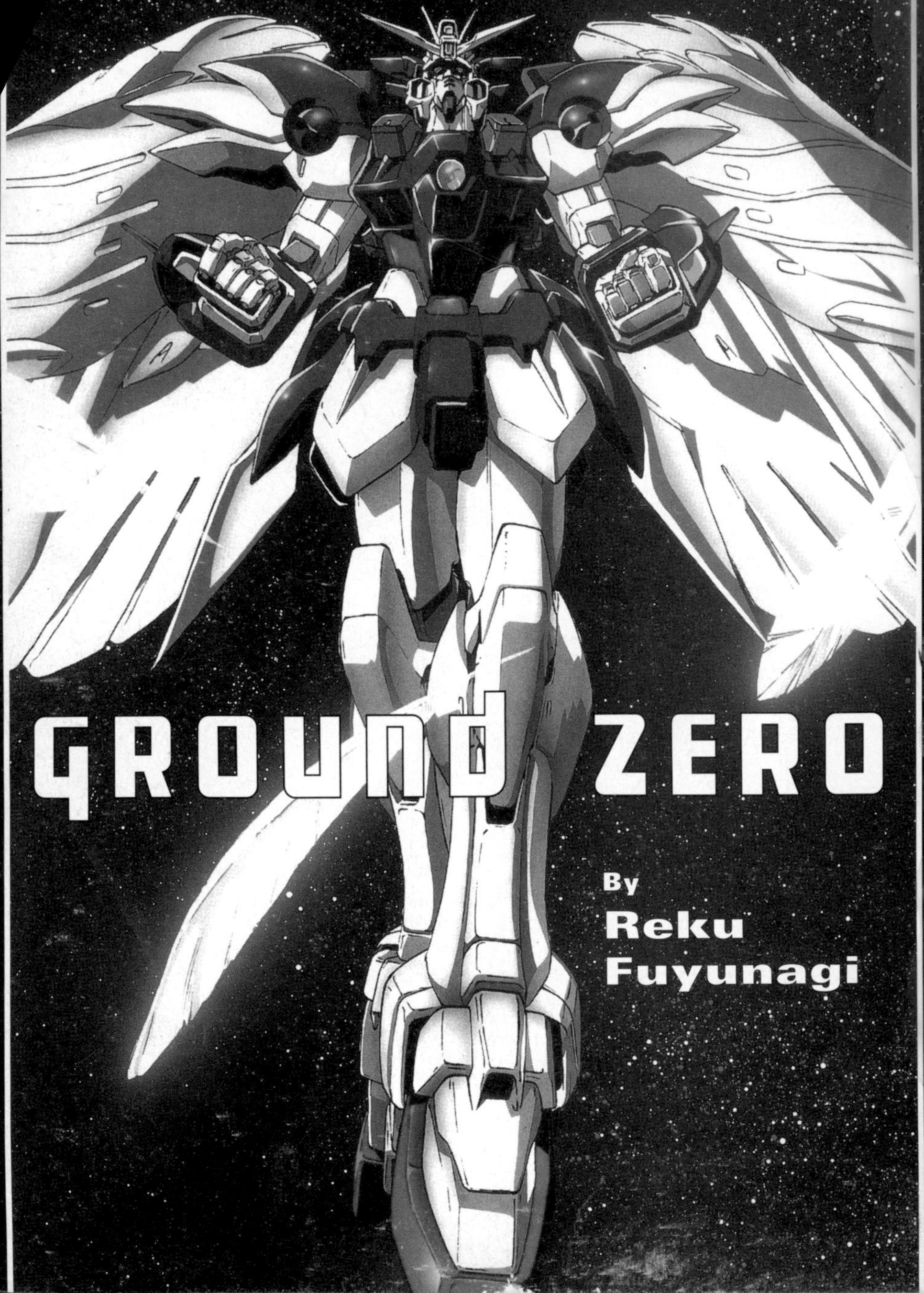

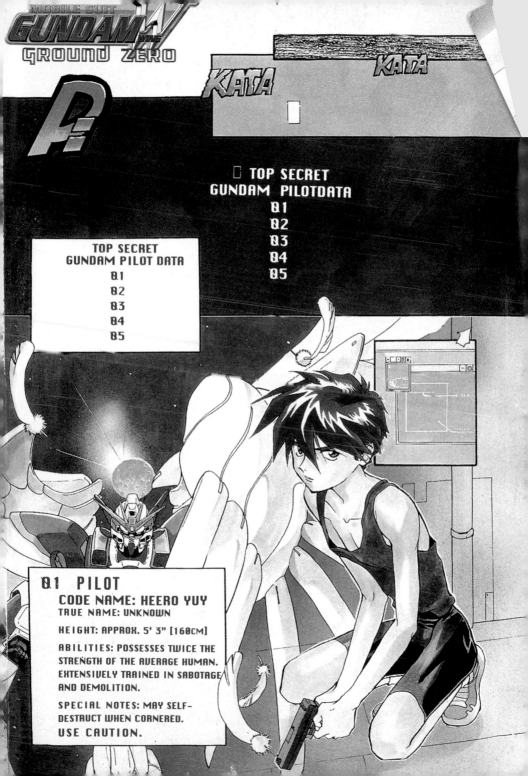

MOBILE SUIT GUNDAM W
GROUND ZERO

KATA

KATA

TOP SECRET
GUNDAM PILOTDATA
01
02
03
04
05

TOP SECRET
GUNDAM PILOT DATA
01
02
03
04
05

01 PILOT

CODE NAME: HEERO YUY
TRUE NAME: UNKNOWN

HEIGHT: APPROX. 5' 3" [160CM]

ABILITIES: POSSESSES TWICE THE
STRENGTH OF THE AVERAGE HUMAN.
EXTENSIVELY TRAINED IN SABOTAGE
AND DEMOLITION.

SPECIAL NOTES: MAY SELF-
DESTRUCT WHEN CORNERED.
USE CAUTION.

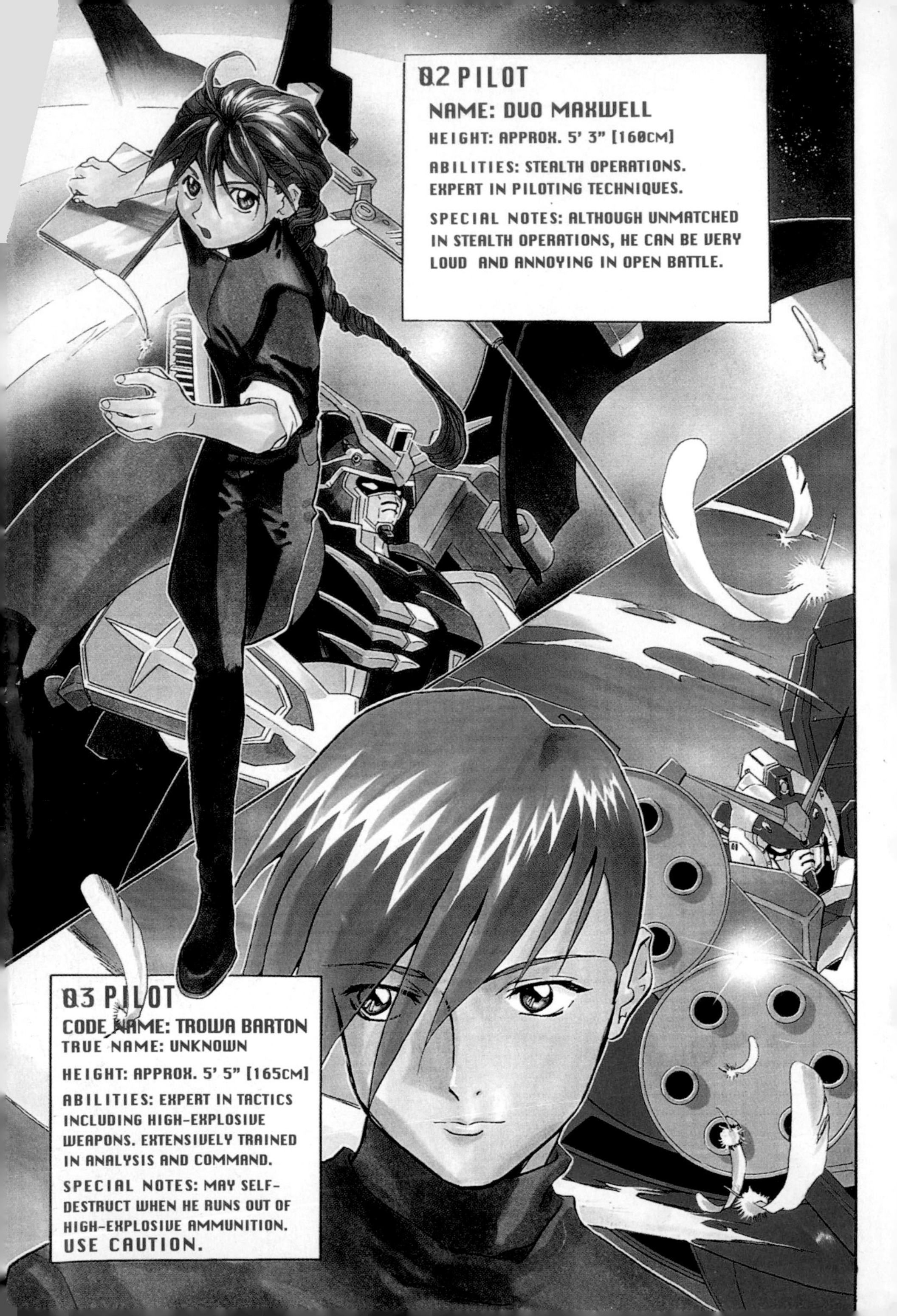
02 PILOT
NAME: DUO MAXWELL
HEIGHT: APPROX. 5' 3" [160CM]
ABILITIES: STEALTH OPERATIONS. EXPERT IN PILOTING TECHNIQUES.
SPECIAL NOTES: ALTHOUGH UNMATCHED IN STEALTH OPERATIONS, HE CAN BE VERY LOUD AND ANNOYING IN OPEN BATTLE.
03 PILOT
CODE NAME: TROWA BARTON
TRUE NAME: UNKNOWN
HEIGHT: APPROX. 5' 5" [165CM]
ABILITIES: EXPERT IN TACTICS INCLUDING HIGH-EXPLOSIVE WEAPONS. EXTENSIVELY TRAINED IN ANALYSIS AND COMMAND.
SPECIAL NOTES: MAY SELF-DESTRUCT WHEN HE RUNS OUT OF HIGH-EXPLOSIVE AMMUNITION. USE CAUTION.

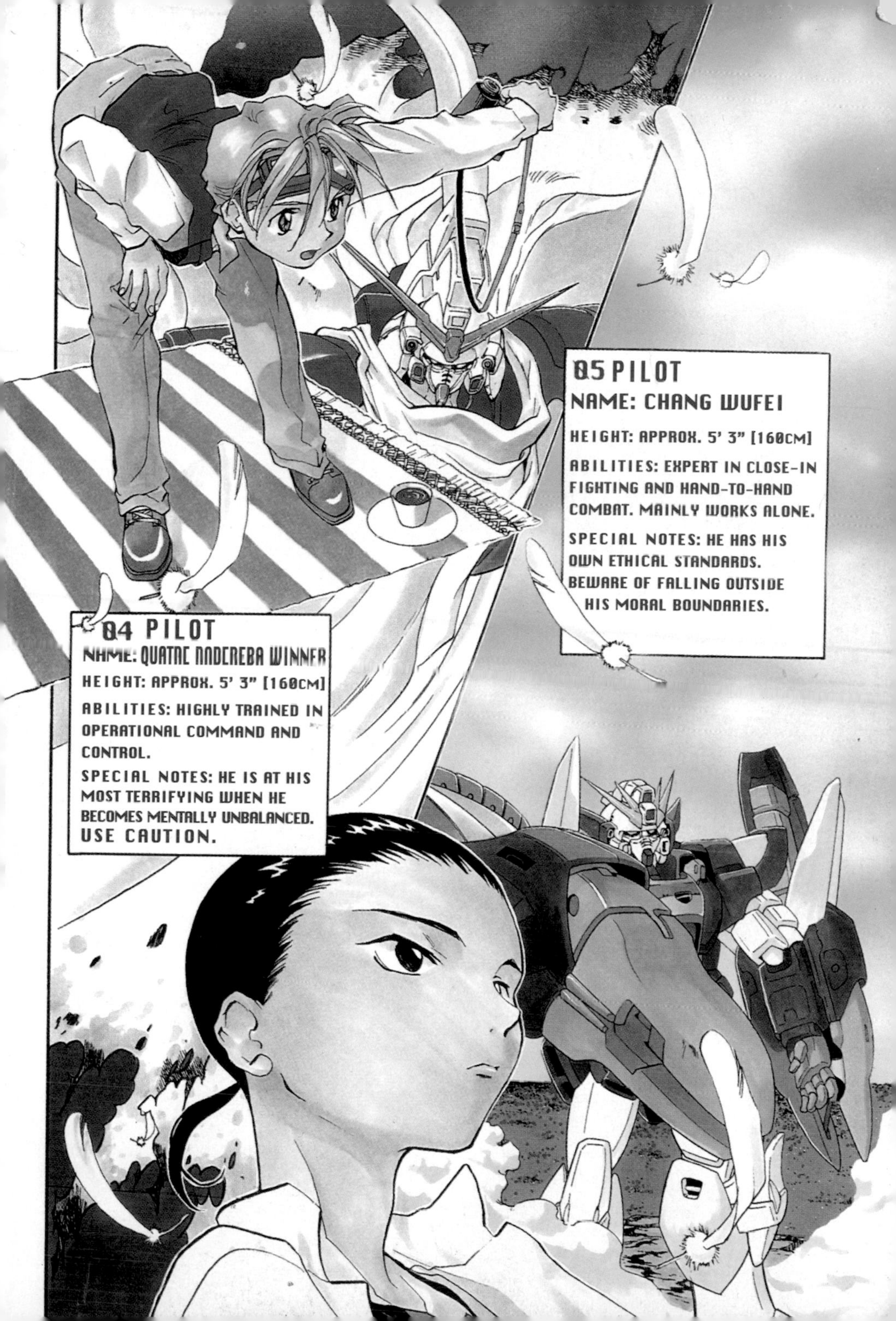
05 PILOT
NAME: CHANG WUFEI
HEIGHT: APPROX. 5' 3" [160CM]
ABILITIES: EXPERT IN CLOSE-IN FIGHTING AND HAND-TO-HAND COMBAT. MAINLY WORKS ALONE.
SPECIAL NOTES: HE HAS HIS OWN ETHICAL STANDARDS. BEWARE OF FALLING OUTSIDE HIS MORAL BOUNDARIES.
04 PILOT
NAME: QUATRE RABERBA WINNER
HEIGHT: APPROX. 5' 3" [160CM]
ABILITIES: HIGHLY TRAINED IN OPERATIONAL COMMAND AND CONTROL.
SPECIAL NOTES: HE IS AT HIS MOST TERRIFYING WHEN HE BECOMES MENTALLY UNBALANCED. USE CAUTION.

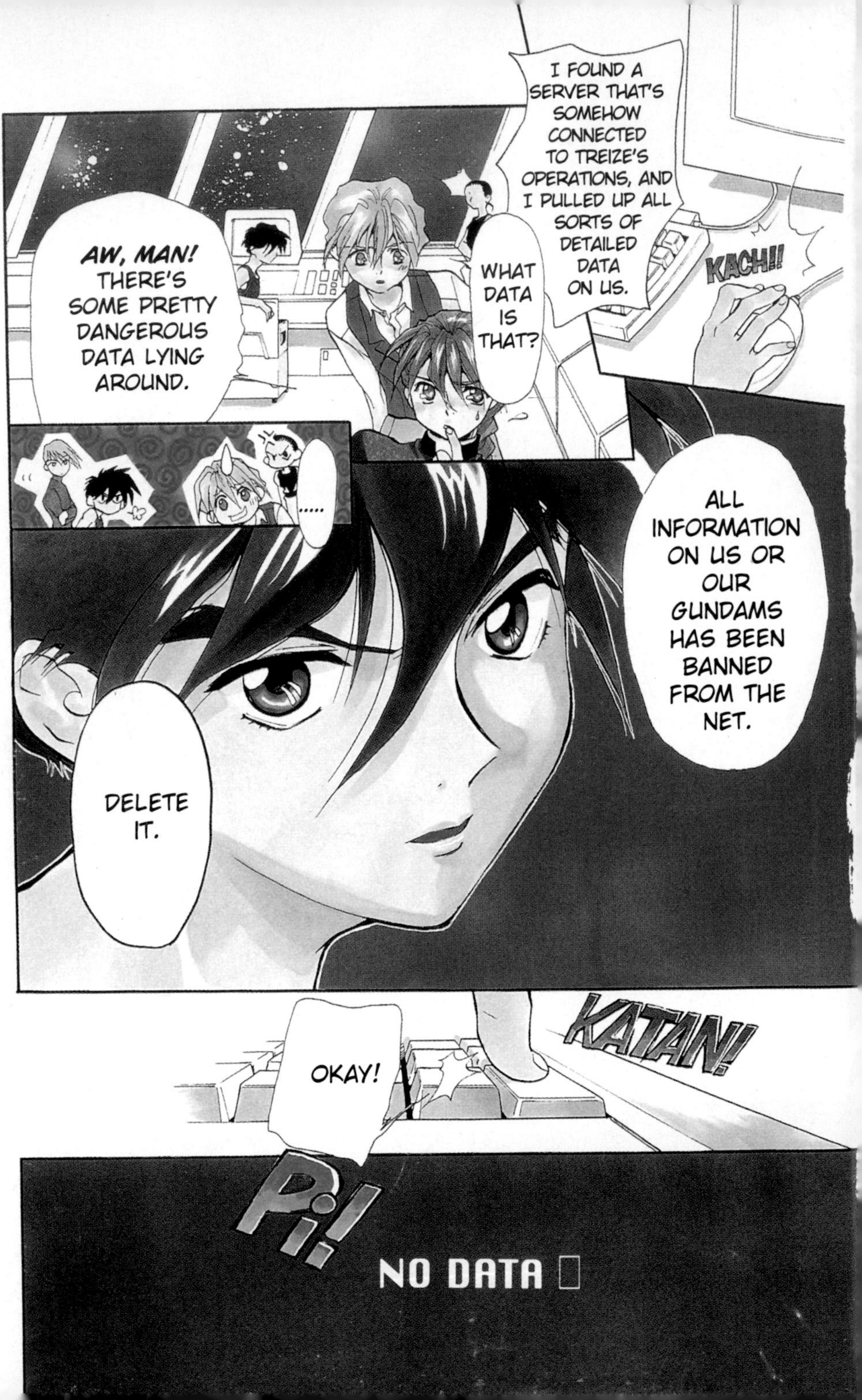
AW, MAN! THERE'S SOME PRETTY DANGEROUS DATA LYING AROUND.
WHAT DATA IS THAT?
I FOUND A SERVER THAT'S SOMEHOW CONNECTED TO TREIZE'S OPERATIONS, AND I PULLED UP ALL SORTS OF DETAILED DATA ON US.
KACH!!
.....
ALL INFORMATION ON US OR OUR GUNDAMS HAS BEEN BANNED FROM THE NET.
DELETE IT.
OKAY!
KATAN!
Pi!
NO DATA

CHAPTER ONE

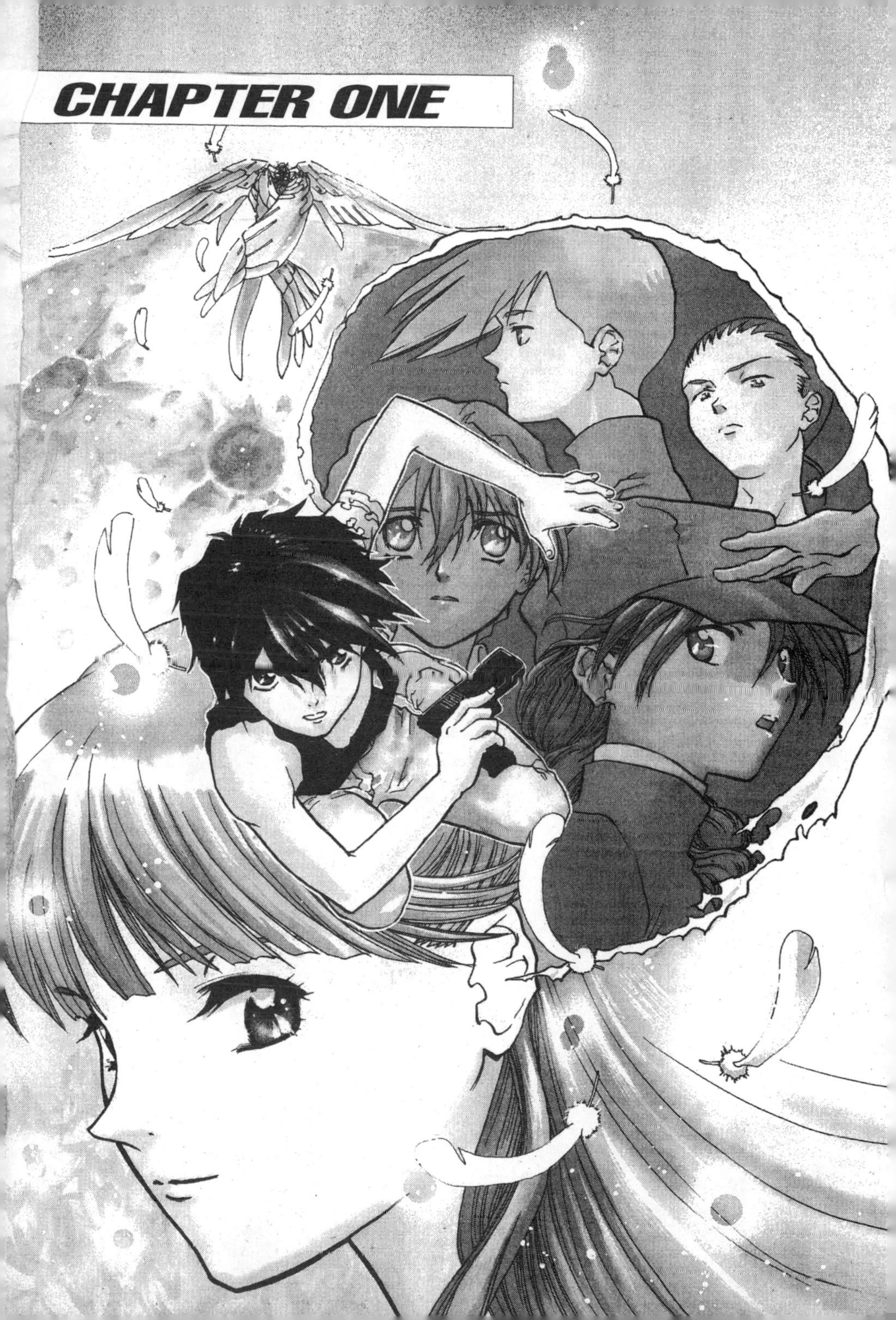

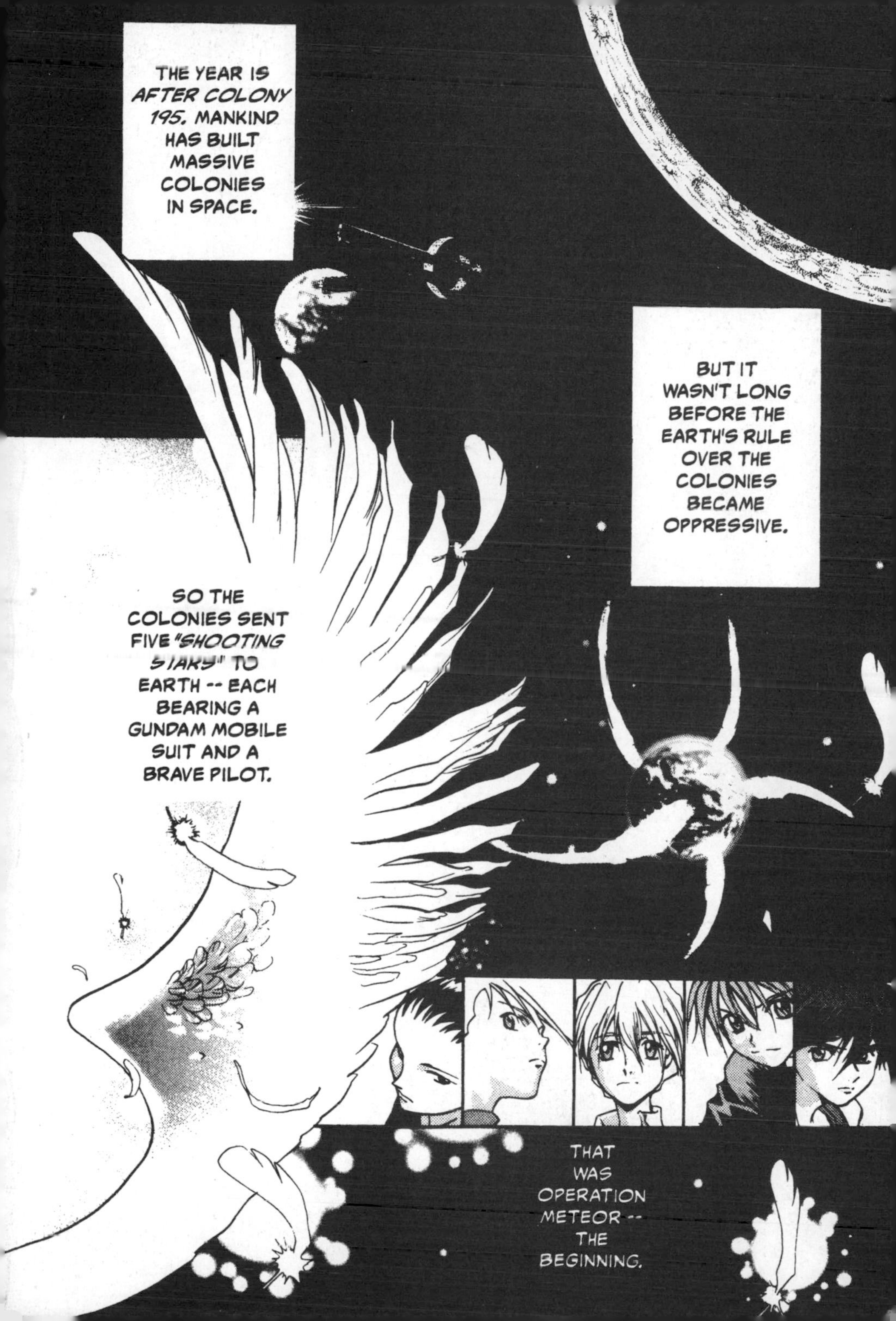
THE YEAR IS AFTER COLONY 195. MANKIND HAS BUILT MASSIVE COLONIES IN SPACE.
BUT IT WASN'T LONG BEFORE THE EARTH'S RULE OVER THE COLONIES BECAME OPPRESSIVE.
SO THE COLONIES SENT FIVE "SHOOTING STARS" TO EARTH -- EACH BEARING A GUNDAM MOBILE SUIT AND A BRAVE PILOT.
THAT WAS OPERATION METEOR -- THE BEGINNING.

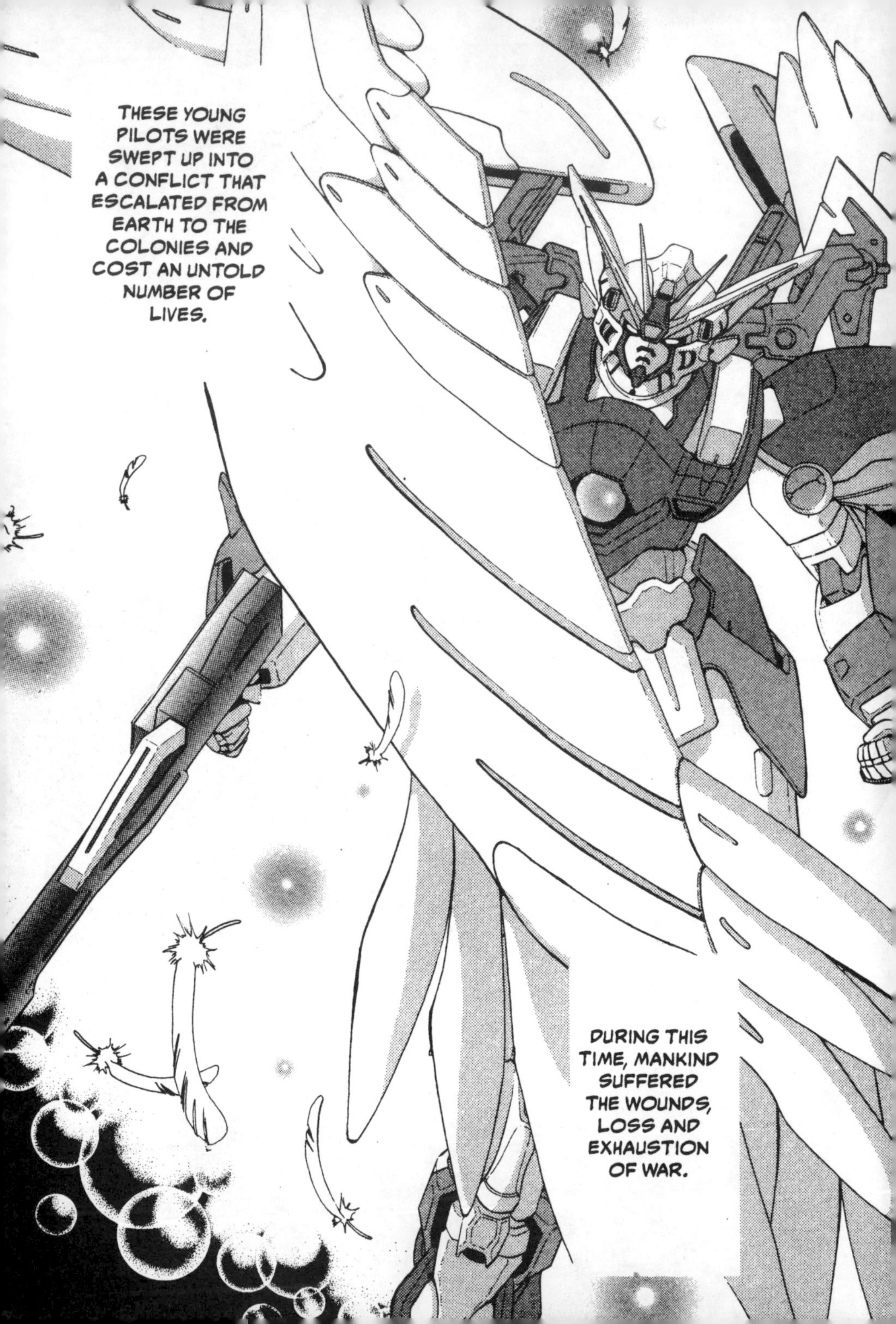
THESE YOUNG PILOTS WERE SWEPT UP INTO A CONFLICT THAT ESCALATED FROM EARTH TO THE COLONIES AND COST AN UNTOLD NUMBER OF LIVES.
DURING THIS TIME, MANKIND SUFFERED THE WOUNDS, LOSS AND EXHAUSTION OF WAR.

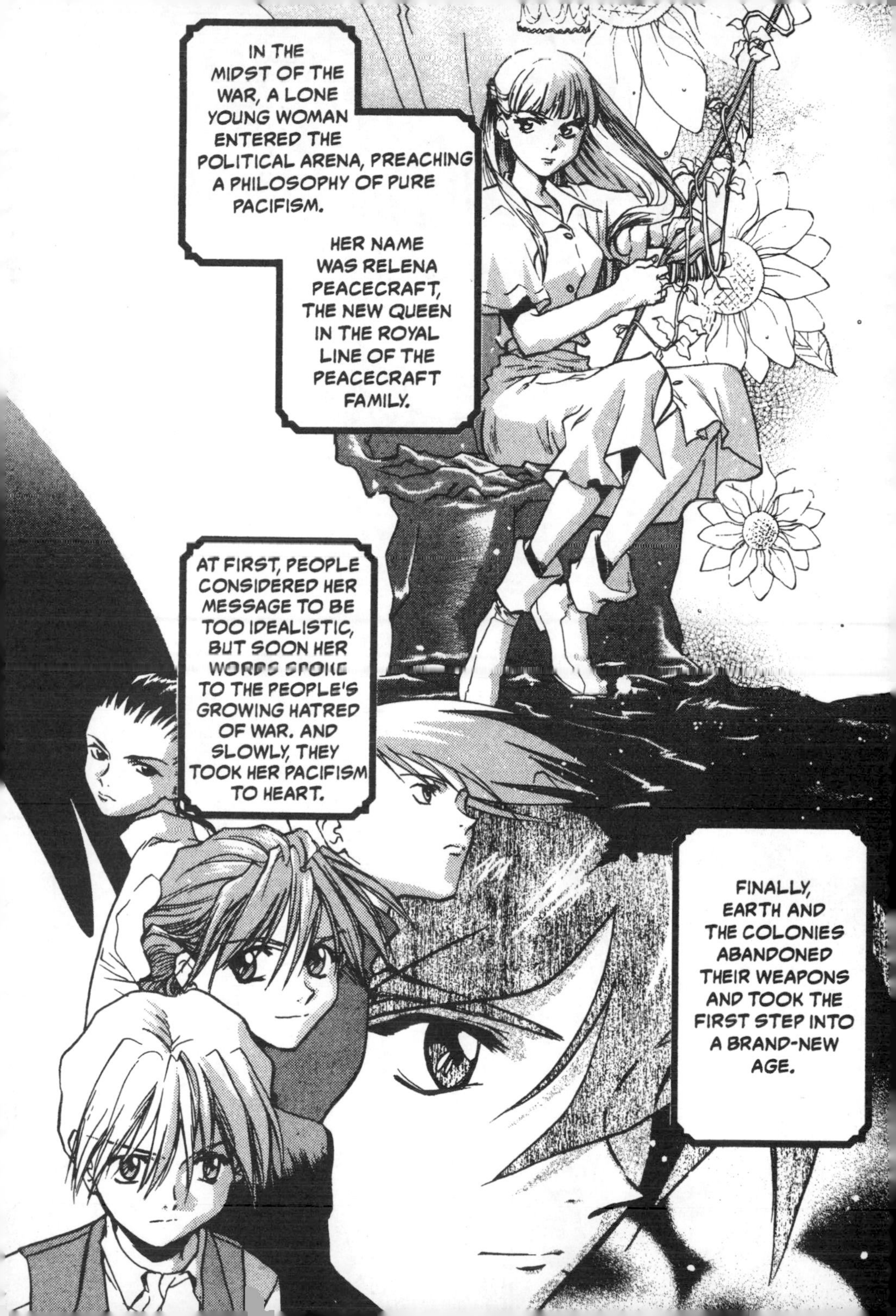
IN THE MIDST OF THE WAR, A LONE YOUNG WOMAN ENTERED THE POLITICAL ARENA, PREACHING A PHILOSOPHY OF PURE PACIFISM.
HER NAME WAS RELENA PEACECRAFT, THE NEW QUEEN IN THE ROYAL LINE OF THE PEACECRAFT FAMILY.
AT FIRST, PEOPLE CONSIDERED HER MESSAGE TO BE TOO IDEALISTIC, BUT SOON HER WORDS SPOKE TO THE PEOPLE'S GROWING HATRED OF WAR. AND SLOWLY, THEY TOOK HER PACIFISM TO HEART.
FINALLY, EARTH AND THE COLONIES ABANDONED THEIR WEAPONS AND TOOK THE FIRST STEP INTO A BRAND-NEW AGE.

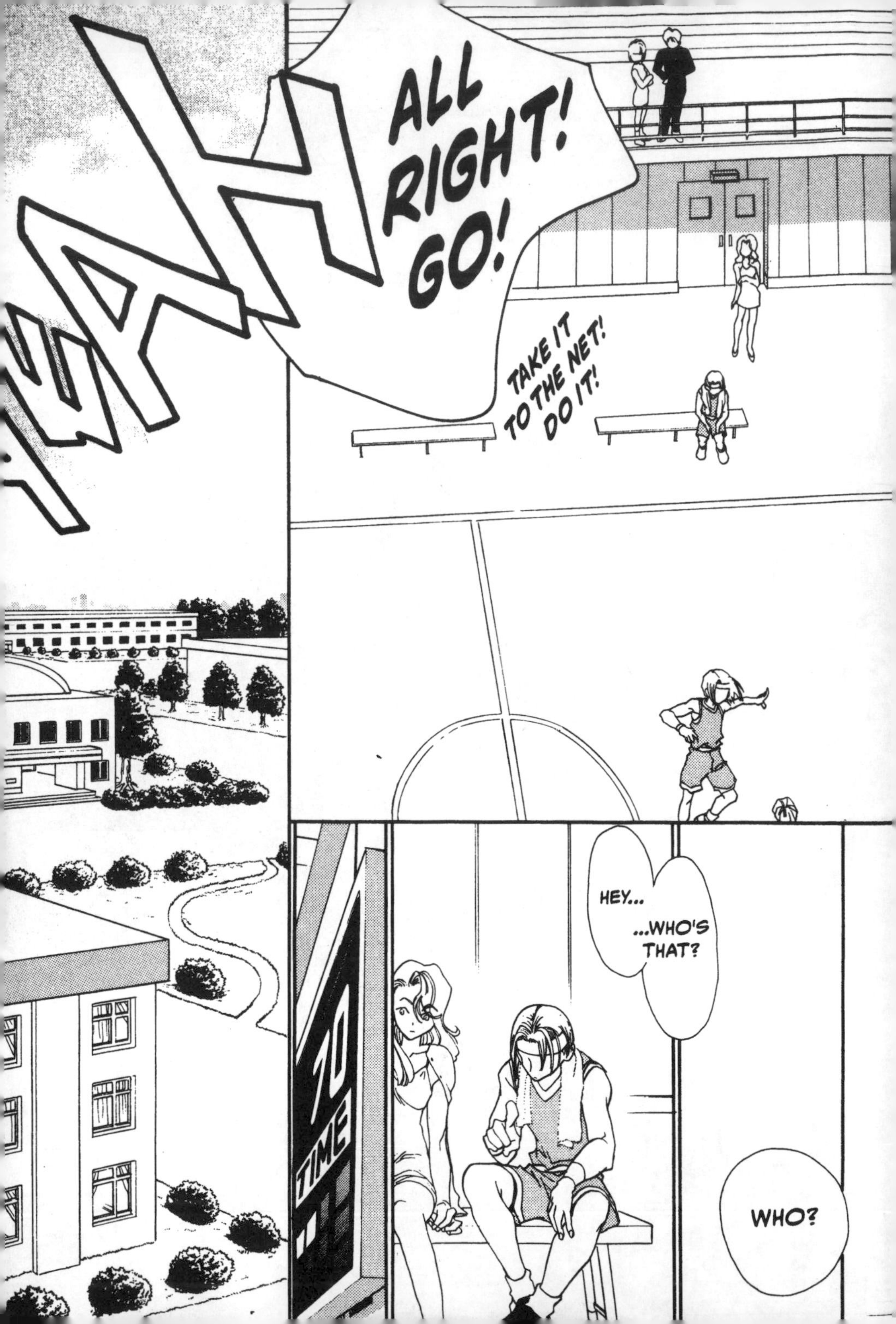
YEAH
ALL RIGHT! GO!
TAKE IT TO THE NET! DO IT!
HEY... ...WHO'S THAT?
TIME
WHO?

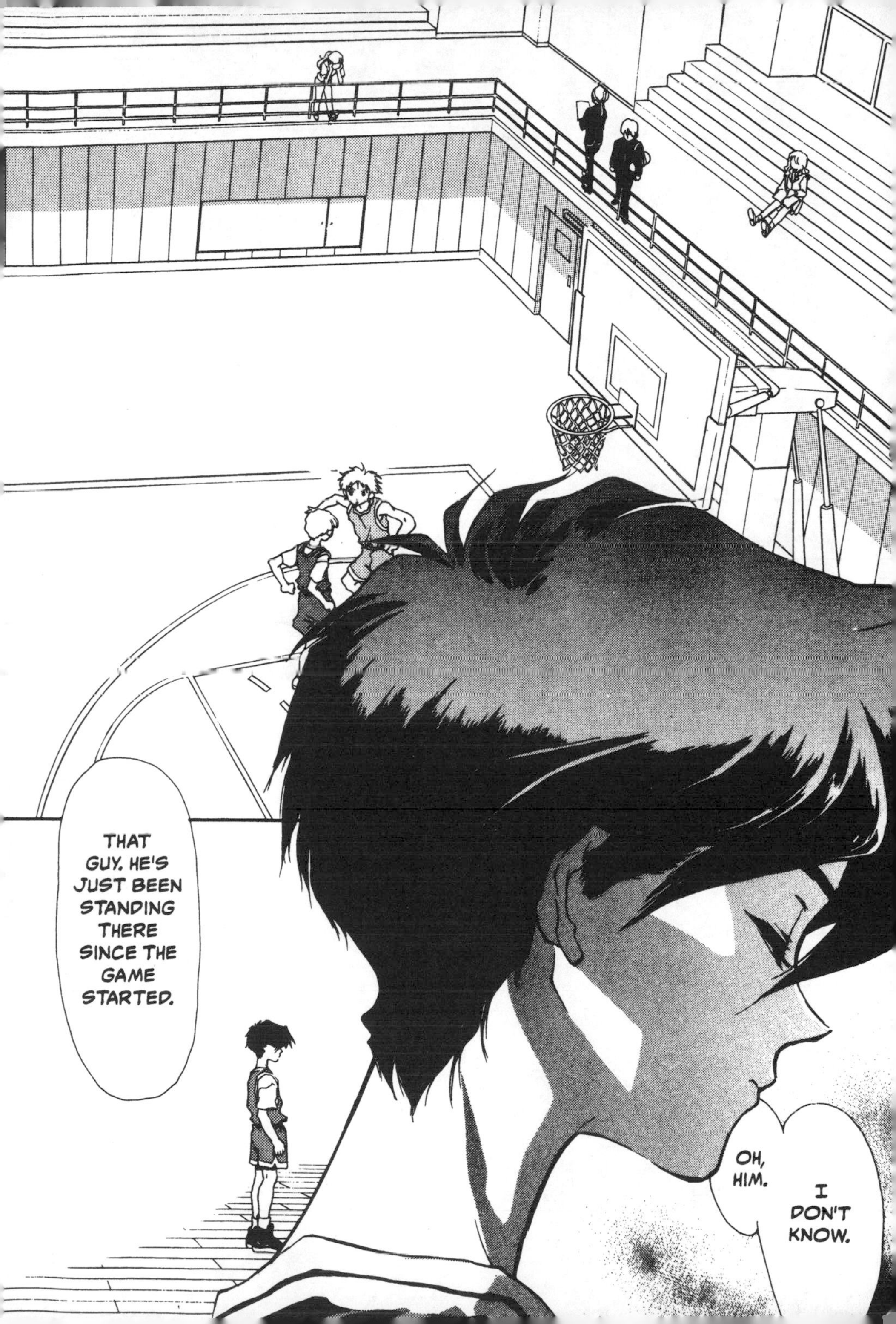
THAT GUY. HE'S JUST BEEN STANDING THERE SINCE THE GAME STARTED.
OH, HIM.
I DON'T KNOW.

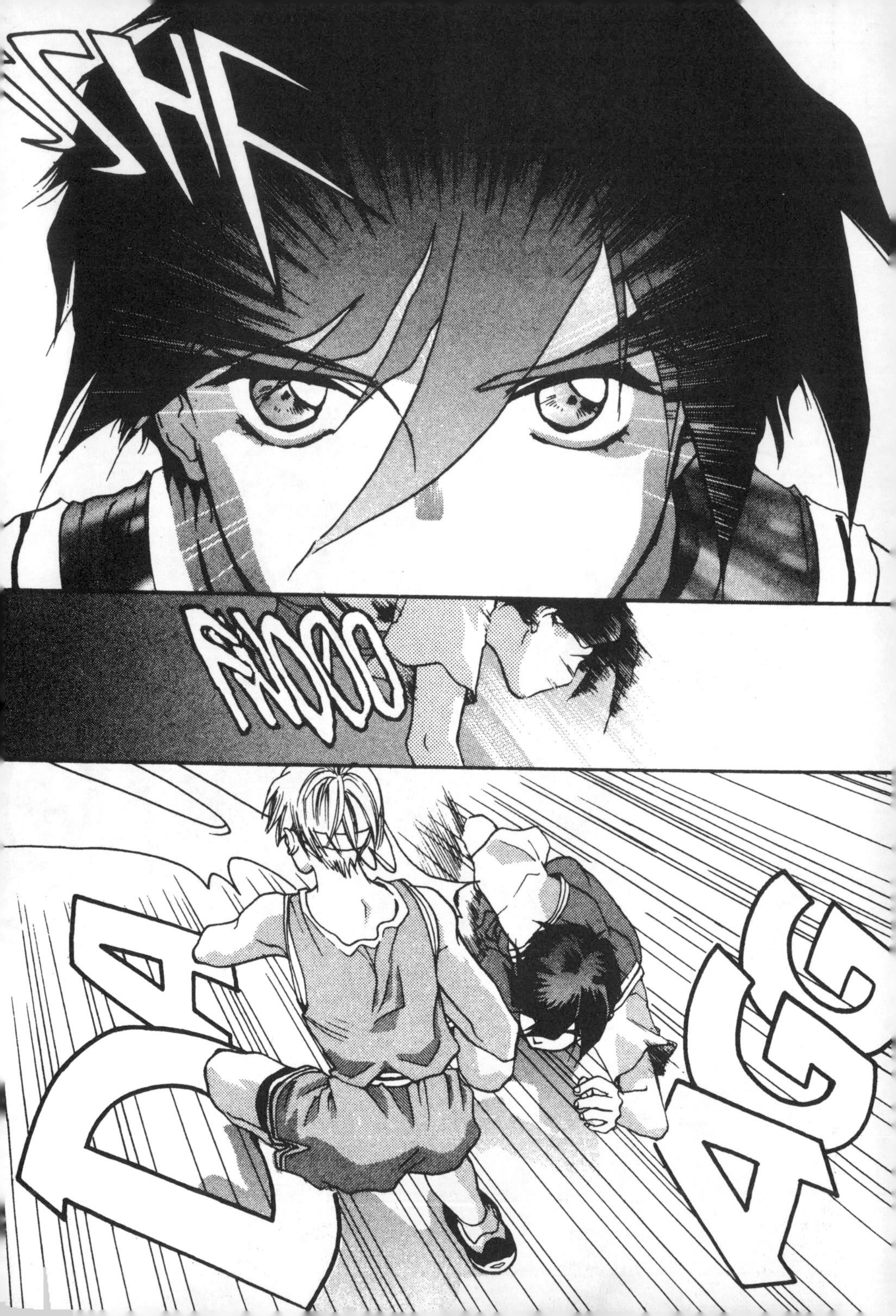
SHF
FWOOO
DA
AGG

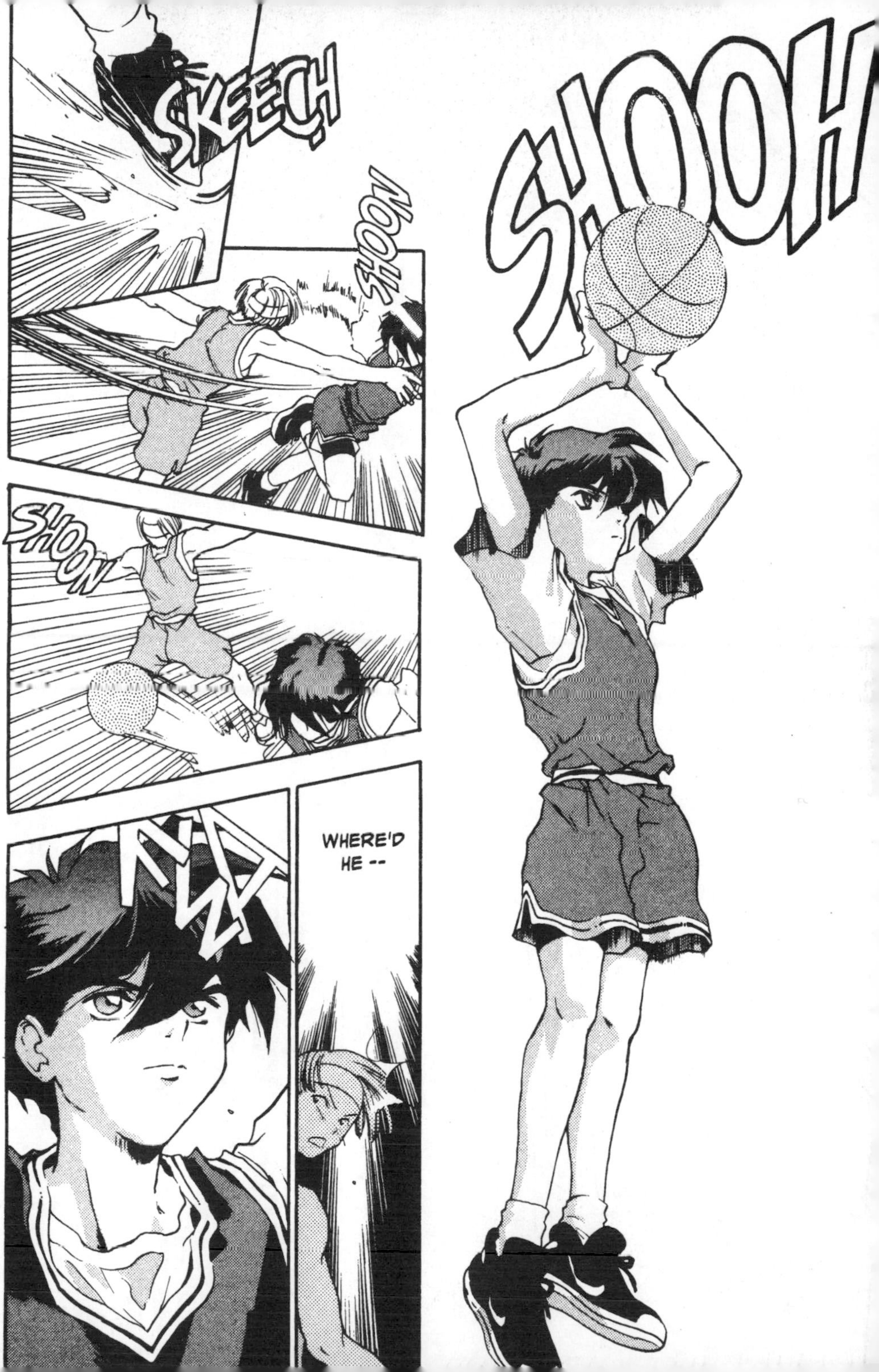
SKEECH
SHOON
SHOON
WHERE'D HE --
SHOOH

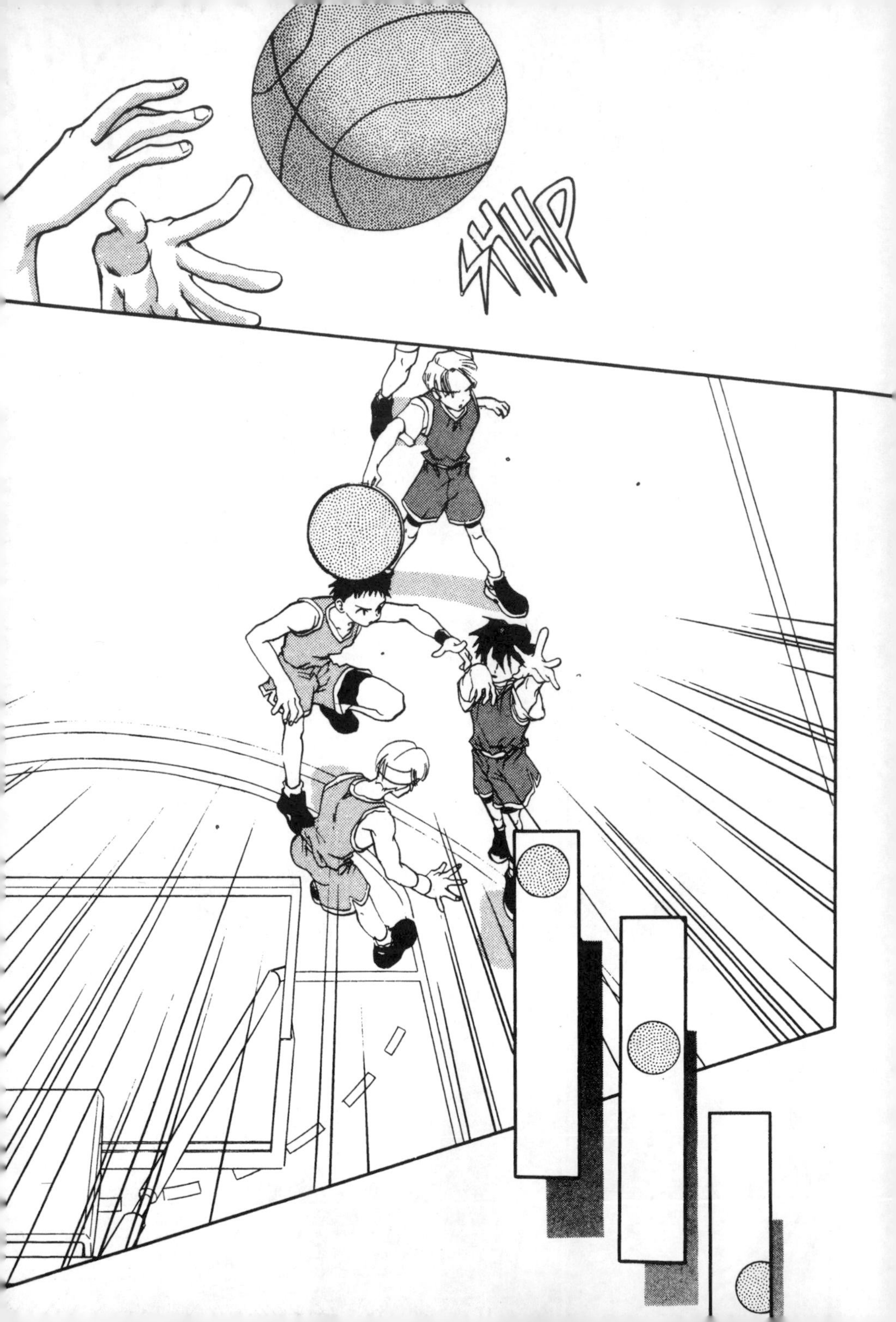

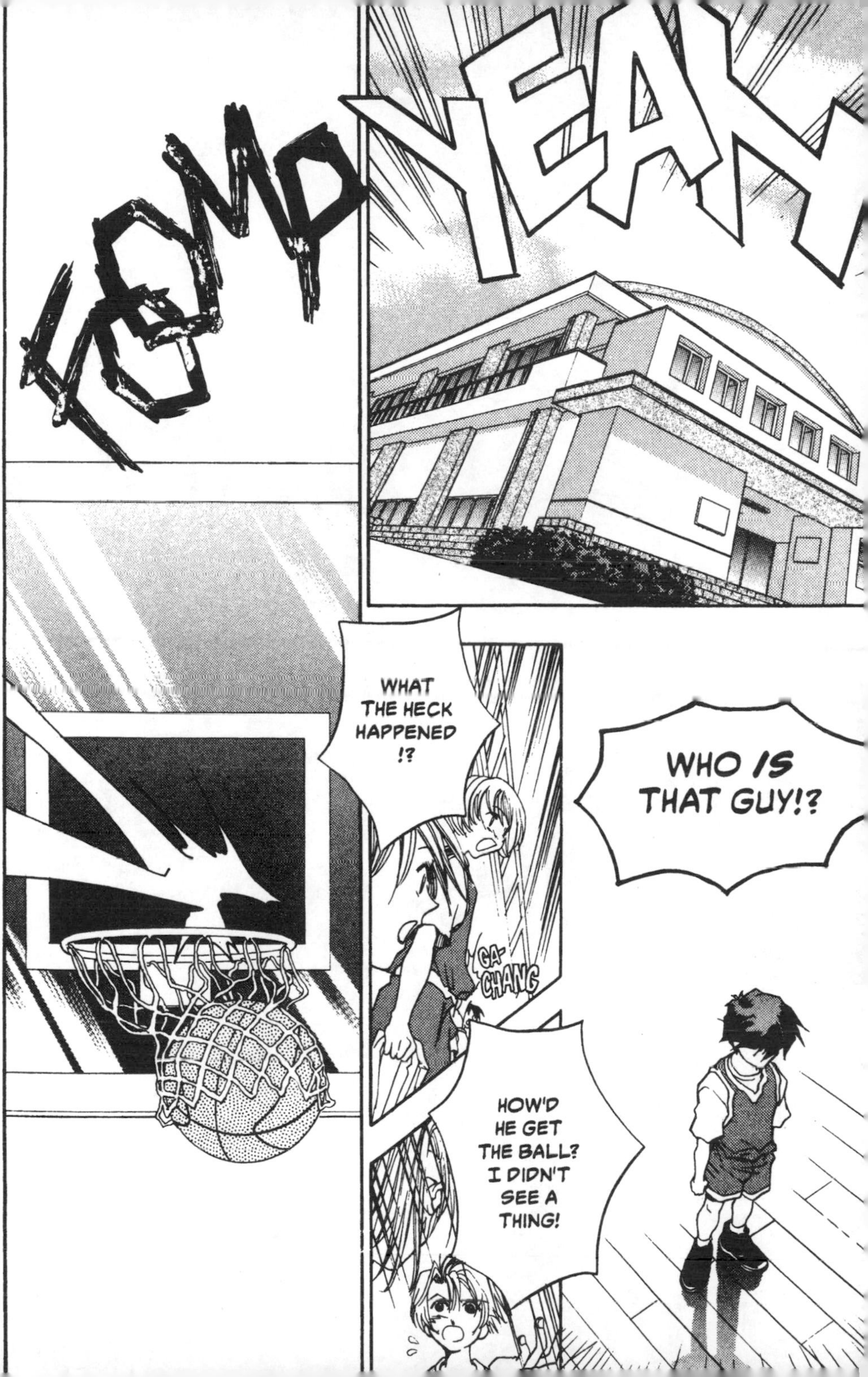
FOMP
YEAH
WHAT THE HECK HAPPENED !?
GA-CHANG
WHO *IS* THAT GUY!?
HOW'D HE GET THE BALL? I DIDN'T SEE A THING!

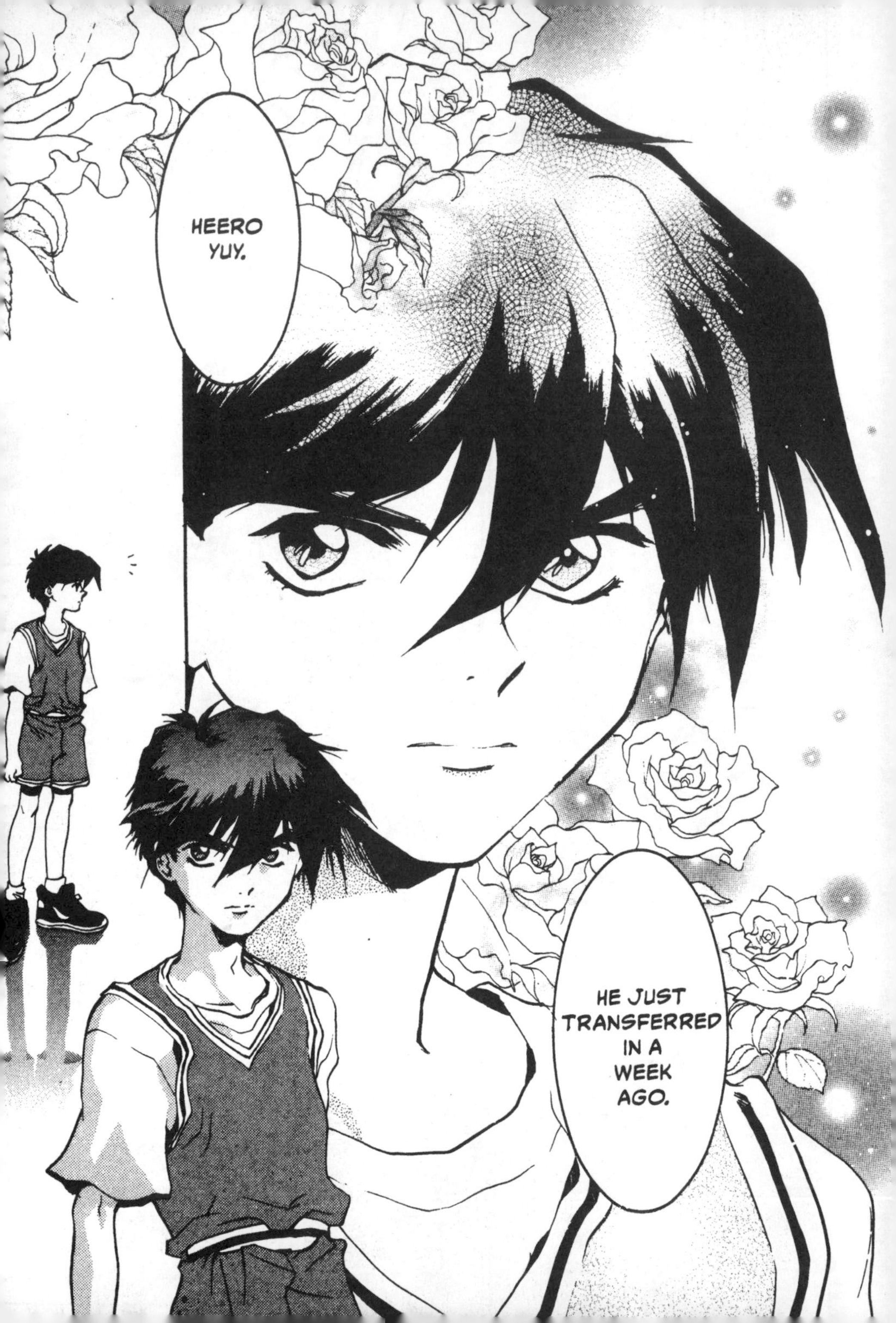
HEERO YUY.
HE JUST TRANSFERRED IN A WEEK AGO.

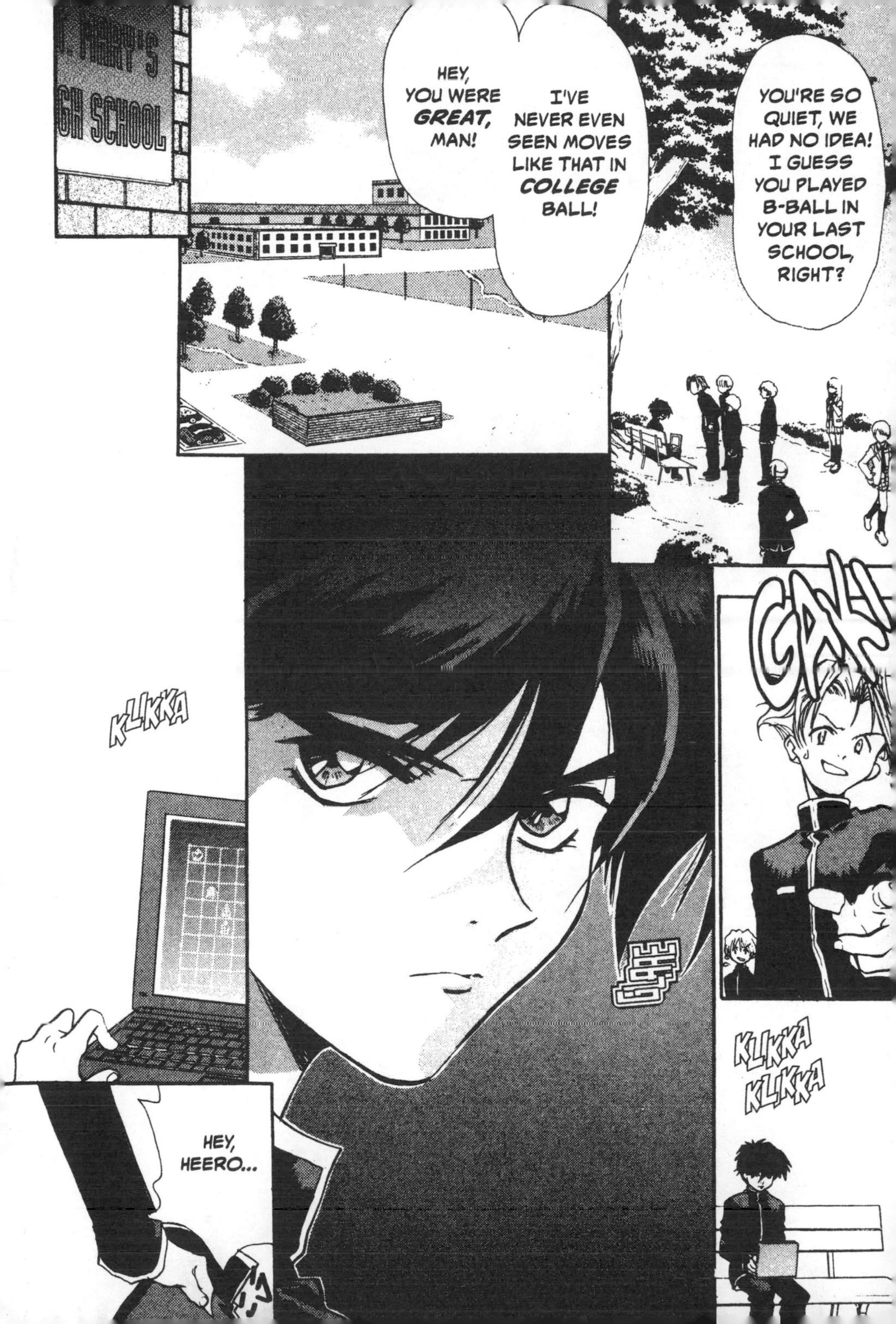
HEY, YOU WERE GREAT, MAN!
I'VE NEVER EVEN SEEN MOVES LIKE THAT IN COLLEGE BALL!
YOU'RE SO QUIET, WE HAD NO IDEA! I GUESS YOU PLAYED B-BALL IN YOUR LAST SCHOOL, RIGHT?
KLIKKA
KLIKKA KLIKKA
HEY, HEERO...

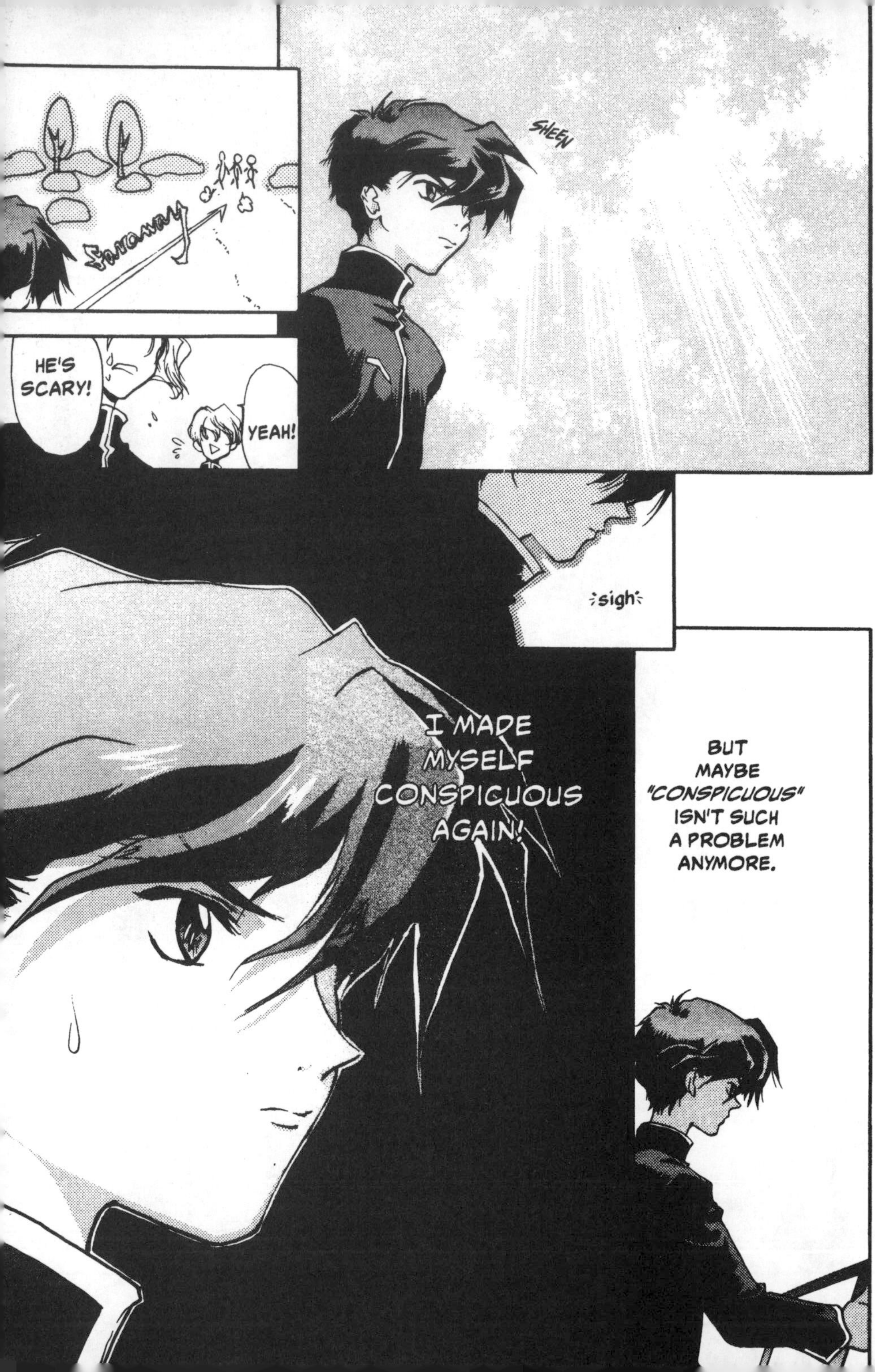
Faraway
HE'S SCARY!
YEAH!
SHEEN
sigh
I MADE MYSELF CONSPICUOUS AGAIN!
BUT MAYBE "CONSPICUOUS" ISN'T SUCH A PROBLEM ANYMORE.

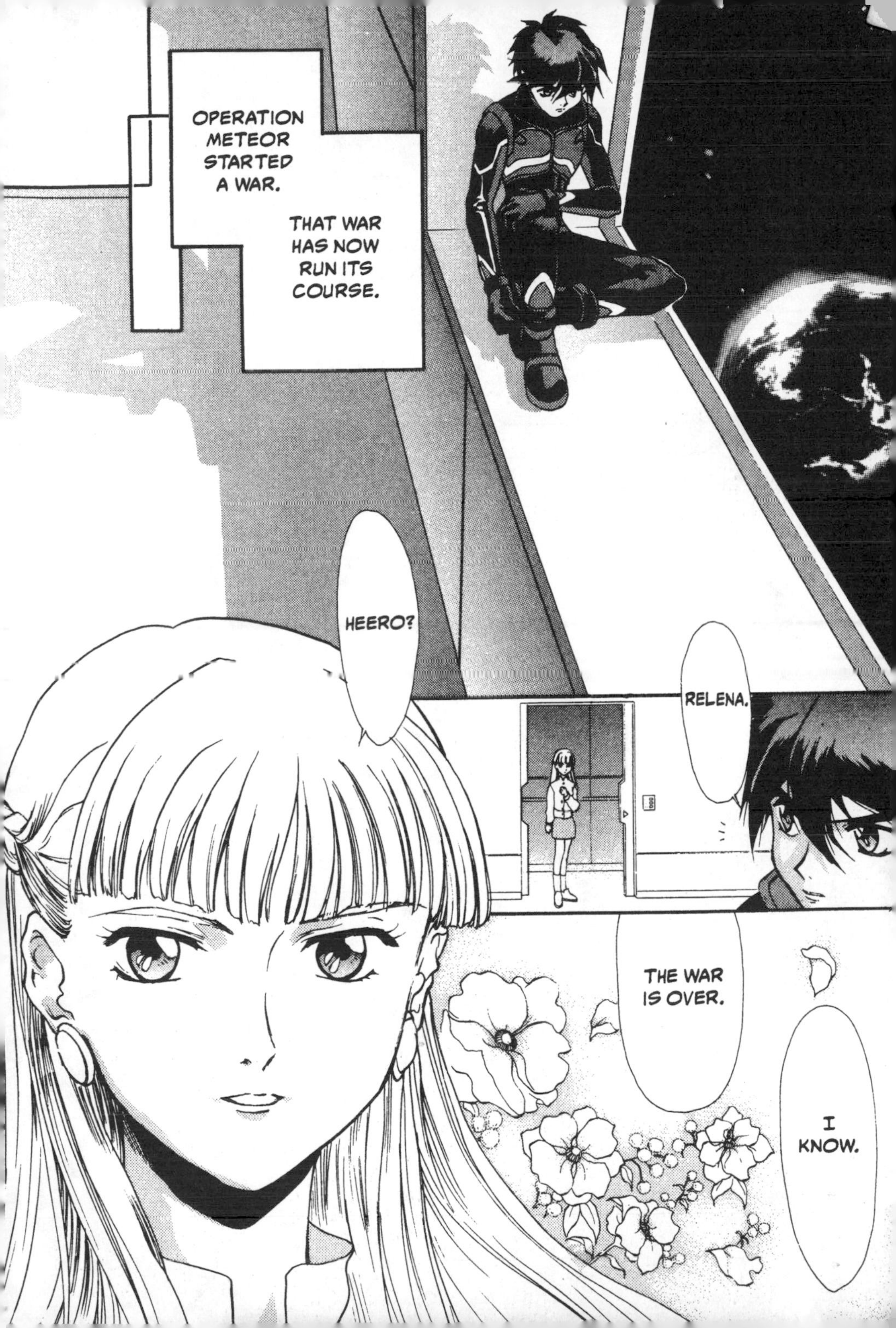
OPERATION METEOR STARTED A WAR.
THAT WAR HAS NOW RUN ITS COURSE.
HEERO?
RELENA.
THE WAR IS OVER.
I KNOW.

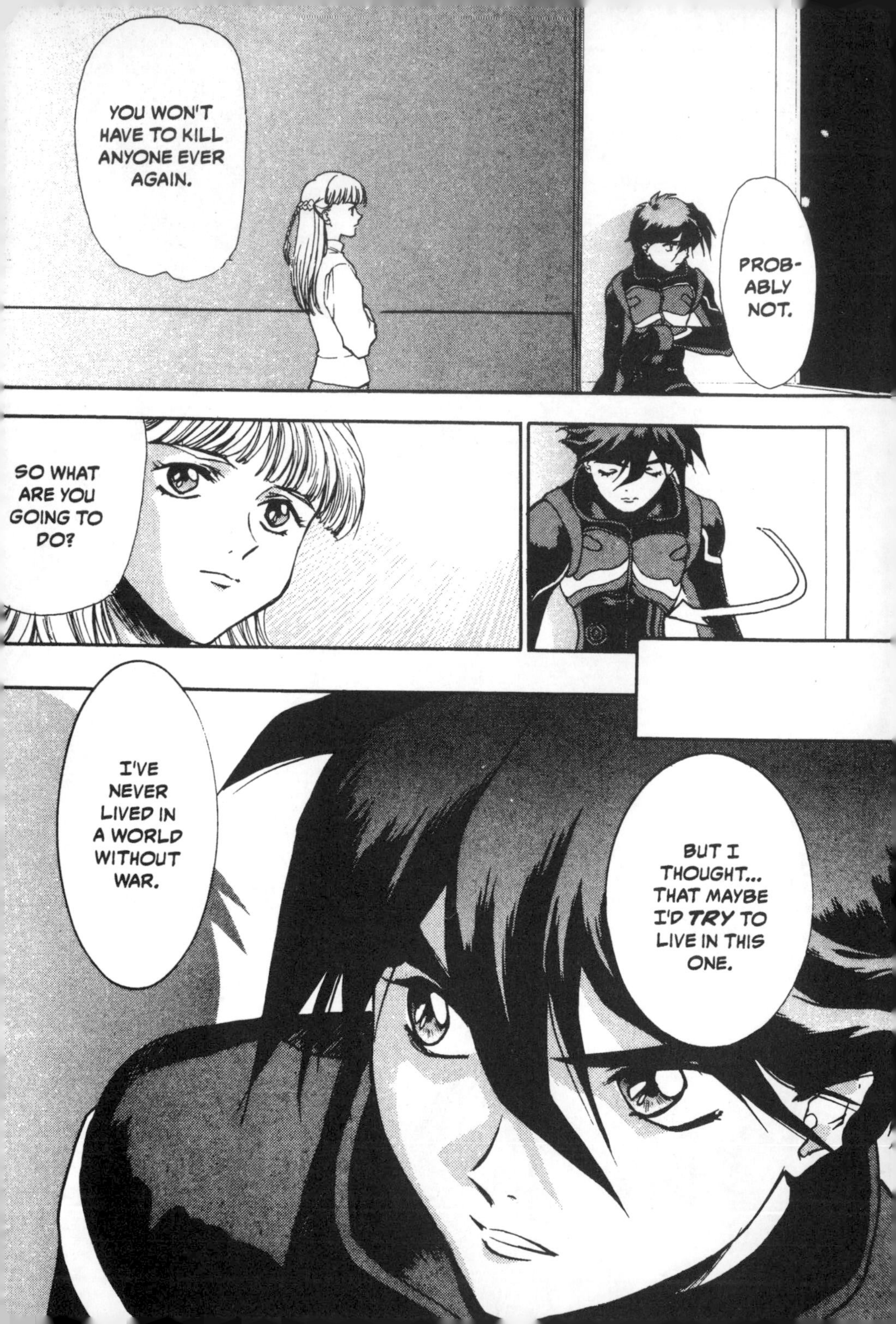

YOU WON'T HAVE TO KILL ANYONE EVER AGAIN.
PROB- ABLY NOT.
SO WHAT ARE YOU GOING TO DO?
I'VE NEVER LIVED IN A WORLD WITHOUT WAR.
BUT I THOUGHT... THAT MAYBE I'D TRY TO LIVE IN THIS ONE.

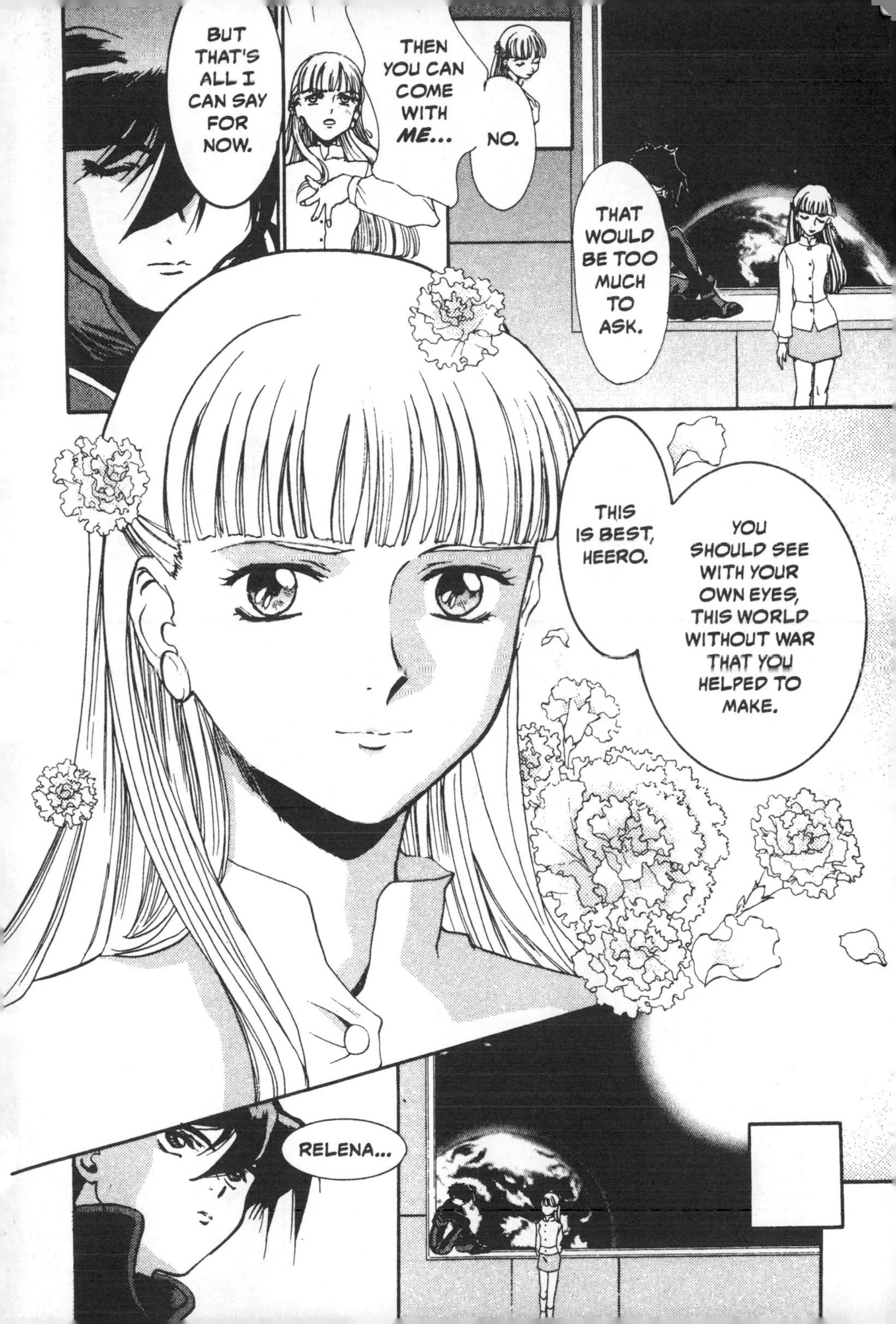
BUT THAT'S ALL I CAN SAY FOR NOW.
THEN YOU CAN COME WITH *ME...*
NO.
THAT WOULD BE TOO MUCH TO ASK.
THIS IS BEST, HEERO.
YOU SHOULD SEE WITH YOUR OWN EYES, THIS WORLD WITHOUT WAR THAT YOU HELPED TO MAKE.
RELENA...

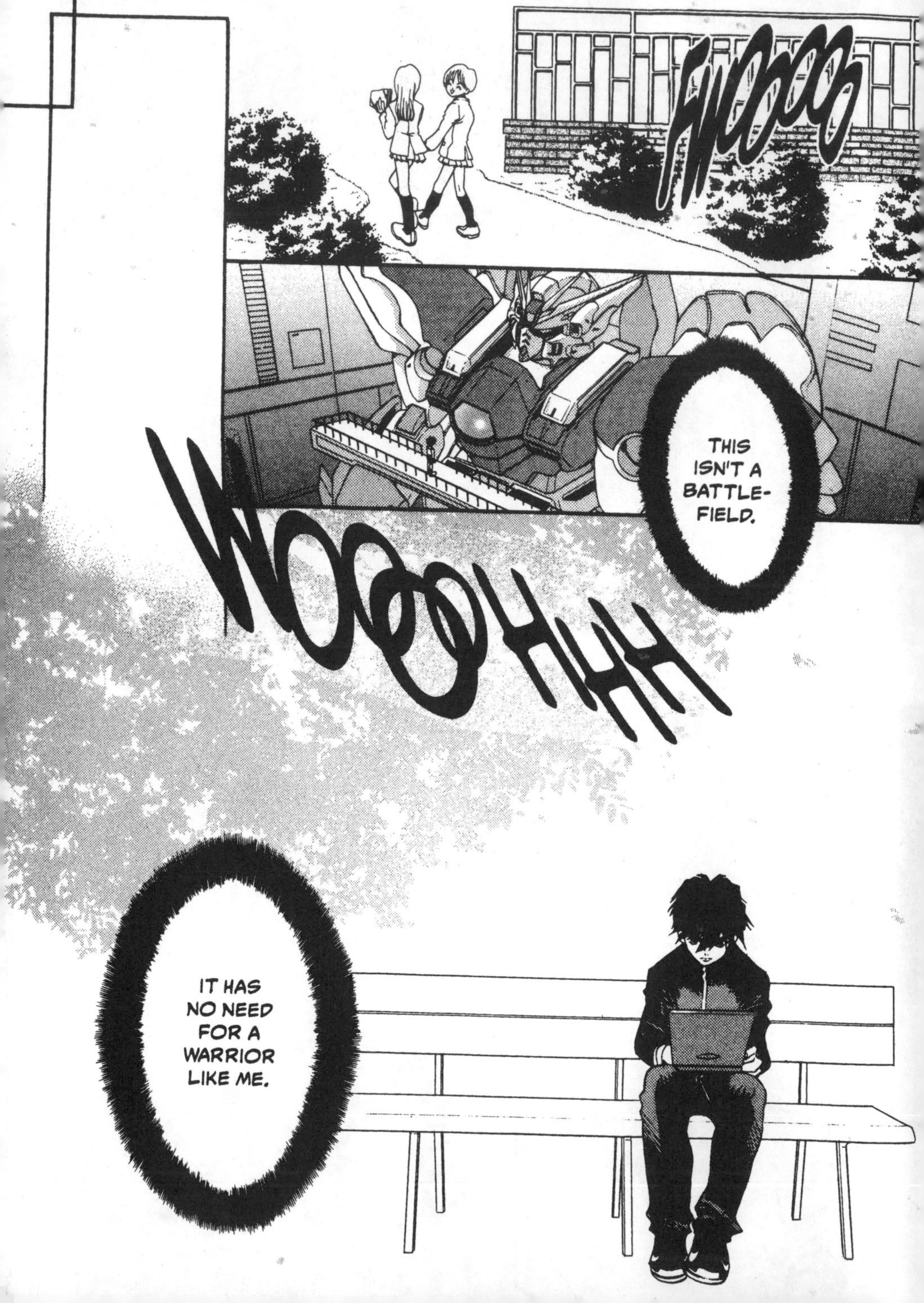
FWOOOO
THIS ISN'T A BATTLE-FIELD.
WOOOOHHH
IT HAS NO NEED FOR A WARRIOR LIKE ME.

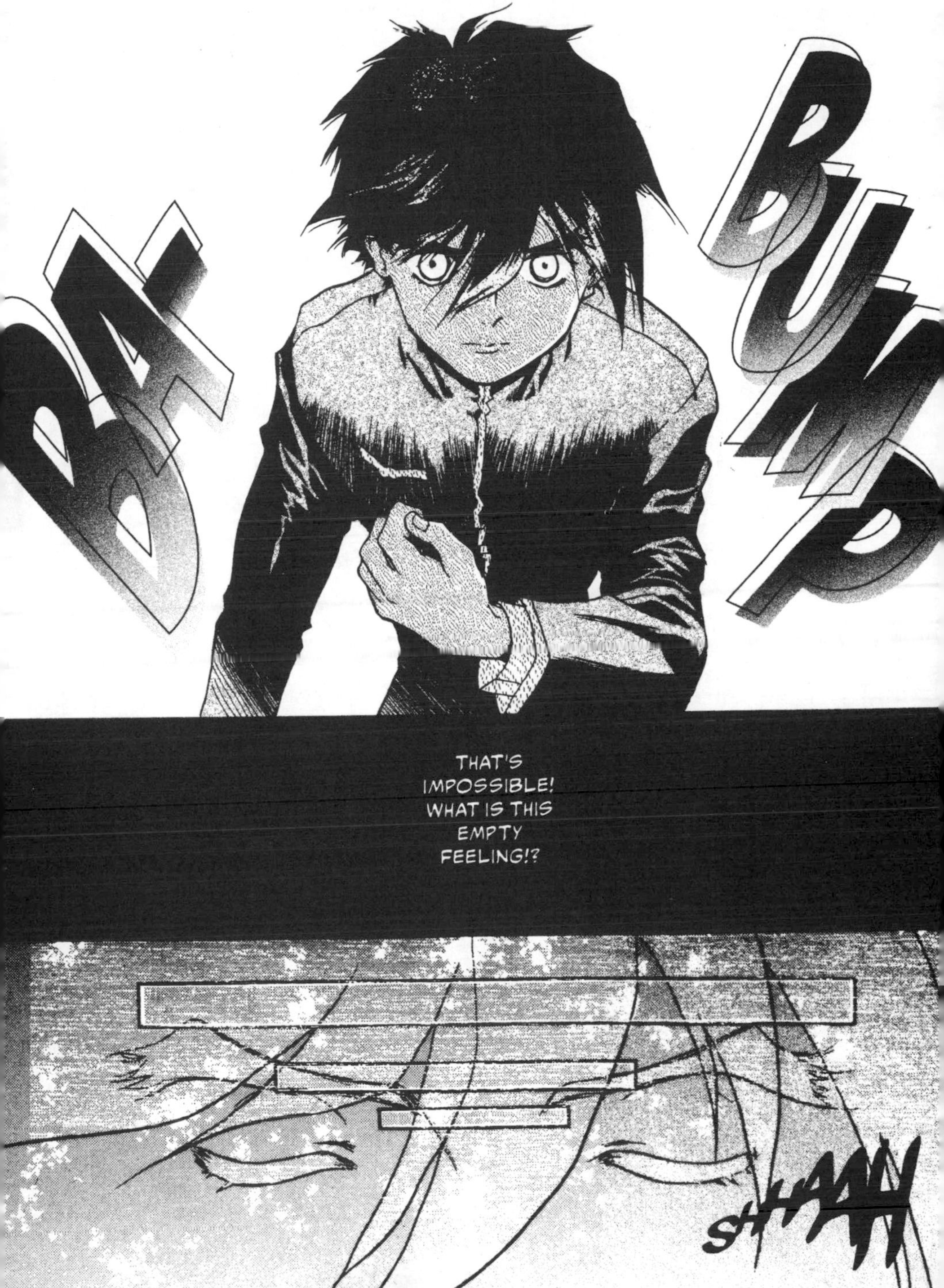
BA-
BUMP
THAT'S IMPOSSIBLE! WHAT IS THIS EMPTY FEELING!?
SHAAH

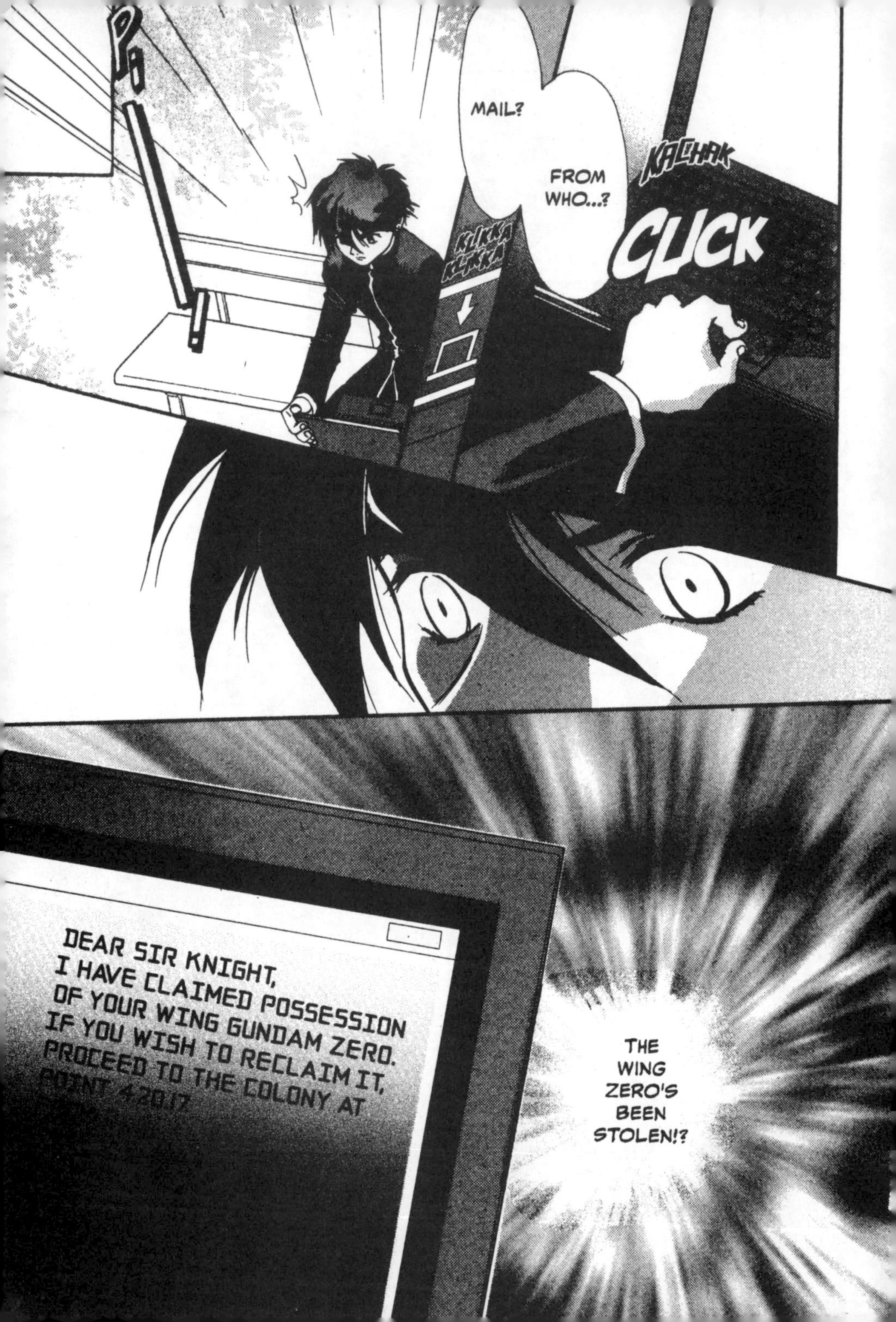
MAIL?
FROM WHO...?
KACHAK
CLICK
KLIKKA KLIKKA
DEAR SIR KNIGHT,
I HAVE CLAIMED POSSESSION
OF YOUR WING GUNDAM ZERO.
IF YOU WISH TO RECLAIM IT,
PROCEED TO THE COLONY AT
POINT 4.20.17
THE WING ZERO'S BEEN STOLEN!?

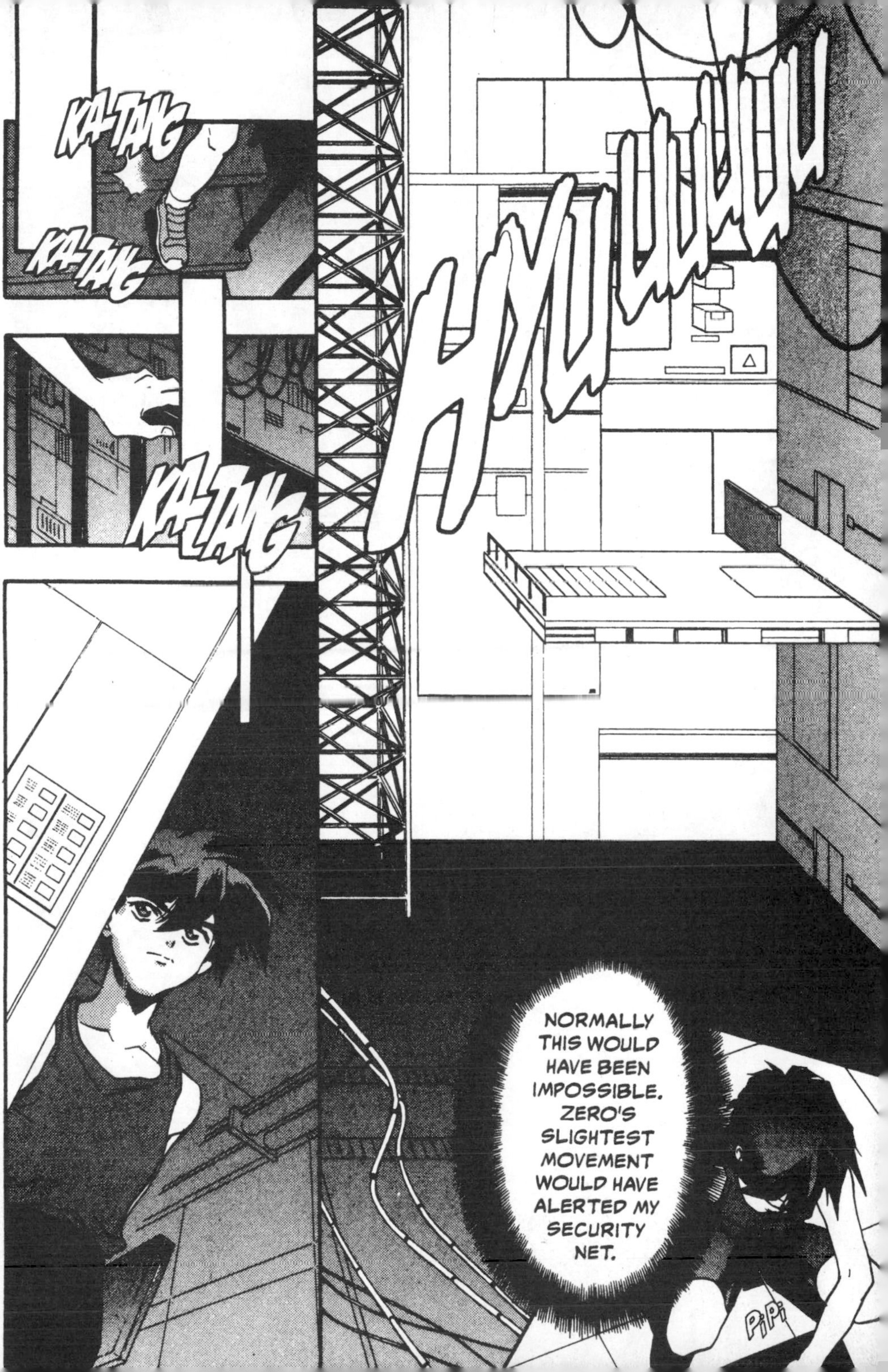
KA-TANG
KA-TANG
KA-TANG
HYUUUUUUU
NORMALLY THIS WOULD HAVE BEEN IMPOSSIBLE. ZERO'S SLIGHTEST MOVEMENT WOULD HAVE ALERTED MY SECURITY NET.
PiPi

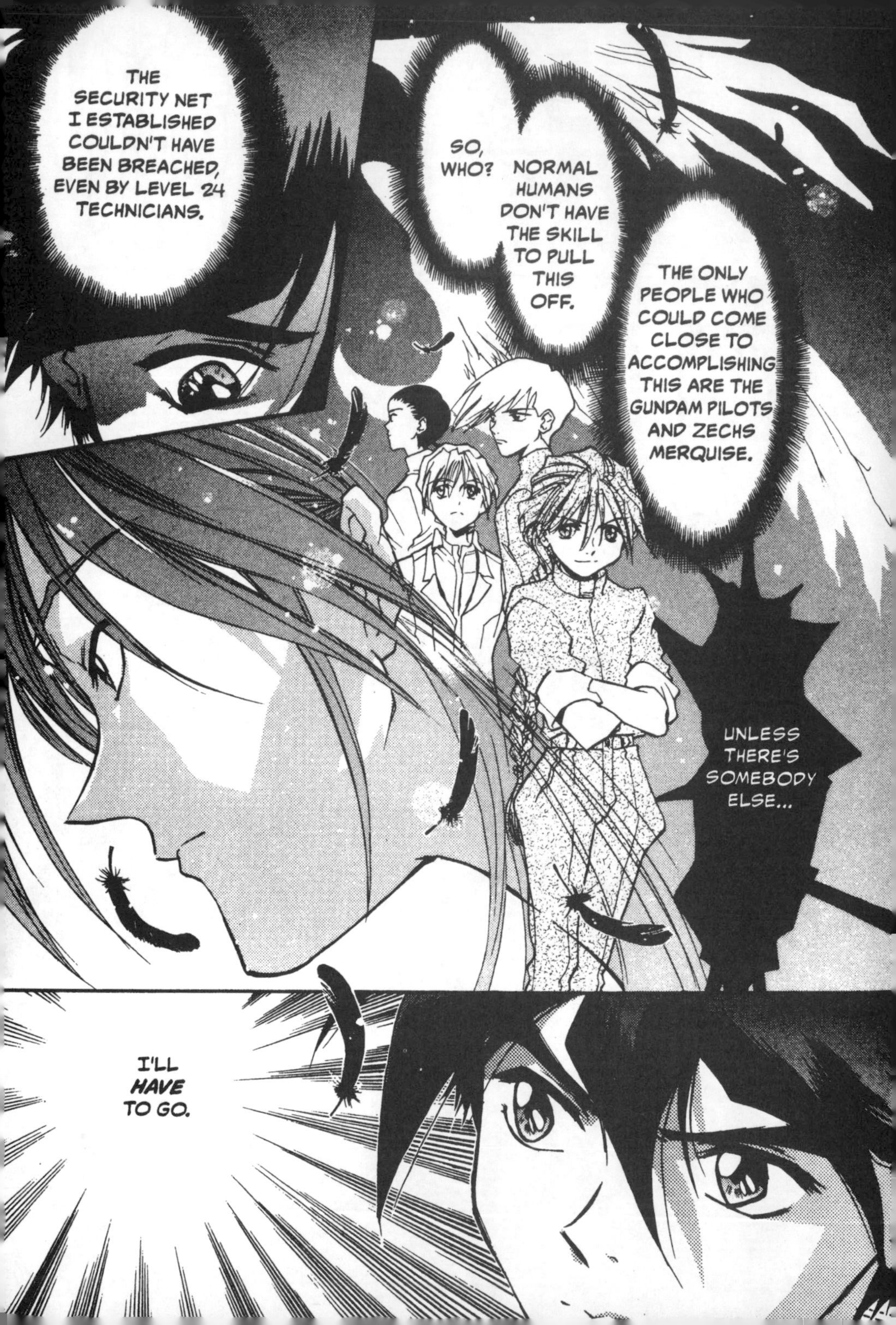
THE SECURITY NET I ESTABLISHED COULDN'T HAVE BEEN BREACHED, EVEN BY LEVEL 24 TECHNICIANS.
SO, WHO?
NORMAL HUMANS DON'T HAVE THE SKILL TO PULL THIS OFF.
THE ONLY PEOPLE WHO COULD COME CLOSE TO ACCOMPLISHING THIS ARE THE GUNDAM PILOTS AND ZECHS MERQUISE.
UNLESS THERE'S SOMEBODY ELSE...
I'LL *HAVE* TO GO.

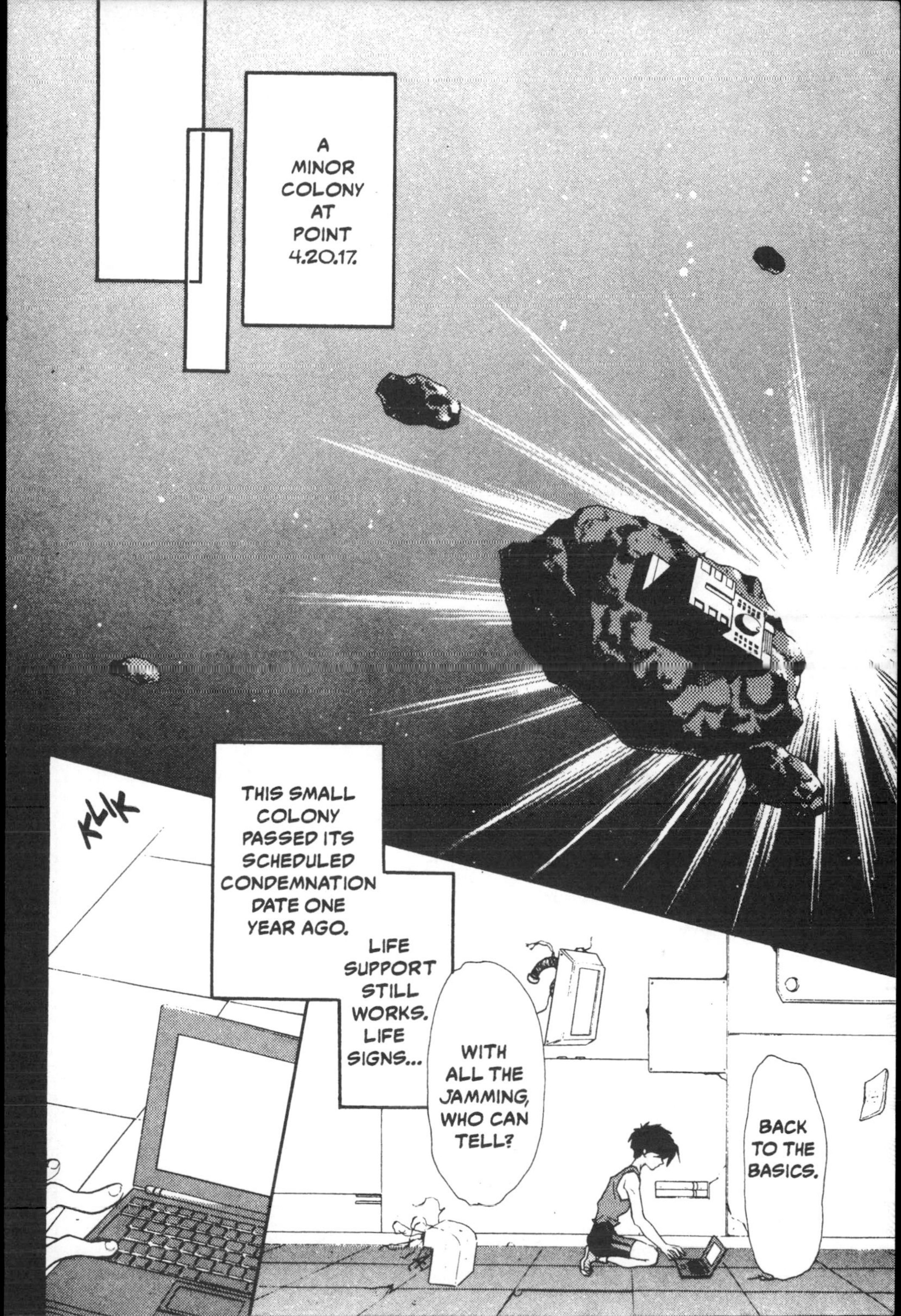
A MINOR COLONY AT POINT 4.20.17.
KLIK
THIS SMALL COLONY PASSED ITS SCHEDULED CONDEMNATION DATE ONE YEAR AGO.
LIFE SUPPORT STILL WORKS. LIFE SIGNS...
WITH ALL THE JAMMING, WHO CAN TELL?
BACK TO THE BASICS.

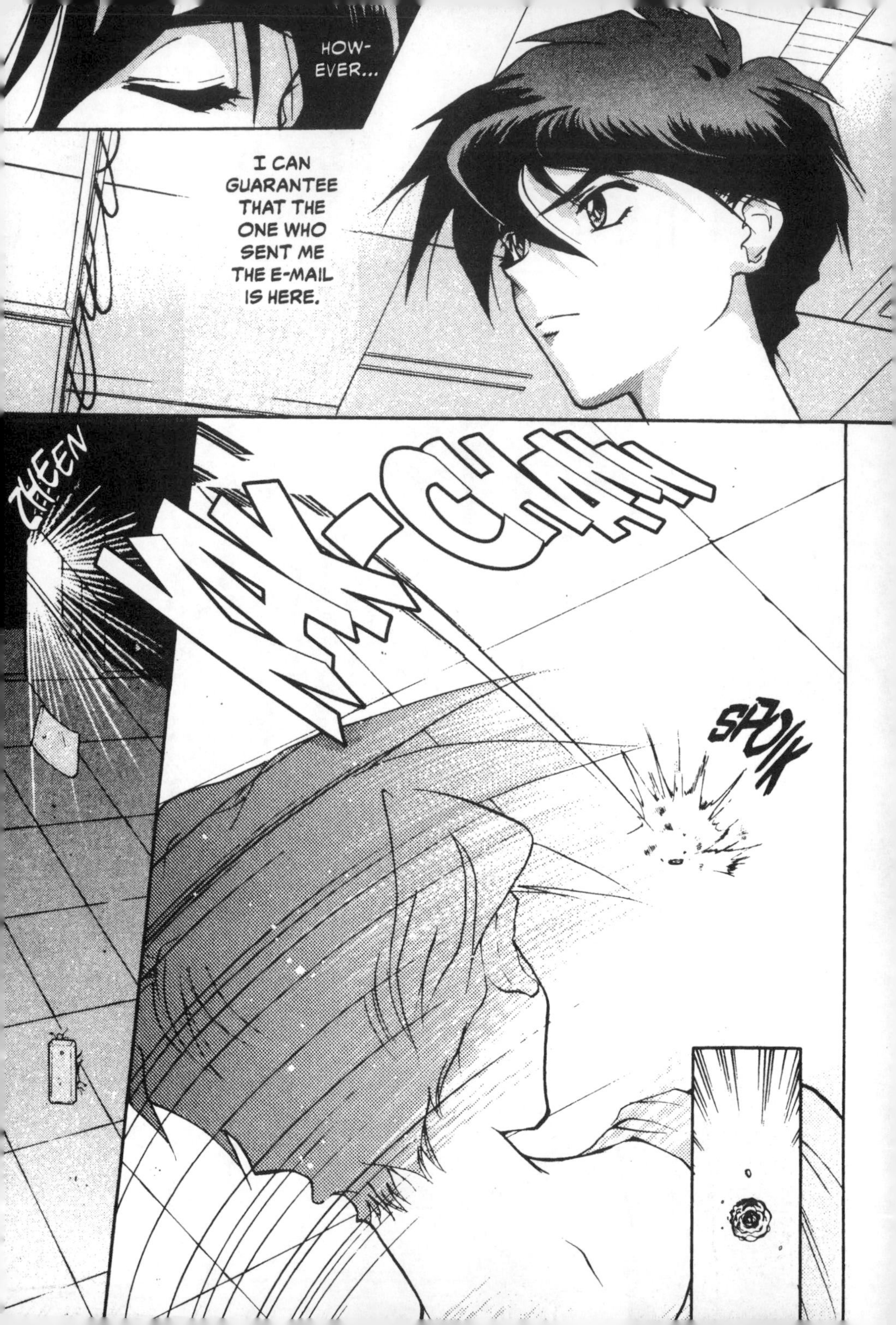
HOW-
EVER...
I CAN
GUARANTEE
THAT THE
ONE WHO
SENT ME
THE E-MAIL
IS HERE.
ZHEEN
SPOIK

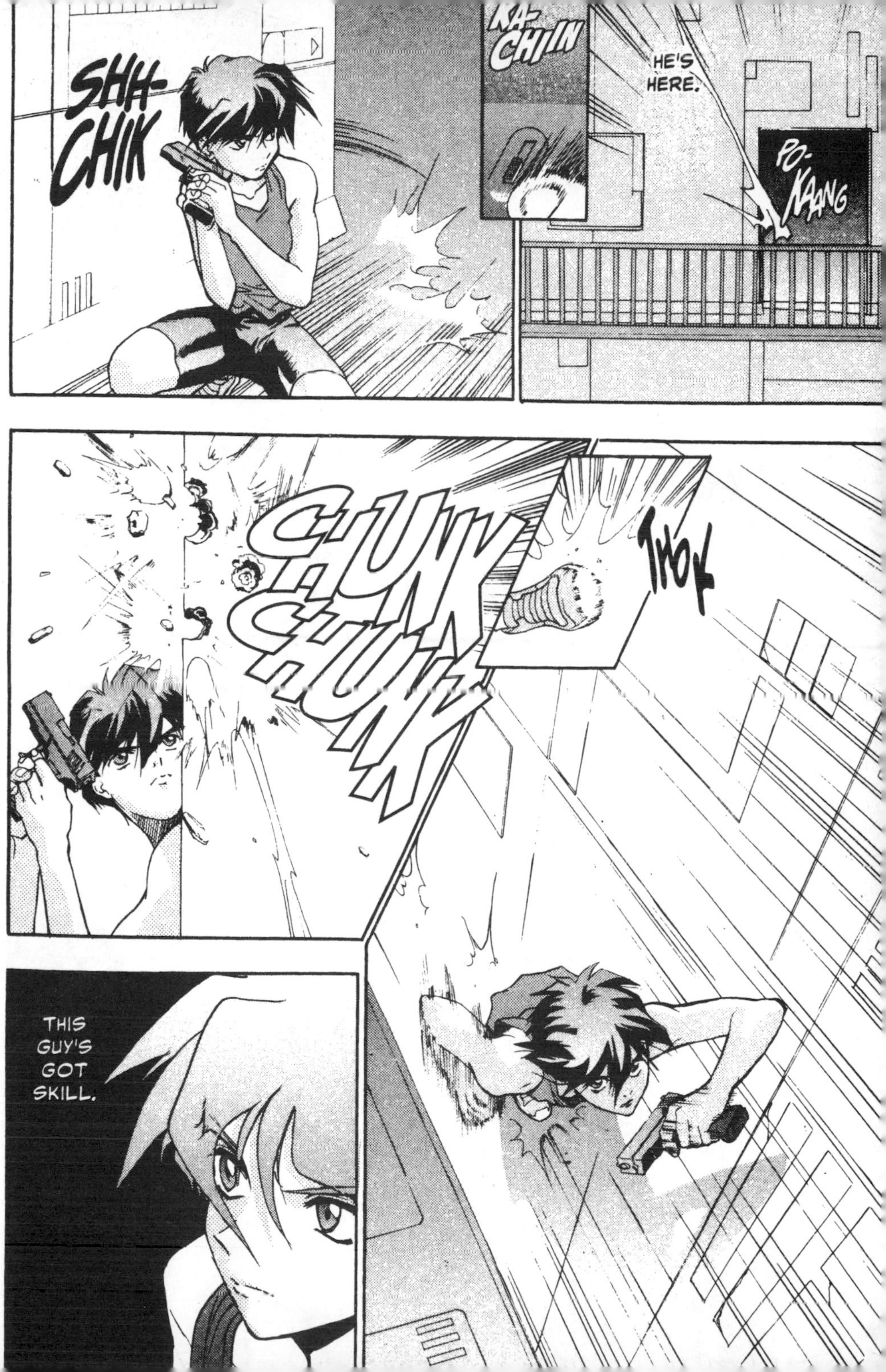
SHH-CHIK
KA-CHIIN
HE'S HERE.
PO-KAANG
CHUNK CHUNK CHUNK
THOK
THIS GUY'S GOT SKILL.

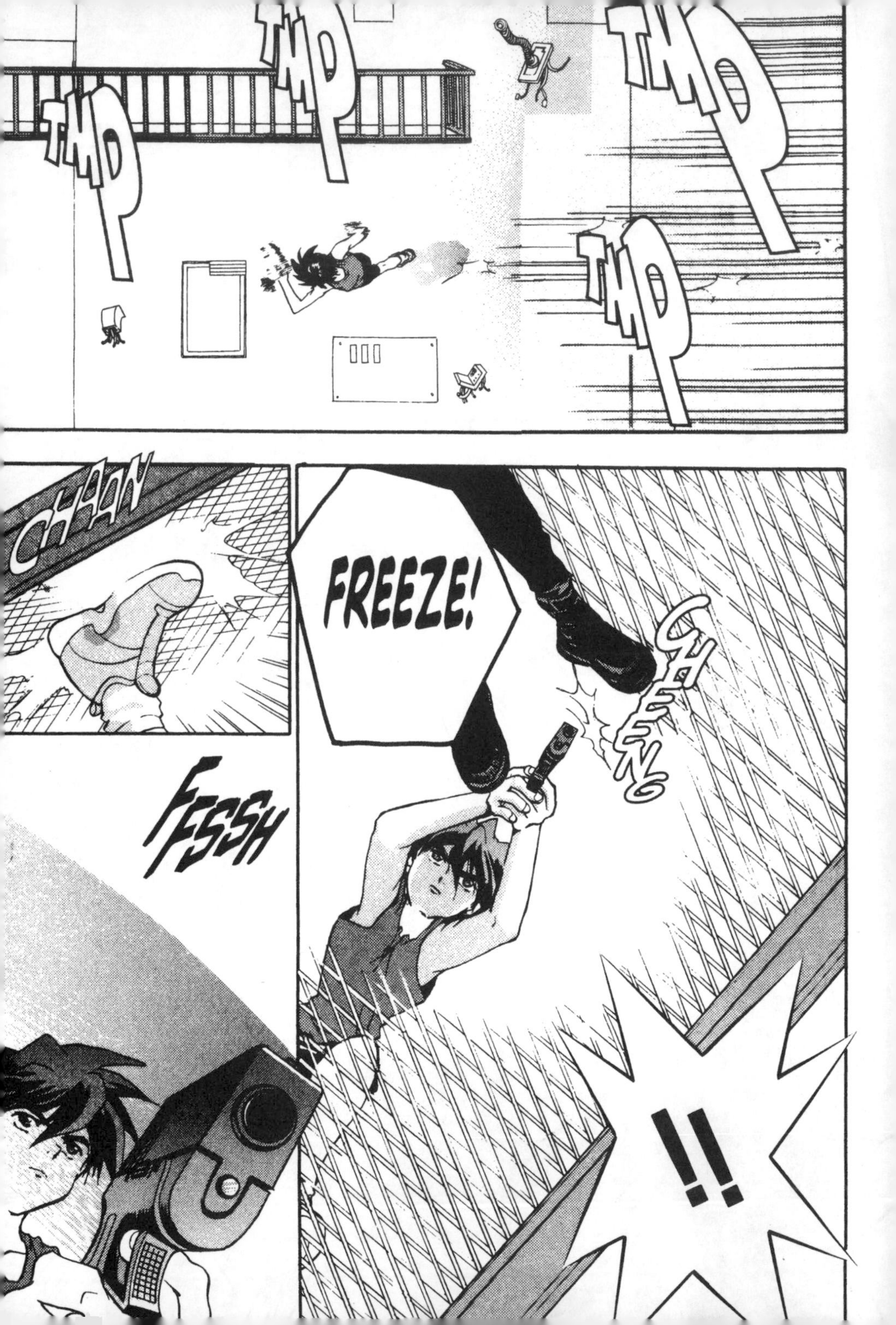
THMP
THMP
THMP
THMP
FREEZE!
CHEENG
CHAAN
FSSH
!!

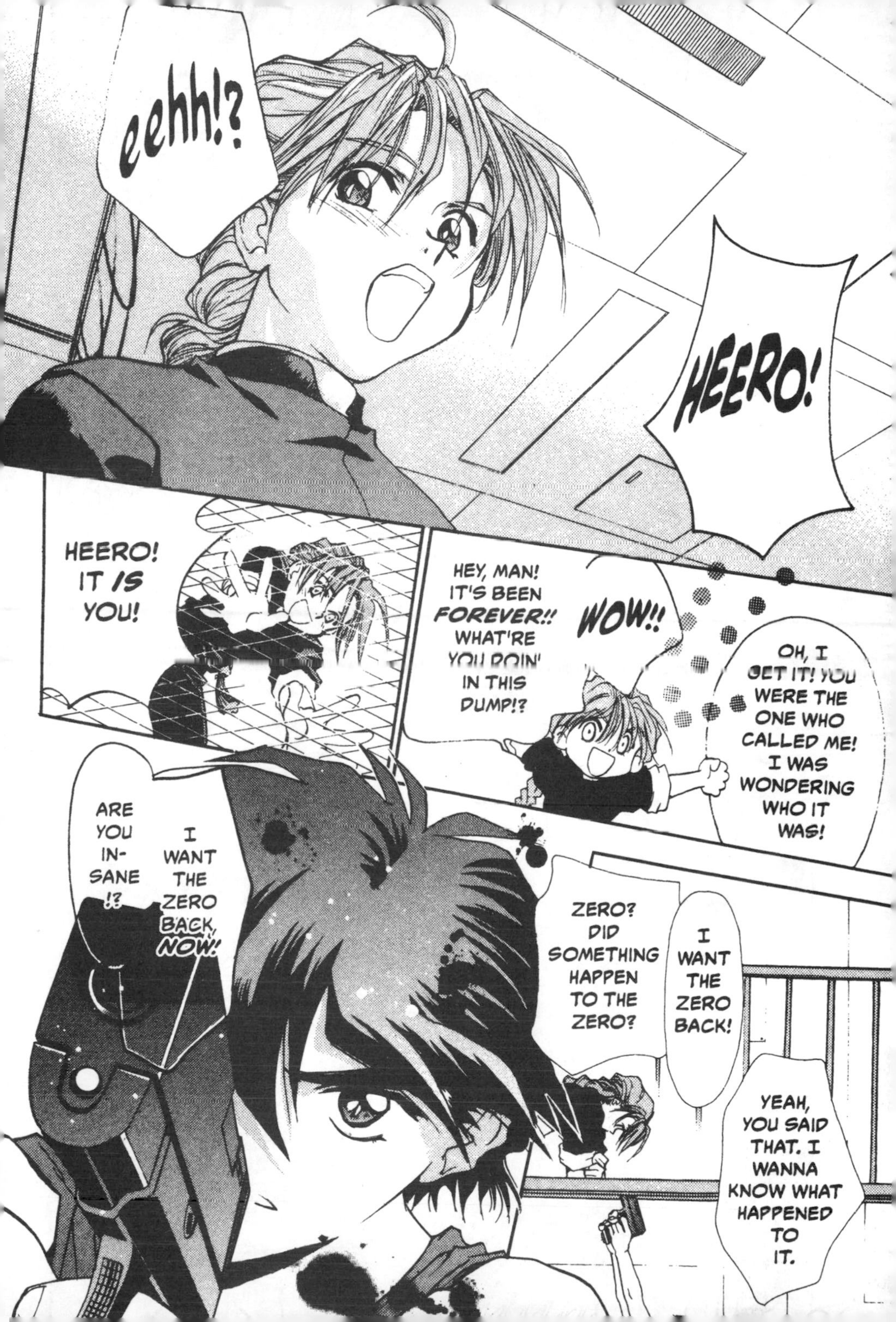
eehh!?
HEERO!
HEERO! IT IS YOU!
HEY, MAN! IT'S BEEN FOREVER!! WHAT'RE YOU DOIN' IN THIS DUMP!?
WOW!!
OH, I GET IT! YOU WERE THE ONE WHO CALLED ME! I WAS WONDERING WHO IT WAS!
ARE YOU IN-SANE !?
I WANT THE ZERO BACK, NOW!
ZERO? DID SOMETHING HAPPEN TO THE ZERO?
I WANT THE ZERO BACK!
YEAH, YOU SAID THAT. I WANNA KNOW WHAT HAPPENED TO IT.

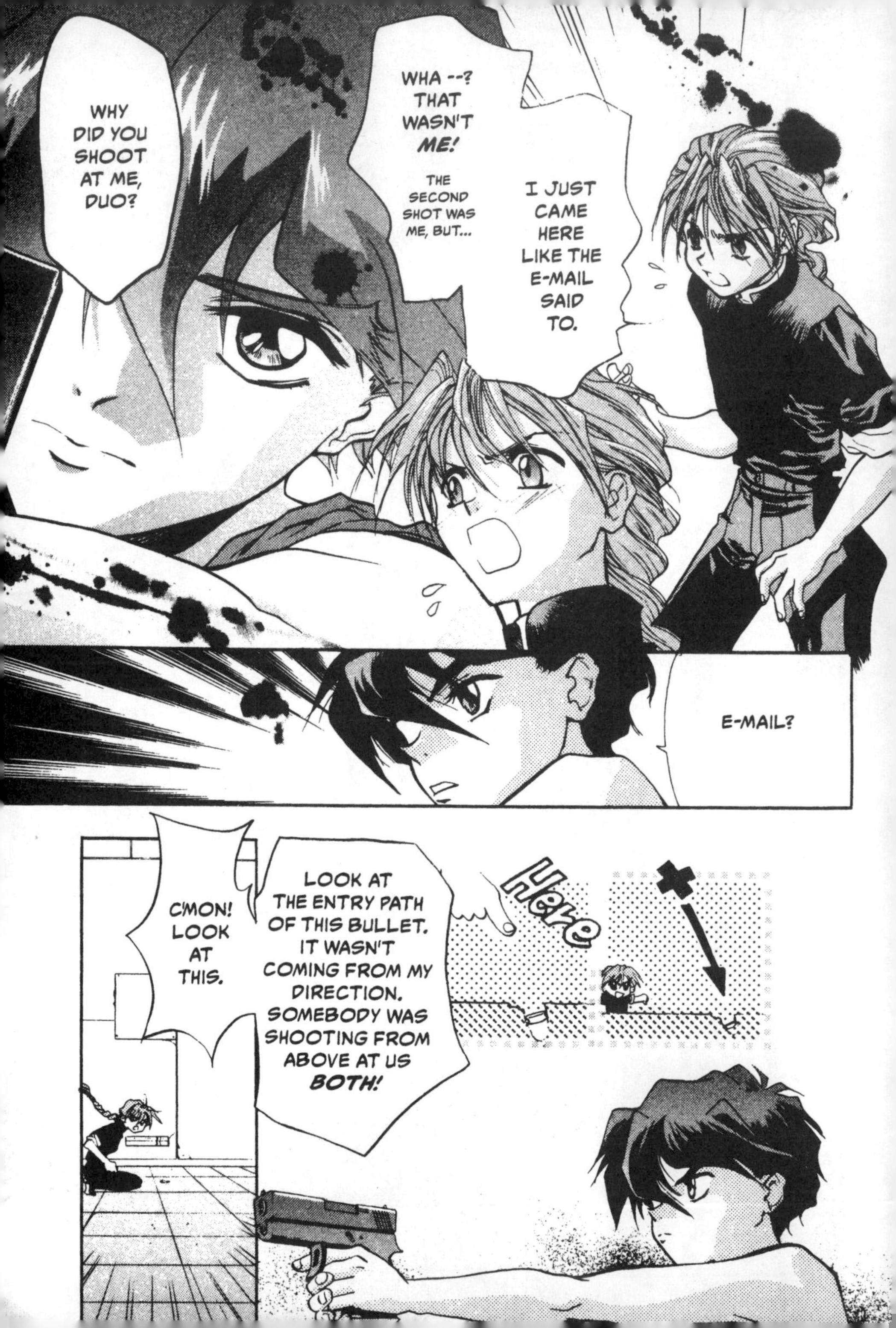
WHY DID YOU SHOOT AT ME, DUO?
WHA --? THAT WASN'T *ME!*
THE SECOND SHOT WAS ME, BUT...
I JUST CAME HERE LIKE THE E-MAIL SAID TO.
E-MAIL?
C'MON! LOOK AT THIS.
LOOK AT THE ENTRY PATH OF THIS BULLET. IT WASN'T COMING FROM MY DIRECTION. SOMEBODY WAS SHOOTING FROM ABOVE AT US *BOTH!*
Here

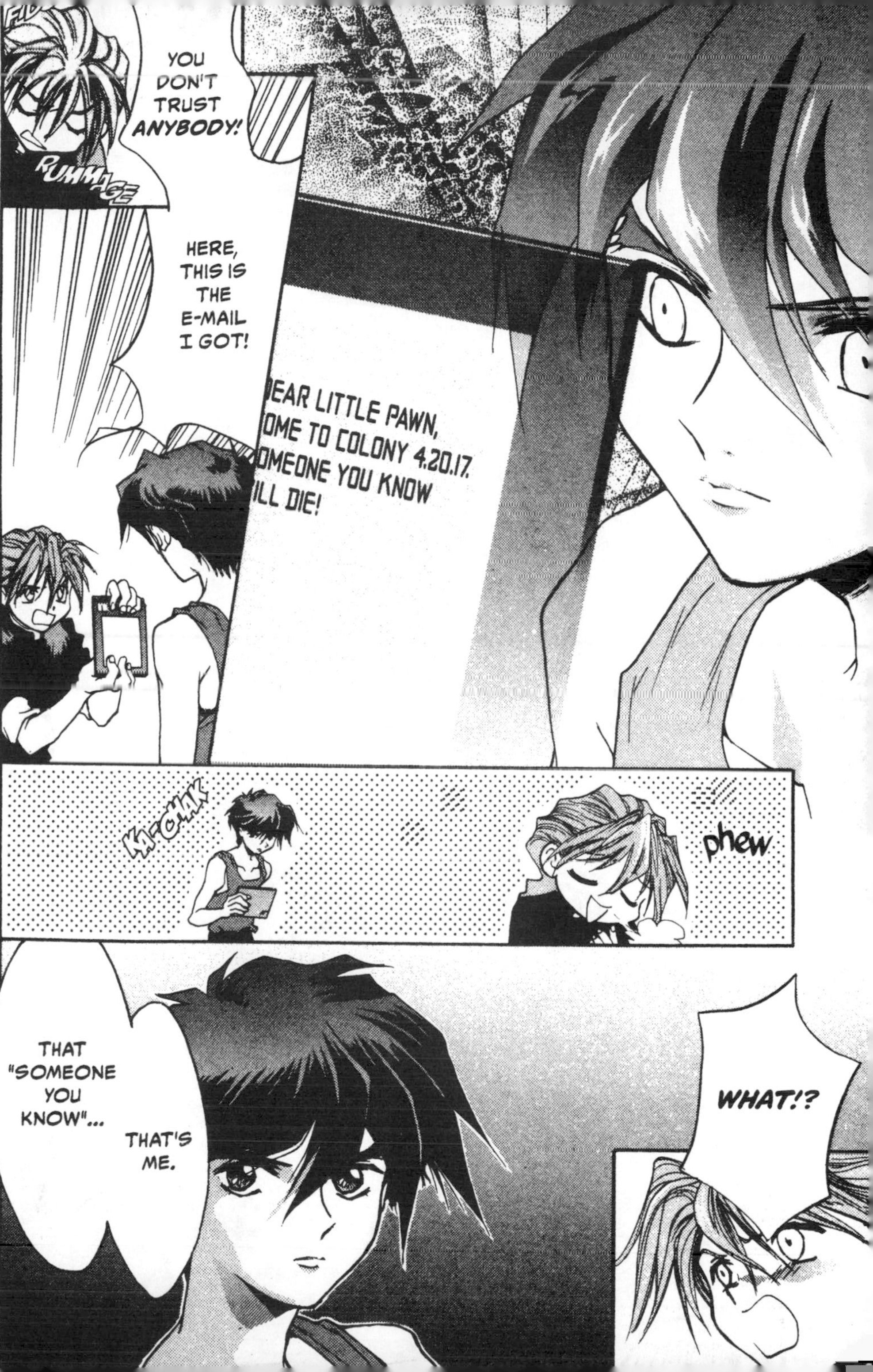
YOU DON'T TRUST ANYBODY!
RUMMAGE
HERE, THIS IS THE E-MAIL I GOT!
EAR LITTLE PAWN,
OME TO COLONY 4.20.17.
OMEONE YOU KNOW
ILL DIE!
KA-CHAK
phew
THAT "SOMEONE YOU KNOW"...
THAT'S ME.
WHAT!?

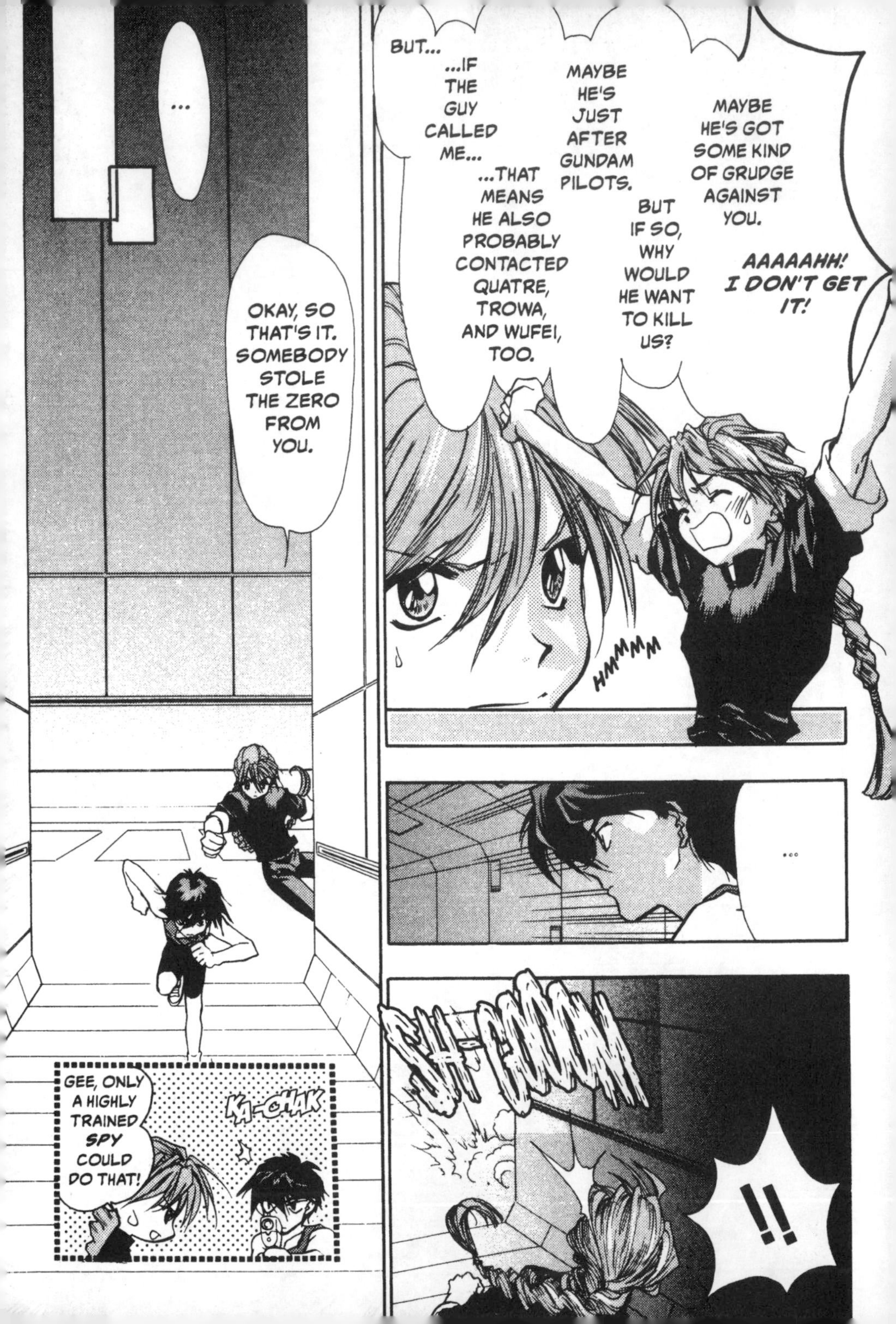
...
OKAY, SO THAT'S IT. SOMEBODY STOLE THE ZERO FROM YOU.
GEE, ONLY A HIGHLY TRAINED *SPY* COULD DO THAT!
KA-CHAK
BUT...
...IF THE GUY CALLED ME...
...THAT MEANS HE ALSO PROBABLY CONTACTED QUATRE, TROWA, AND WUFEI, TOO.
MAYBE HE'S JUST AFTER GUNDAM PILOTS.
BUT IF SO, WHY WOULD HE WANT TO KILL US?
MAYBE HE'S GOT SOME KIND OF GRUDGE AGAINST YOU.
AAAAAHH! I DON'T GET IT!
HMMMMM
...
SH-OOOOM
!!

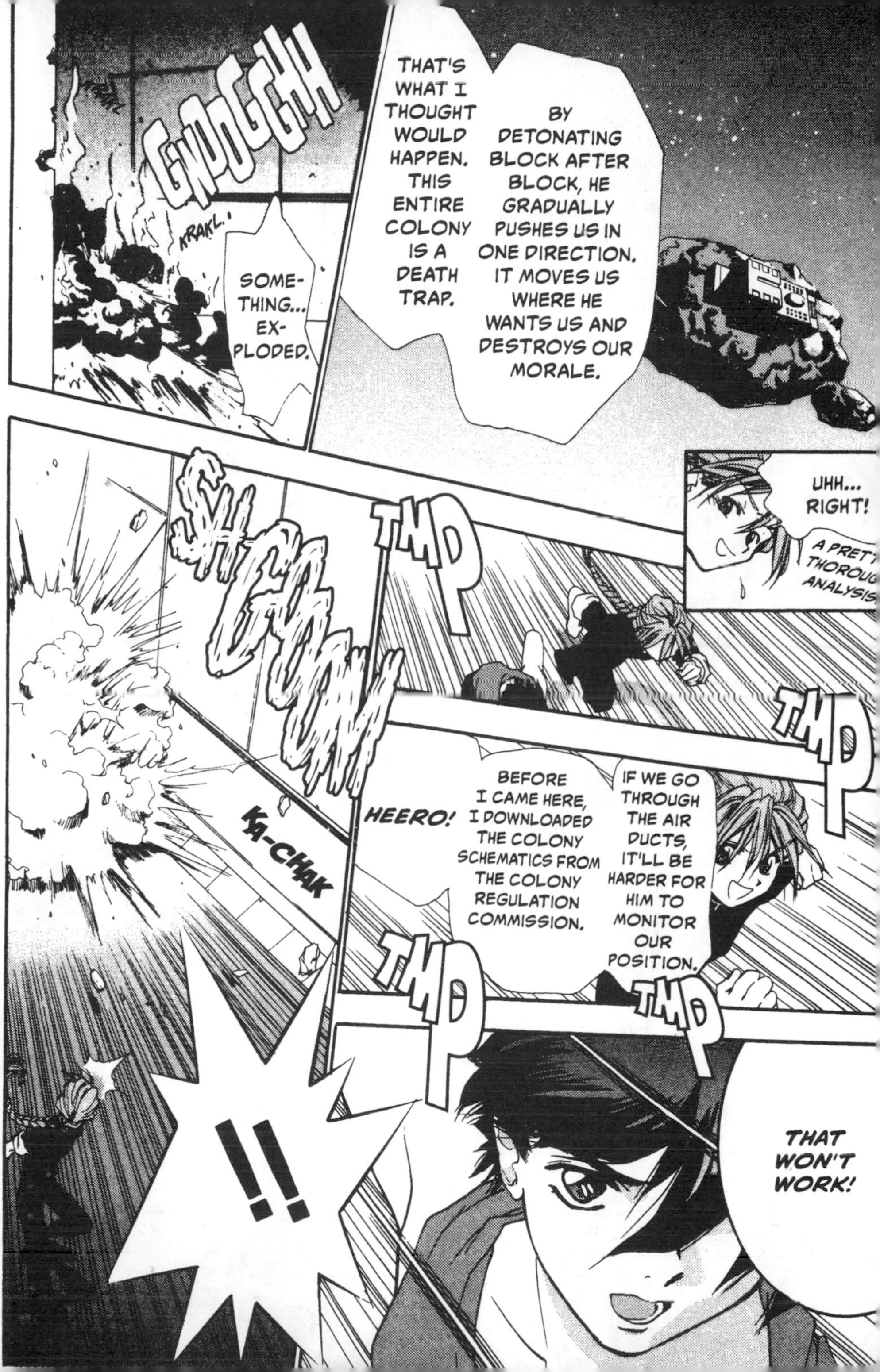
KRAKL
GNOOGCHH
KRAKL.
SOME-THING... EX-PLODED.
THAT'S WHAT I THOUGHT WOULD HAPPEN. THIS ENTIRE COLONY IS A DEATH TRAP.
BY DETONATING BLOCK AFTER BLOCK, HE GRADUALLY PUSHES US IN ONE DIRECTION. IT MOVES US WHERE HE WANTS US AND DESTROYS OUR MORALE.
SHGOOM
KA-CHAK
TMP
UHH... RIGHT!
A PRETT THOROUG ANALYSIS
TMP
HEERO!
BEFORE I CAME HERE, I DOWNLOADED THE COLONY SCHEMATICS FROM THE COLONY REGULATION COMMISSION.
IF WE GO THROUGH THE AIR DUCTS, IT'LL BE HARDER FOR HIM TO MONITOR OUR POSITION.
TMP
TMP
!!
THAT WON'T WORK!

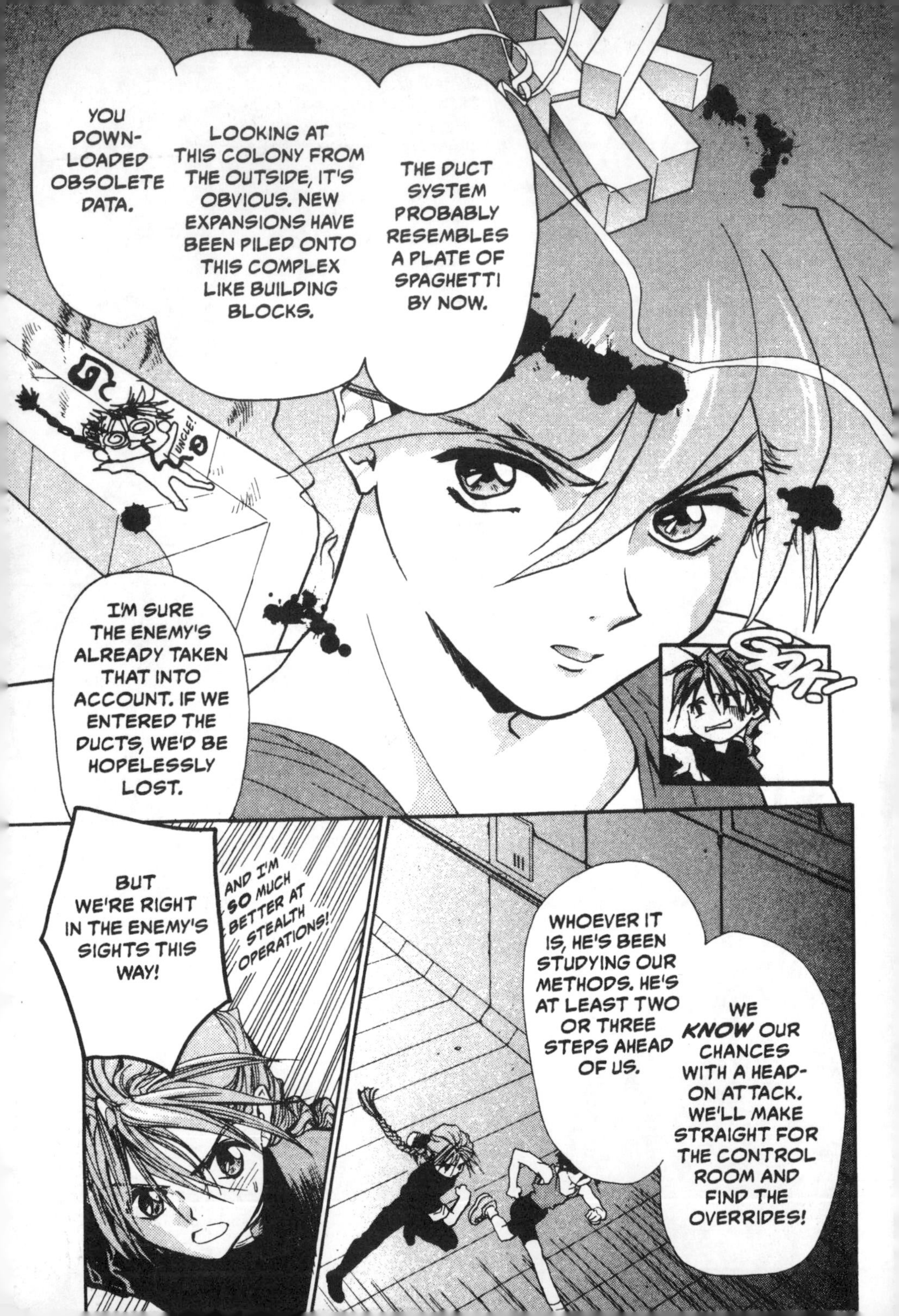

YOU DOWN-LOADED OBSOLETE DATA.
LOOKING AT THIS COLONY FROM THE OUTSIDE, IT'S OBVIOUS. NEW EXPANSIONS HAVE BEEN PILED ONTO THIS COMPLEX LIKE BUILDING BLOCKS.
THE DUCT SYSTEM PROBABLY RESEMBLES A PLATE OF SPAGHETTI BY NOW.
UNCLE!
I'M SURE THE ENEMY'S ALREADY TAKEN THAT INTO ACCOUNT. IF WE ENTERED THE DUCTS, WE'D BE HOPELESSLY LOST.
GAK!
BUT WE'RE RIGHT IN THE ENEMY'S SIGHTS THIS WAY!
AND I'M SO MUCH BETTER AT STEALTH OPERATIONS!
WHOEVER IT IS, HE'S BEEN STUDYING OUR METHODS. HE'S AT LEAST TWO OR THREE STEPS AHEAD OF US.
WE KNOW OUR CHANCES WITH A HEAD-ON ATTACK. WE'LL MAKE STRAIGHT FOR THE CONTROL ROOM AND FIND THE OVERRIDES!

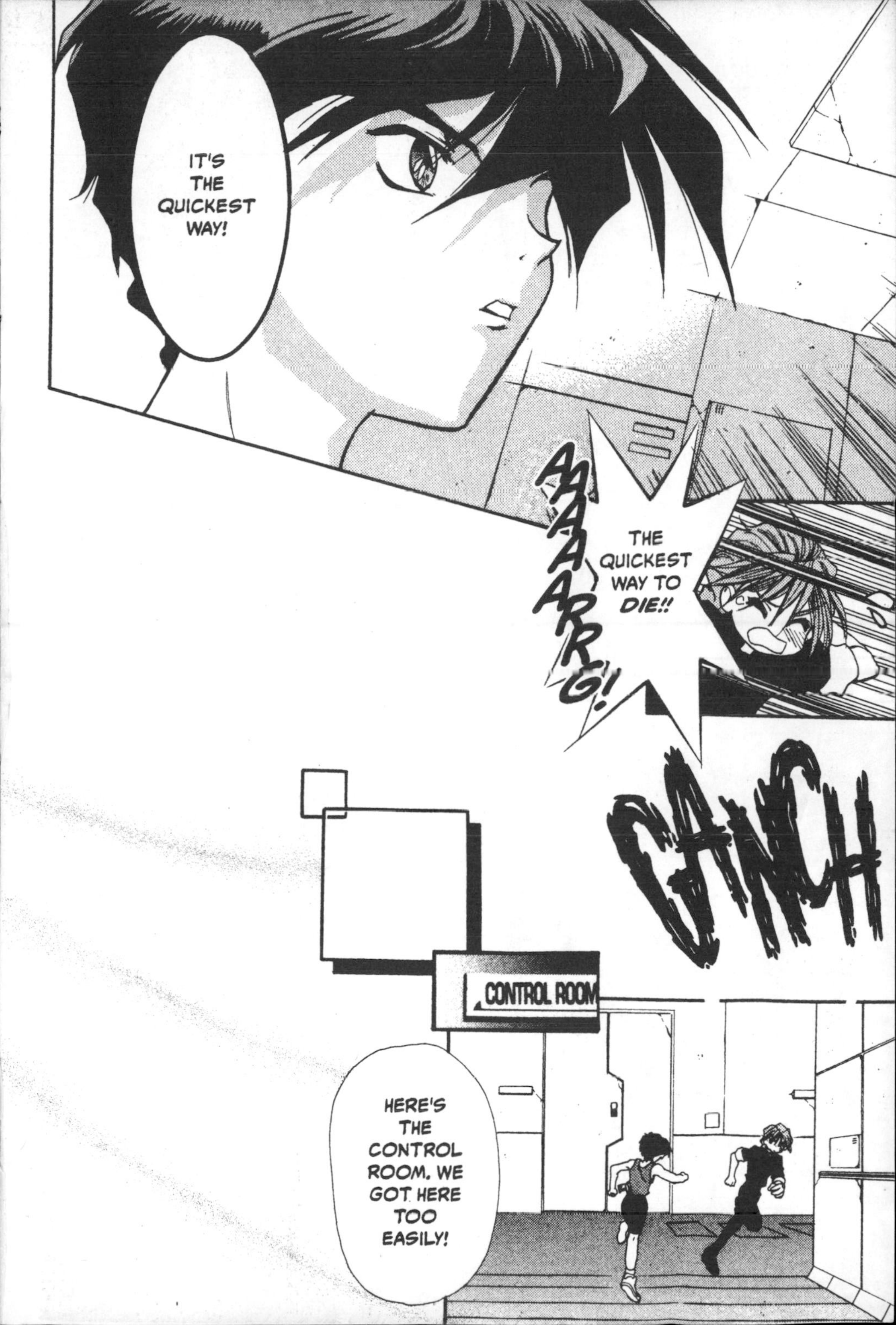
IT'S THE QUICKEST WAY!
AAAAAARRG!
THE QUICKEST WAY TO DIE!!
GANCH
CONTROL ROOM
HERE'S THE CONTROL ROOM. WE GOT HERE TOO EASILY!

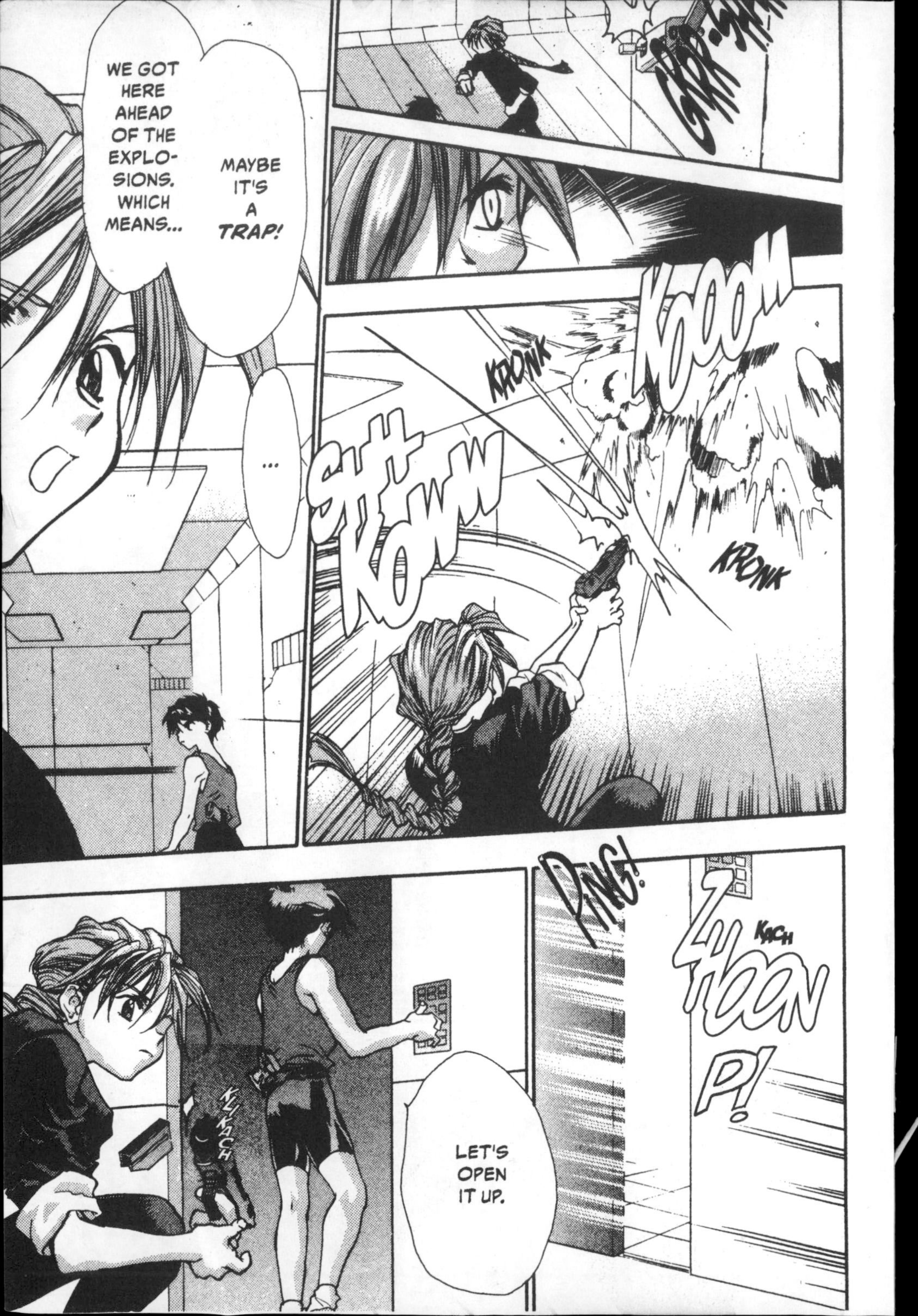
WE GOT HERE AHEAD OF THE EXPLOSIONS. WHICH MEANS...
MAYBE IT'S A TRAP!
...
KRONK
KRONK
KLIKACH
LET'S OPEN IT UP.
DING!
KACH

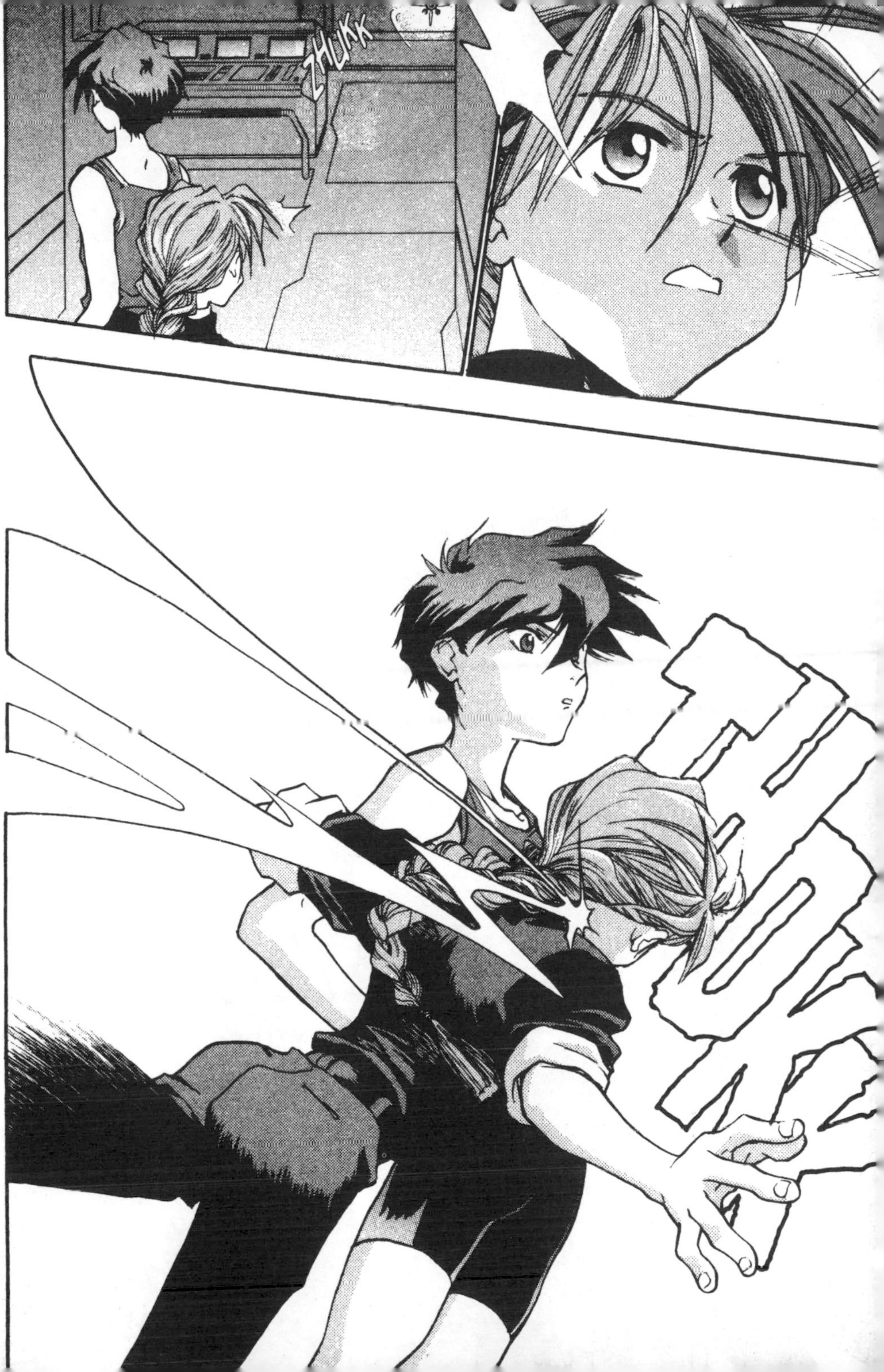
ZHUKK

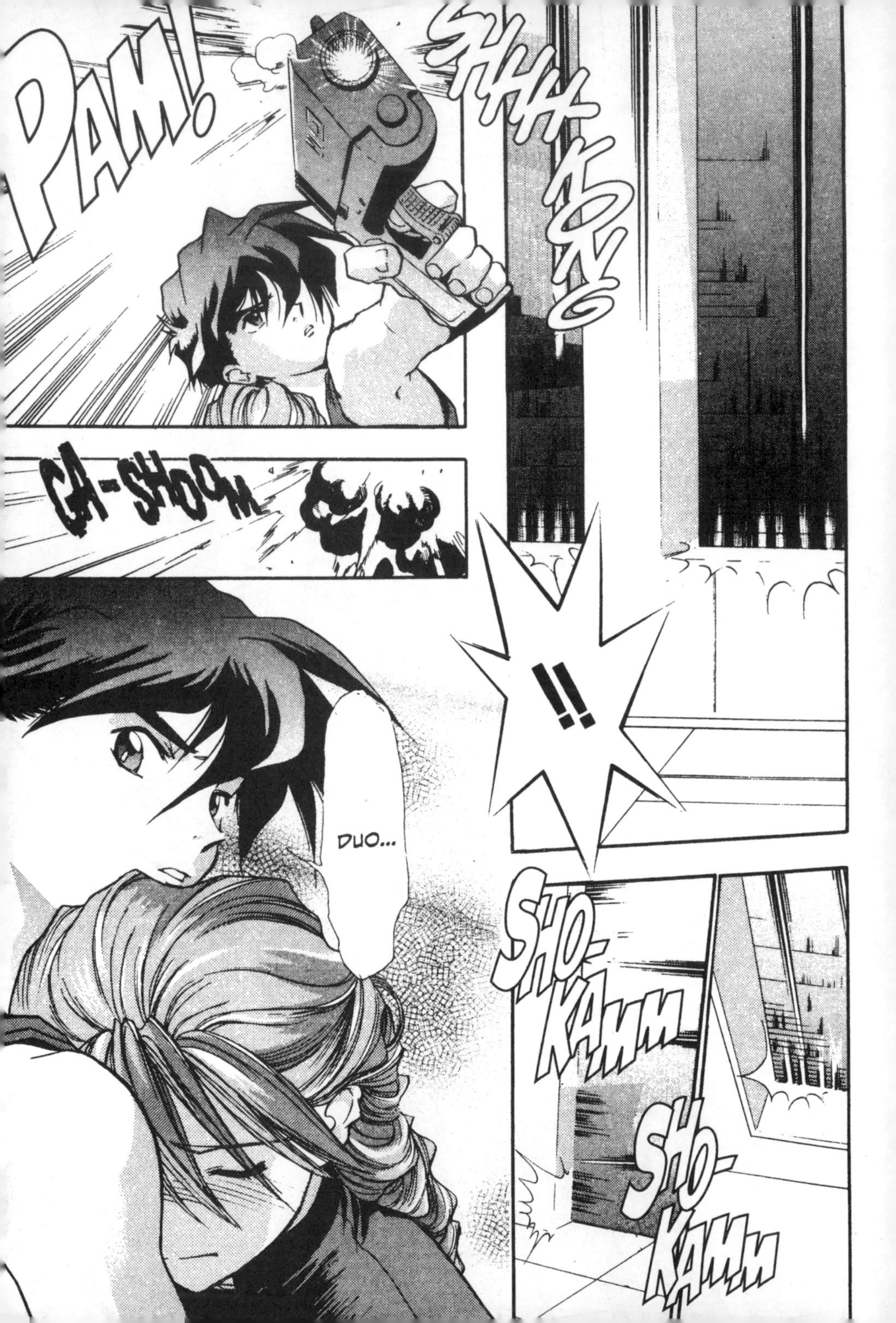
PAM!
SHHH KONG
GA-SHOOM
!!
DUO...
SHO-KAMM
SHO-KAMM

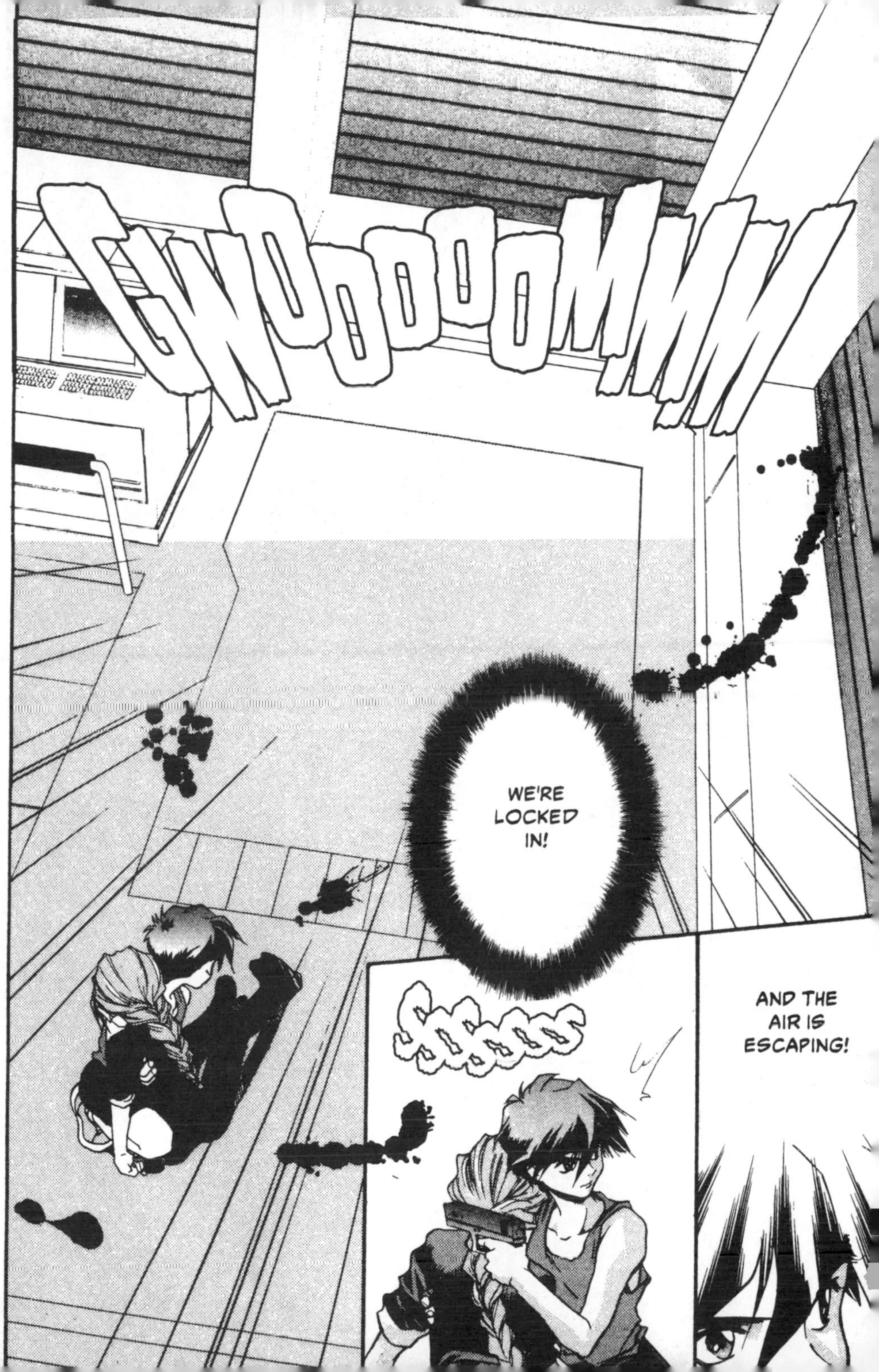
GWOOOOOMMMM
WE'RE LOCKED IN!
SSSSSS
AND THE AIR IS ESCAPING!

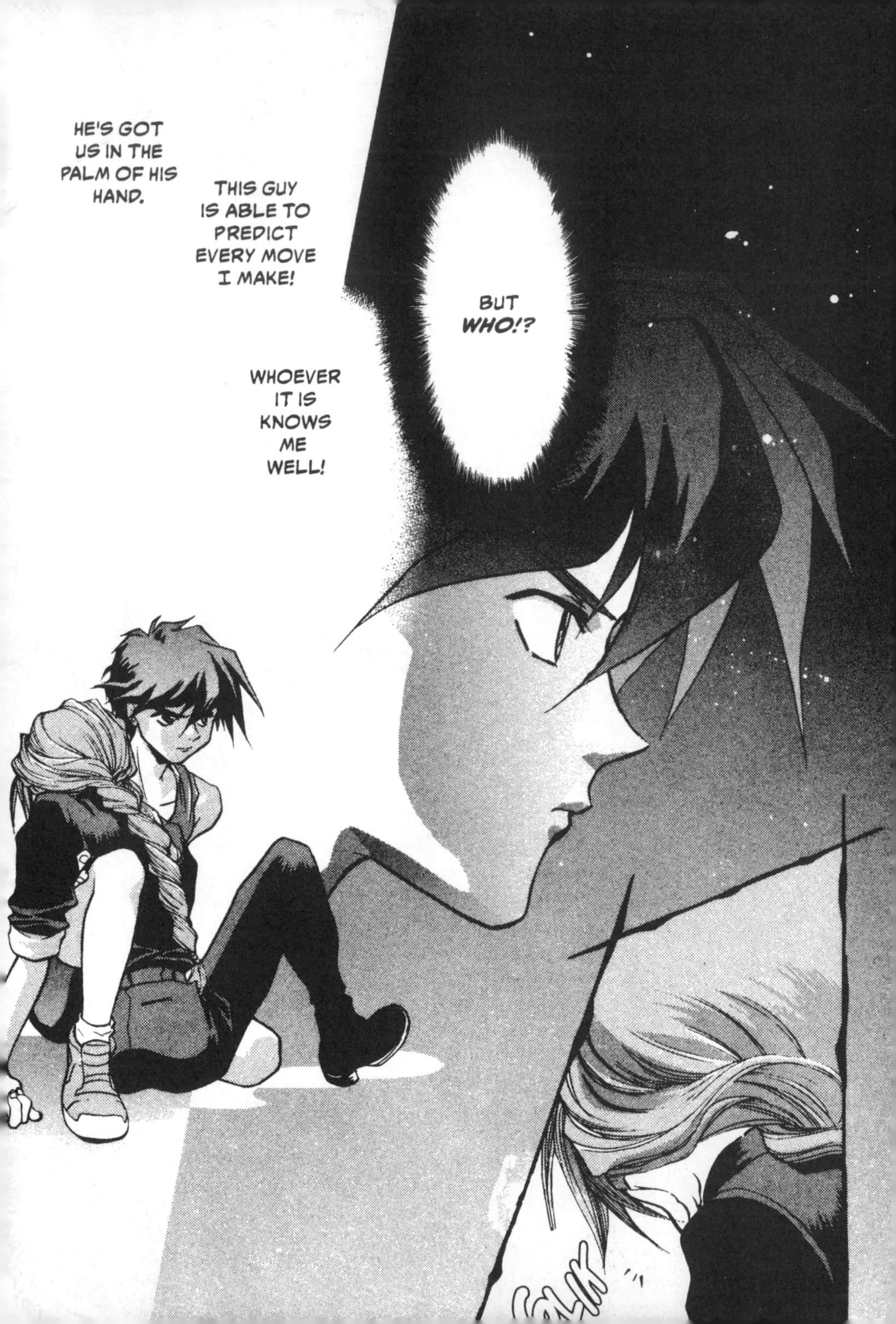
HE'S GOT US IN THE PALM OF HIS HAND.
THIS GUY IS ABLE TO PREDICT EVERY MOVE I MAKE!
BUT *WHO!?*
WHOEVER IT IS KNOWS ME WELL!

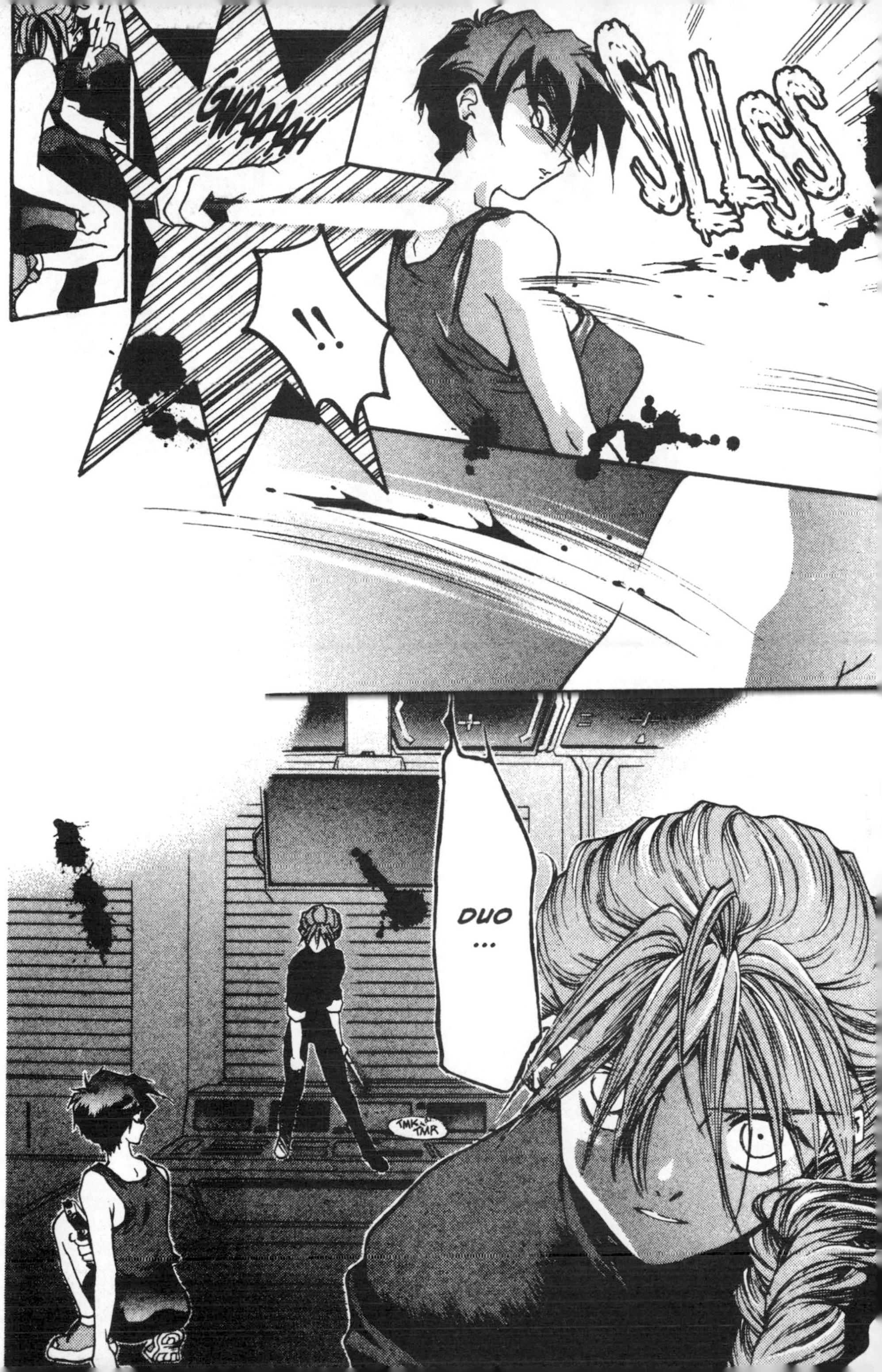
GWAAAAH
!!
DUO
...
TMK TMR

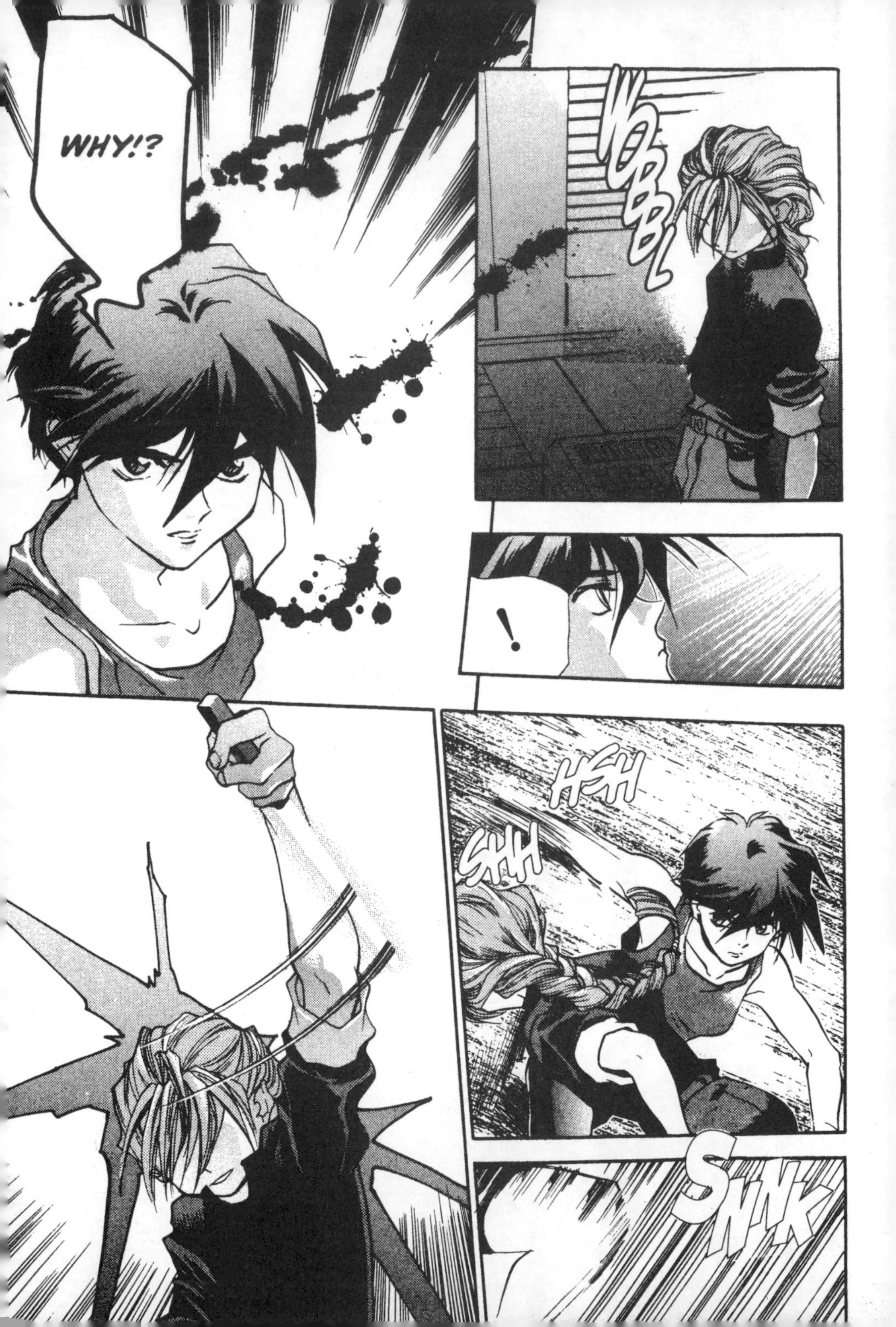
WHY!?
WOBBL
!
HSH
SHH
SNK

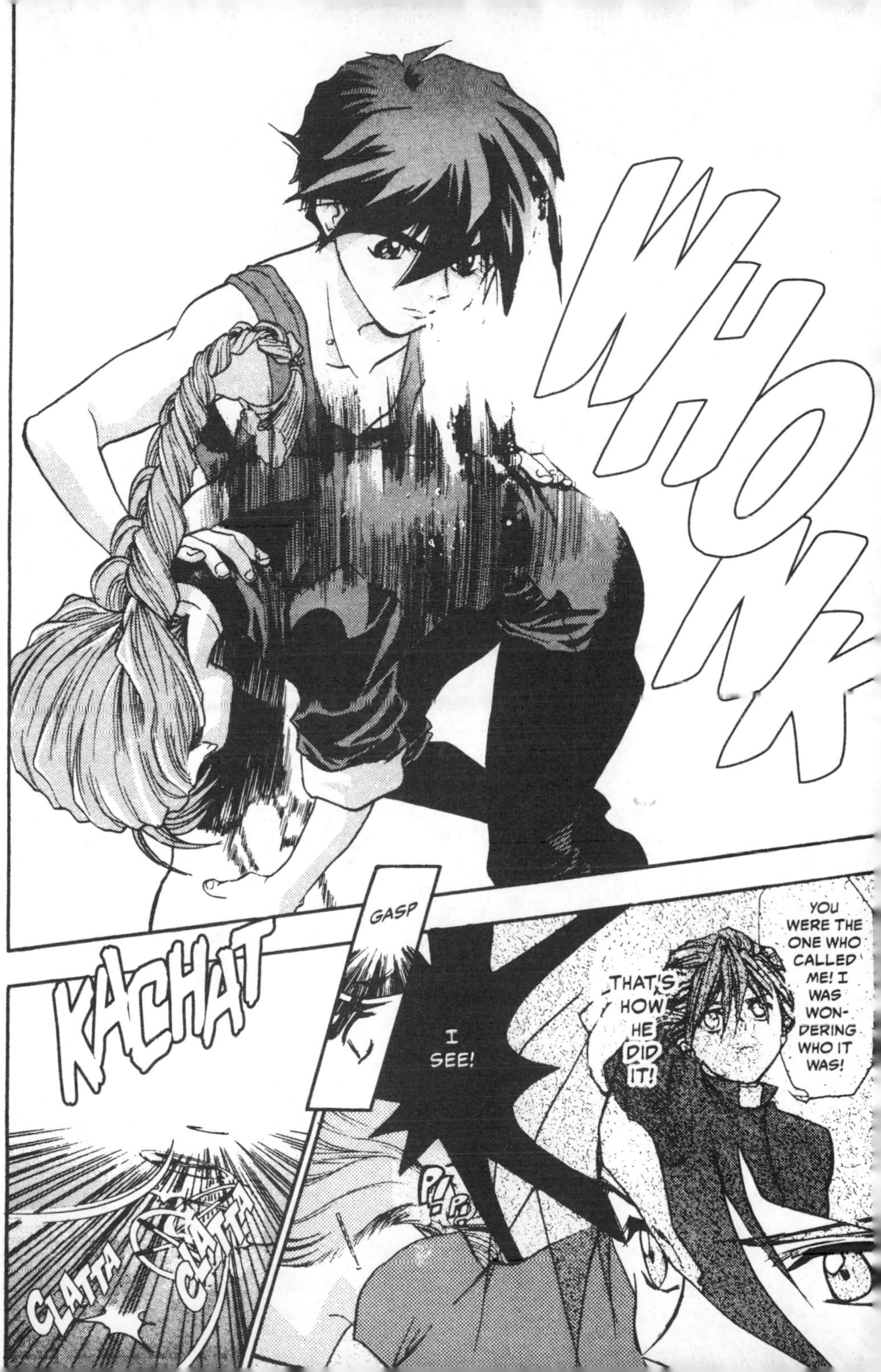
WHONK
KACHAT
CLATTA CLATTA
GASP
I SEE!
PI PI
THAT'S HOW HE DID IT!
YOU WERE THE ONE WHO CALLED ME! I WAS WONDERING WHO IT WAS!

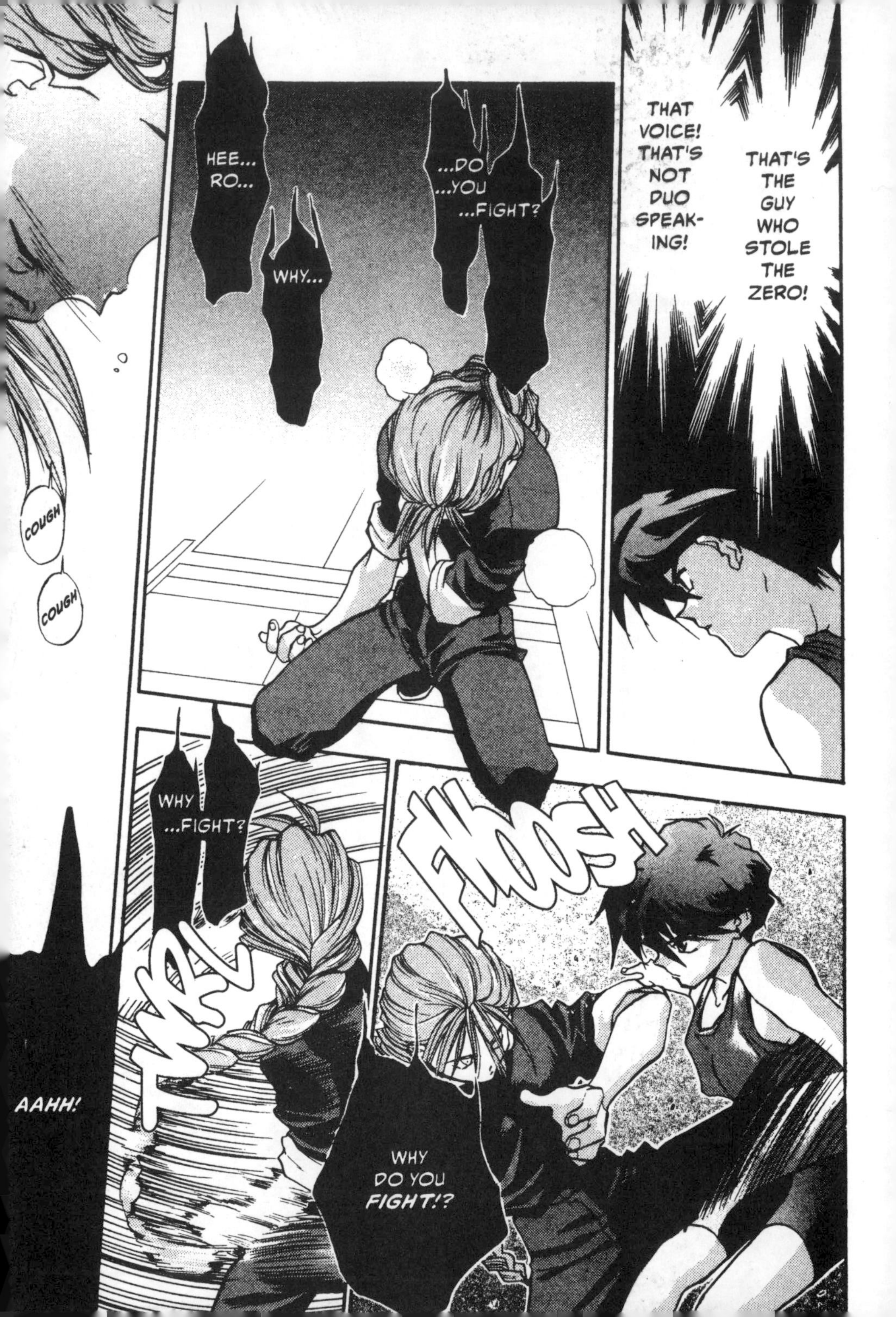

COUGH
COUGH
HEE... RO...
WHY...
...DO ...YOU ...FIGHT?
THAT VOICE! THAT'S NOT DUO SPEAKING!
THAT'S THE GUY WHO STOLE THE ZERO!
AAHH!
WHY ...FIGHT?
TWRL
WHOOSH
WHY DO YOU *FIGHT!?*

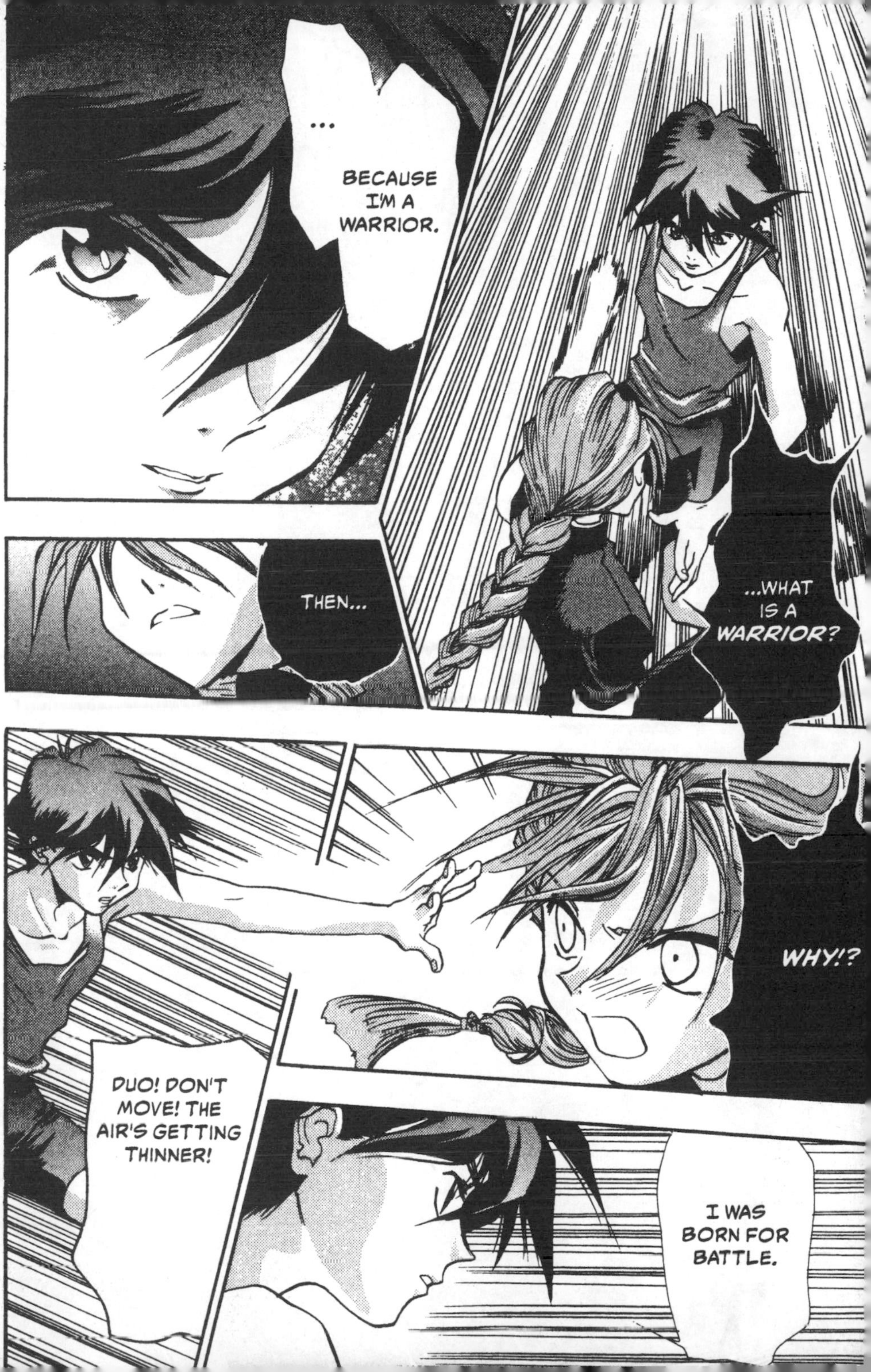
...
BECAUSE I'M A WARRIOR.
THEN...
...WHAT IS A *WARRIOR?*
DUO! DON'T MOVE! THE AIR'S GETTING THINNER!
WHY!?
I WAS BORN FOR BATTLE.

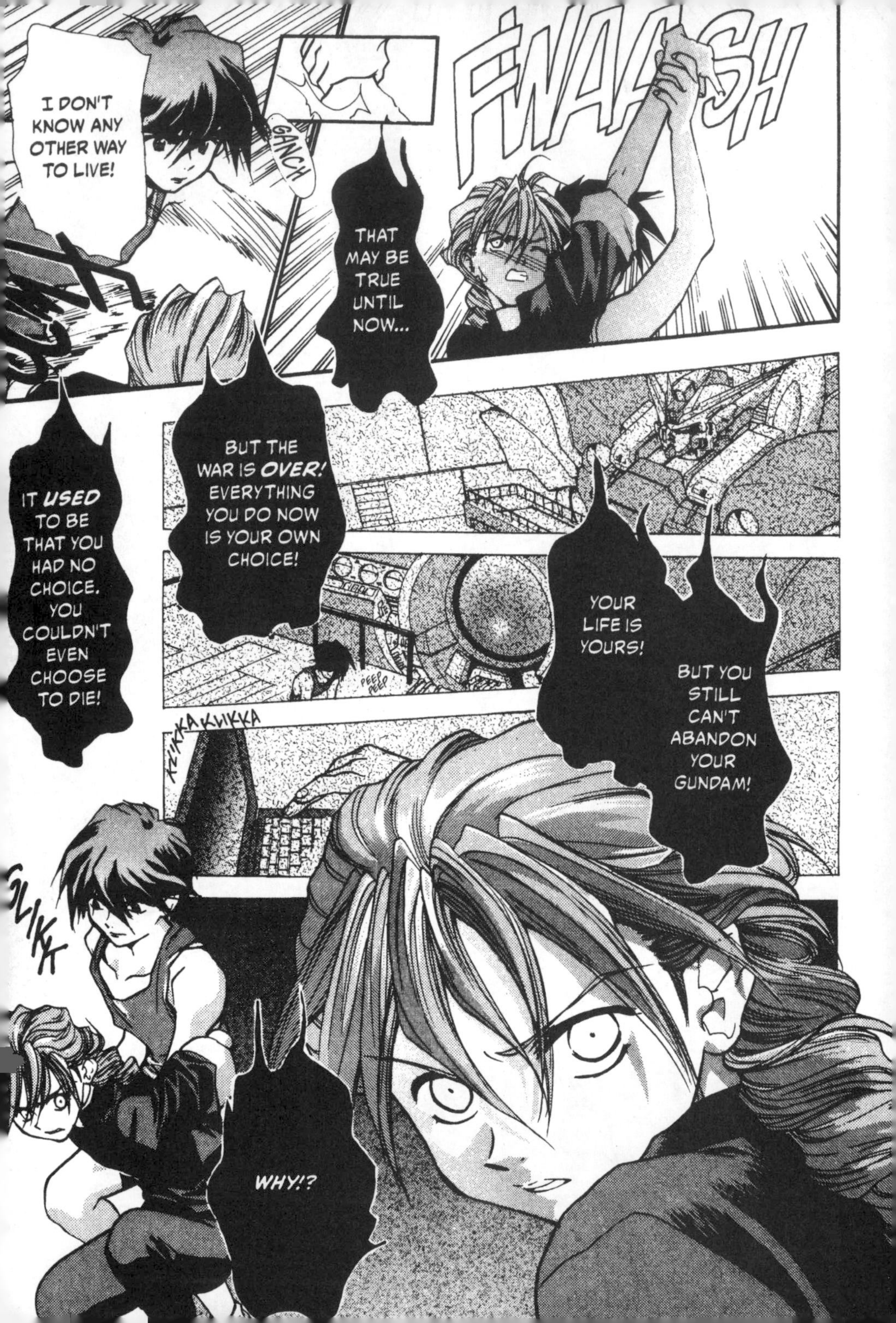
I DON'T KNOW ANY OTHER WAY TO LIVE!
GANCH
FWAASH
THAT MAY BE TRUE UNTIL NOW...
IT USED TO BE THAT YOU HAD NO CHOICE. YOU COULDN'T EVEN CHOOSE TO DIE!
BUT THE WAR IS OVER! EVERYTHING YOU DO NOW IS YOUR OWN CHOICE!
PEEP PEEP
YOUR LIFE IS YOURS!
BUT YOU STILL CAN'T ABANDON YOUR GUNDAM!
KLIKKA KLIKKA
GLIKK
WHY!?

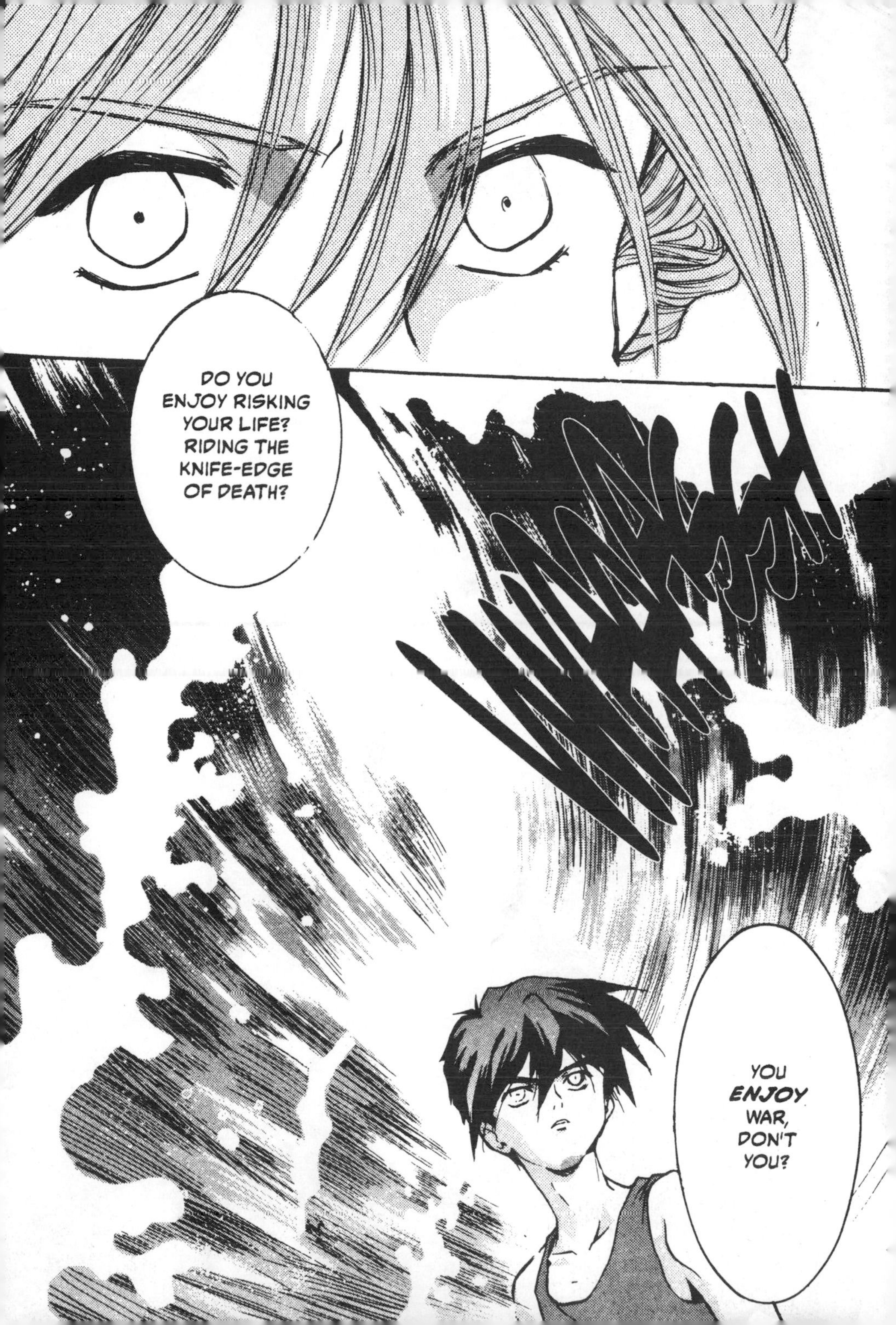
DO YOU ENJOY RISKING YOUR LIFE? RIDING THE KNIFE-EDGE OF DEATH?
YOU ENJOY WAR, DON'T YOU?

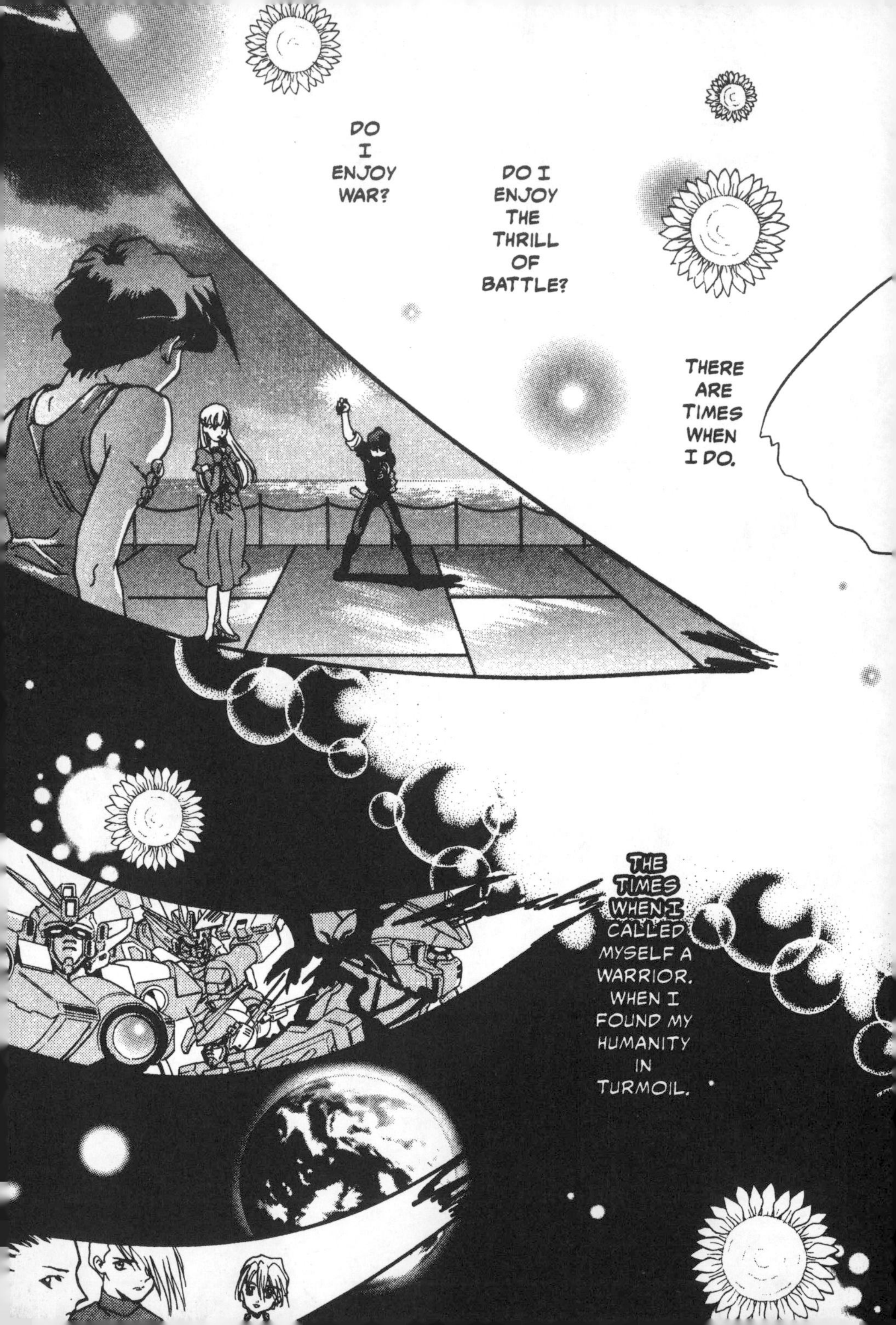
DO I ENJOY WAR?
DO I ENJOY THE THRILL OF BATTLE?
THERE ARE TIMES WHEN I DO.
THE TIMES WHEN I CALLED MYSELF A WARRIOR. WHEN I FOUND MY HUMANITY IN TURMOIL.

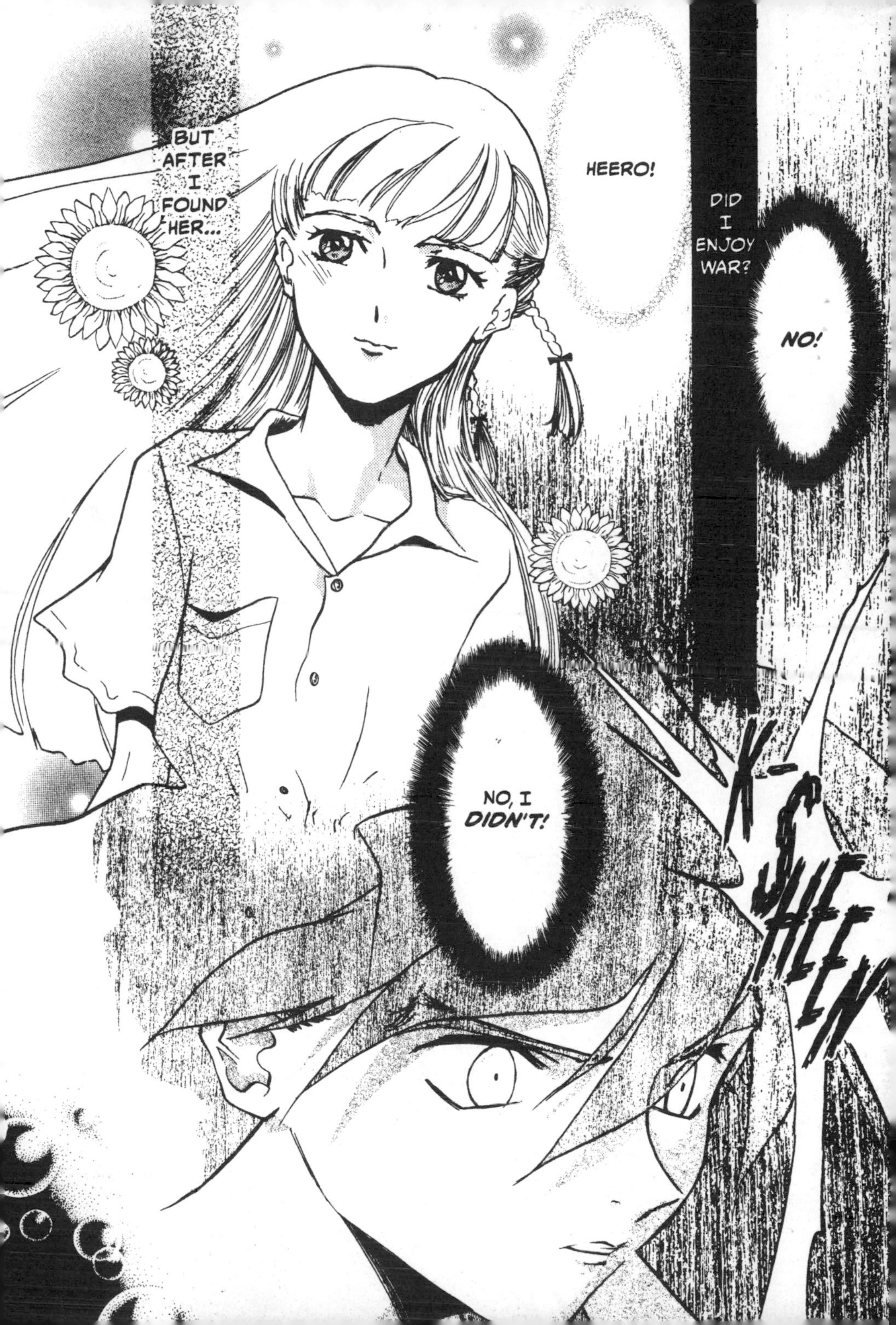
BUT AFTER I FOUND HER...
HEERO!
DID I ENJOY WAR?
NO!
NO, I DIDN'T!
K-SHEEN

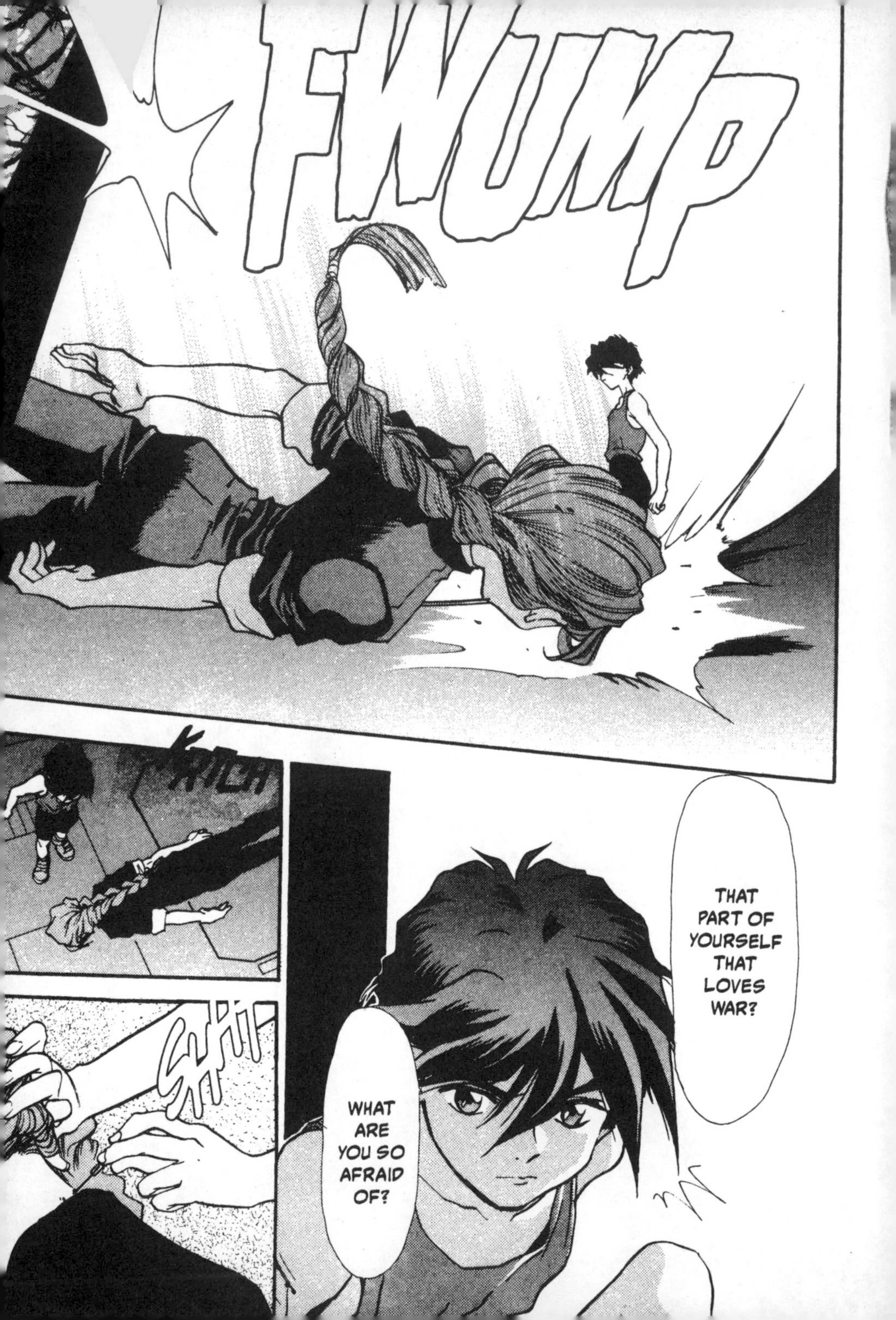
FWUMP
WHAT ARE YOU SO AFRAID OF?
THAT PART OF YOURSELF THAT LOVES WAR?

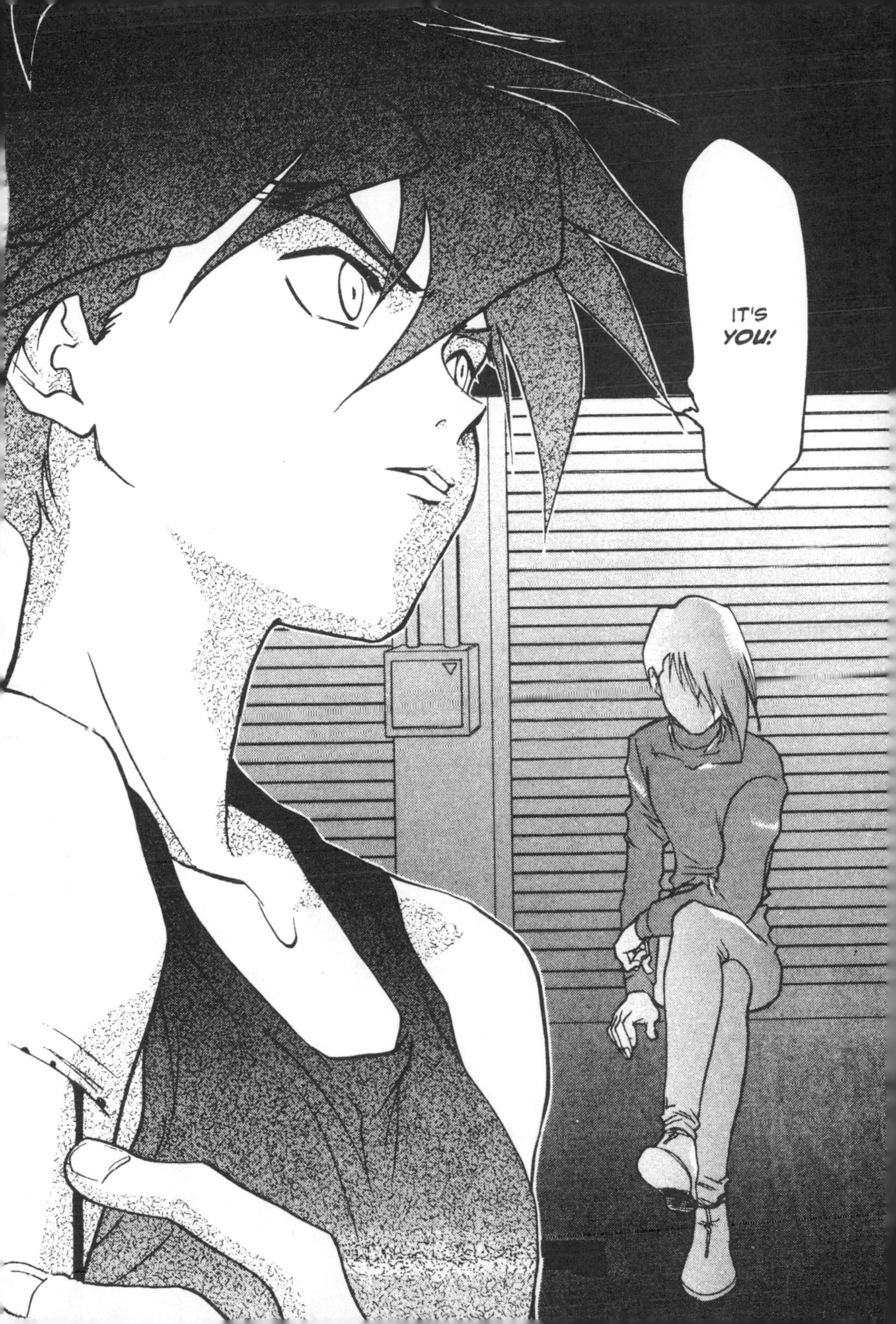
IT'S YOU!

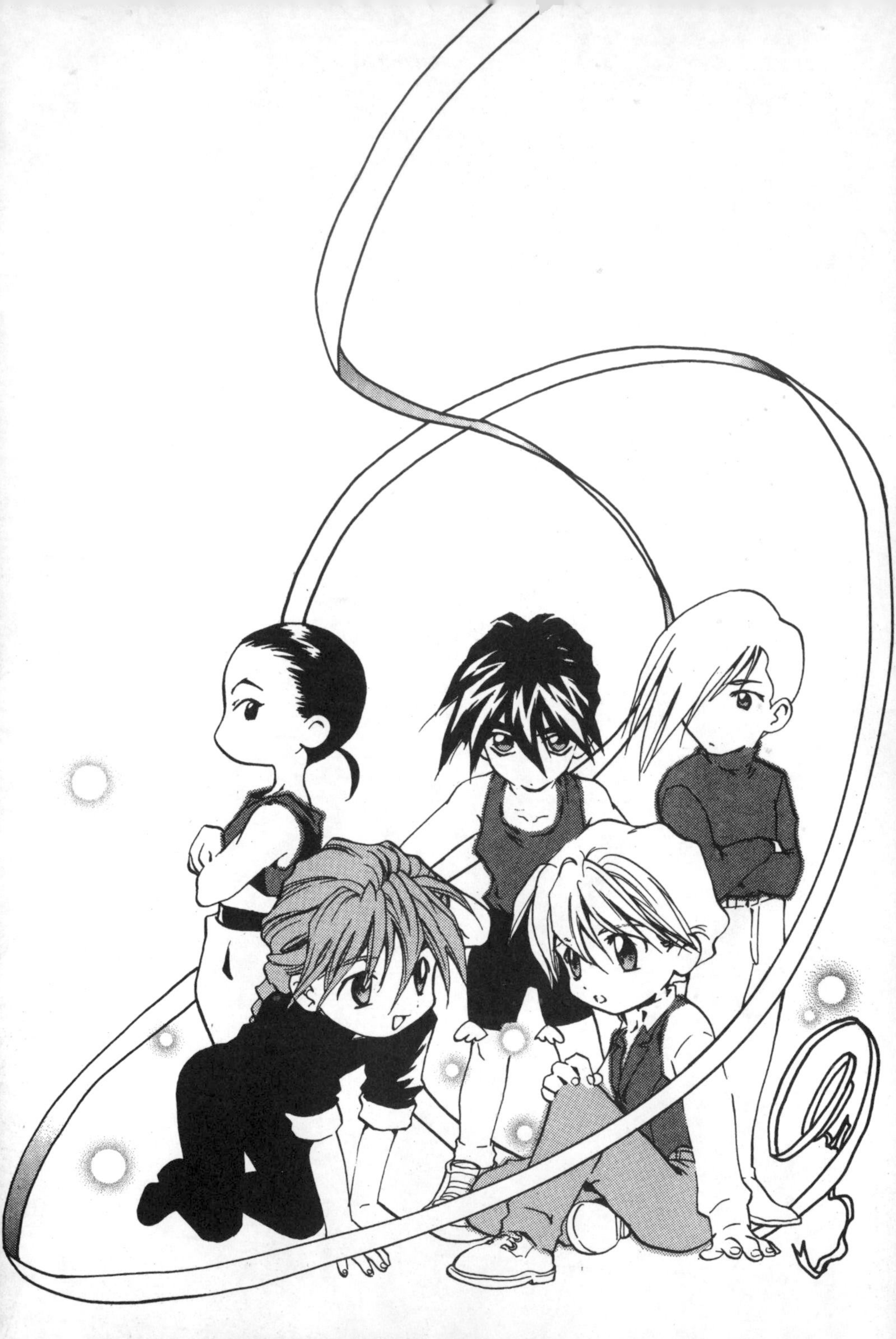

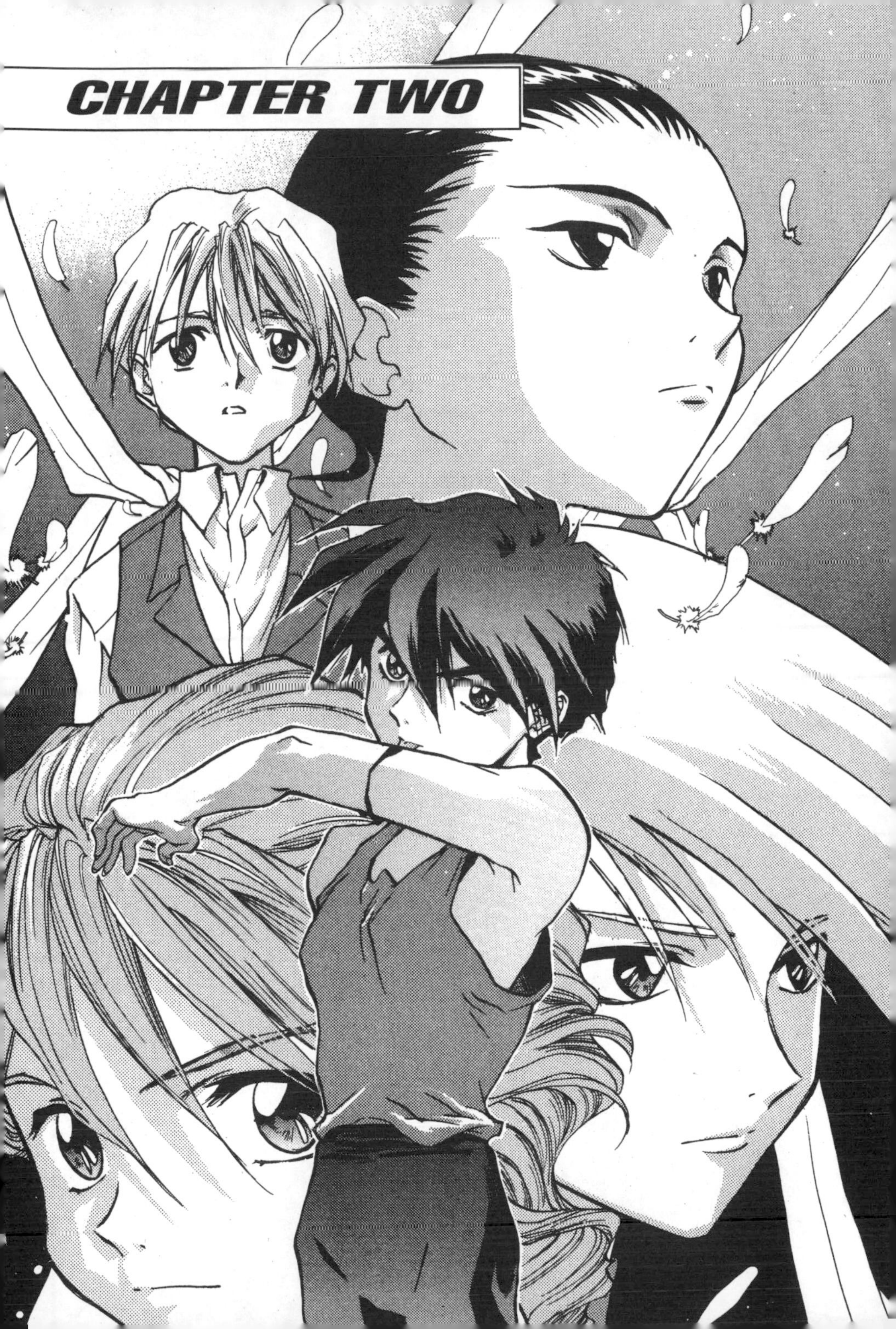
CHAPTER TWO

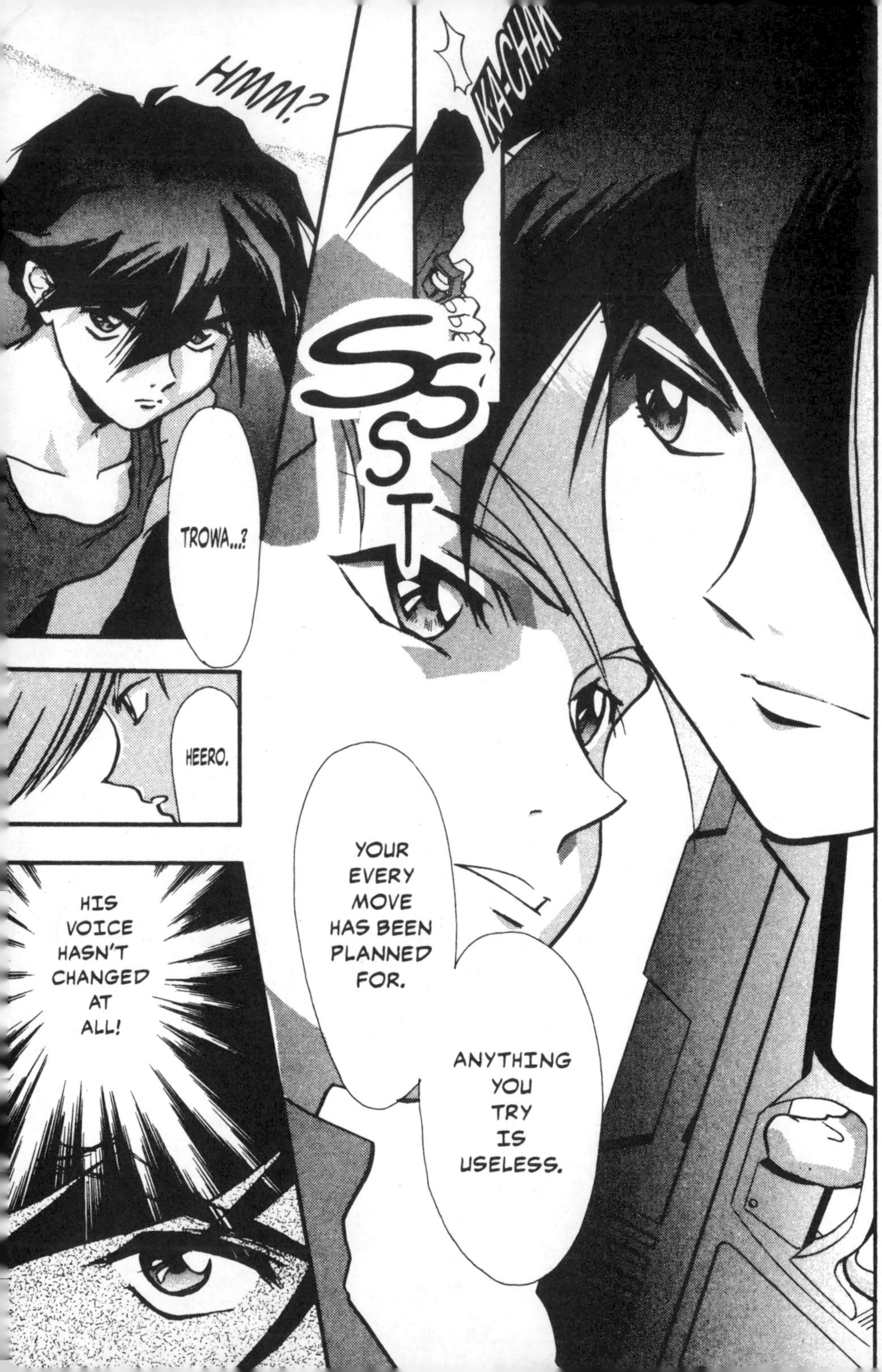
HMM?
TROWA...?
HEERO.
HIS VOICE HASN'T CHANGED AT ALL!
KA-CHAK
SSST
YOUR EVERY MOVE HAS BEEN PLANNED FOR.
ANYTHING YOU TRY IS USELESS.

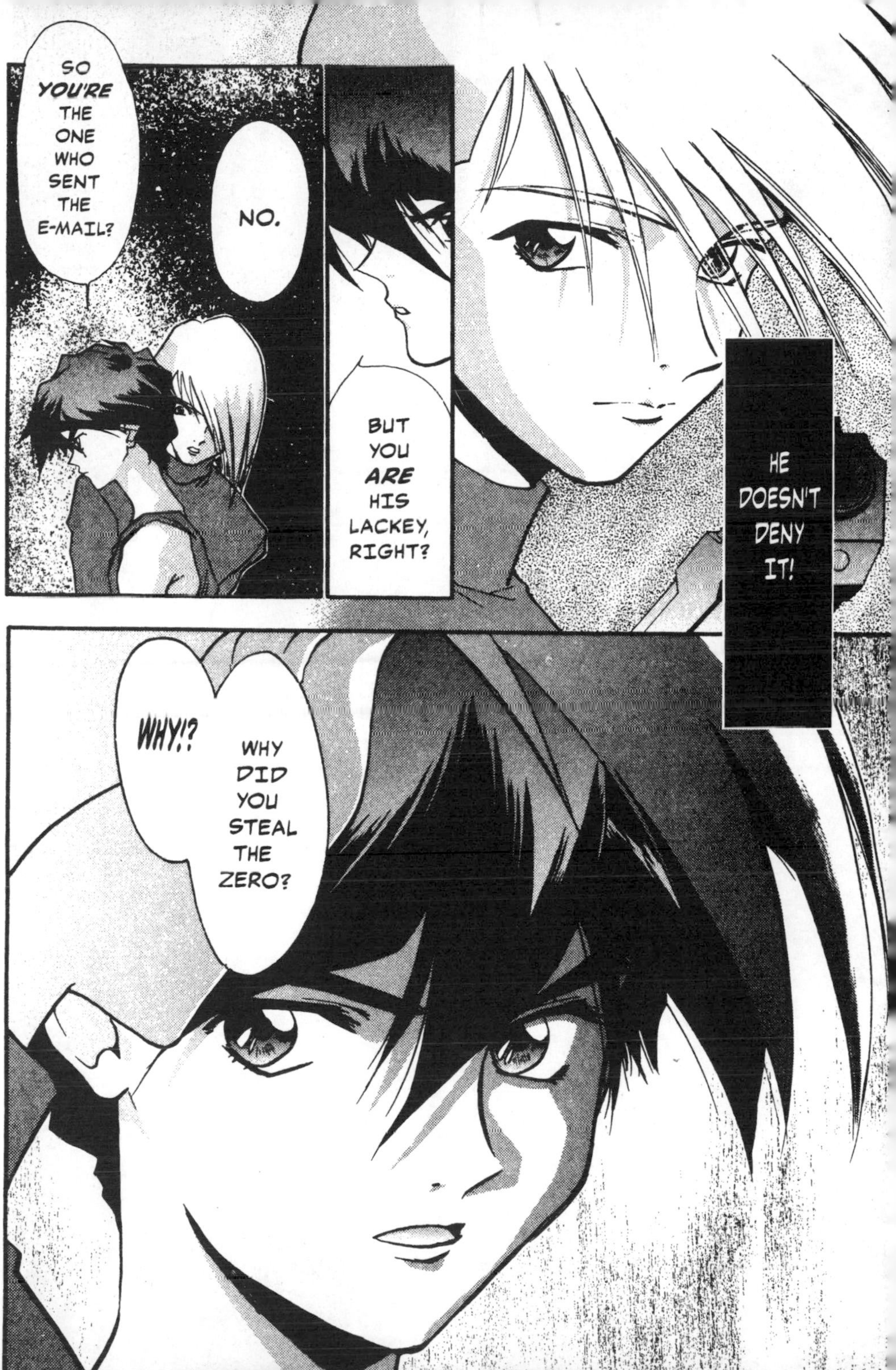
SO YOU'RE THE ONE WHO SENT THE E-MAIL?
NO.
BUT YOU ARE HIS LACKEY, RIGHT?
HE DOESN'T DENY IT!
WHY!?
WHY DID YOU STEAL THE ZERO?

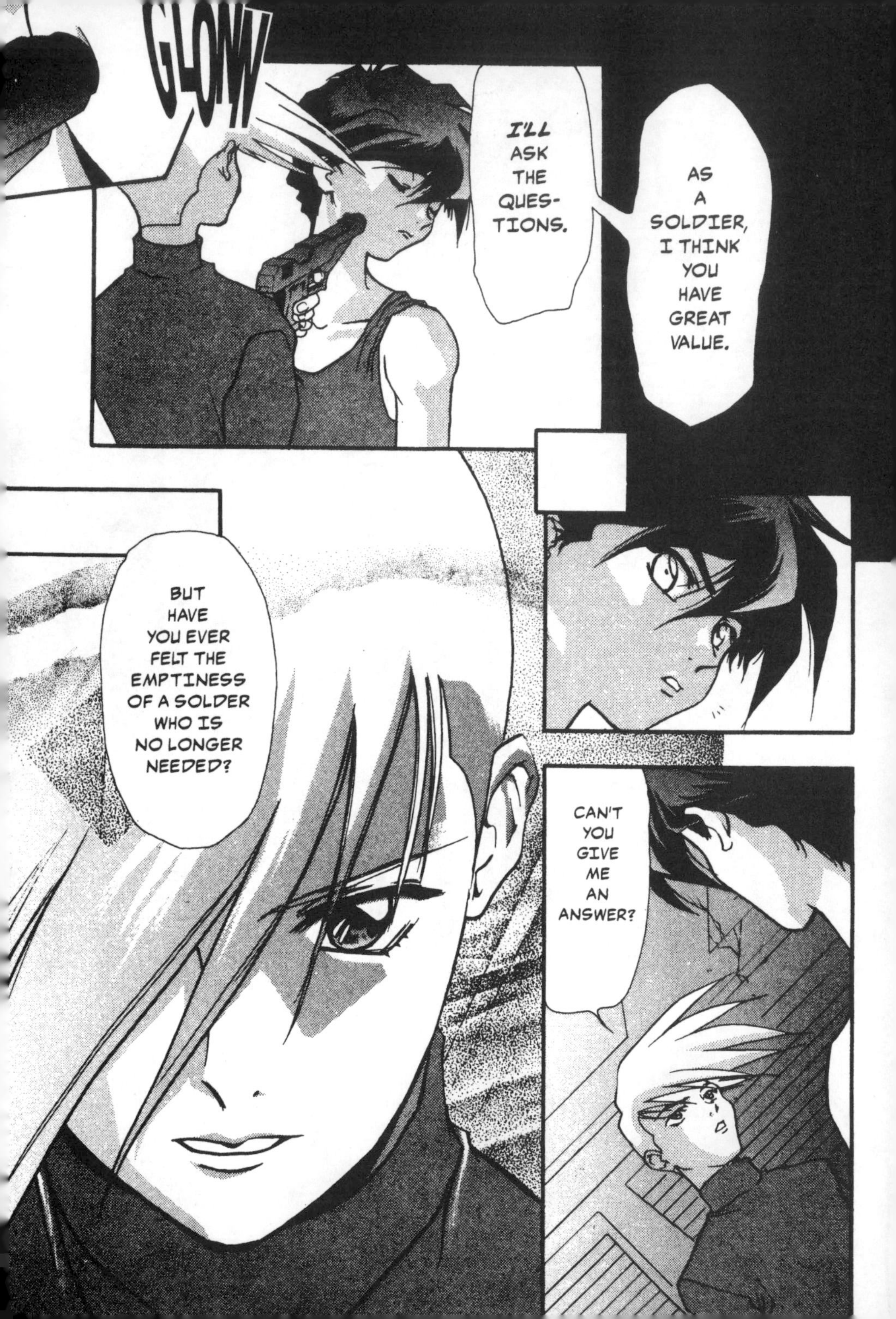
GLOWW
I'LL ASK THE QUES- TIONS.
AS A SOLDIER, I THINK YOU HAVE GREAT VALUE.
BUT HAVE YOU EVER FELT THE EMPTINESS OF A SOLDER WHO IS NO LONGER NEEDED?
CAN'T YOU GIVE ME AN ANSWER?

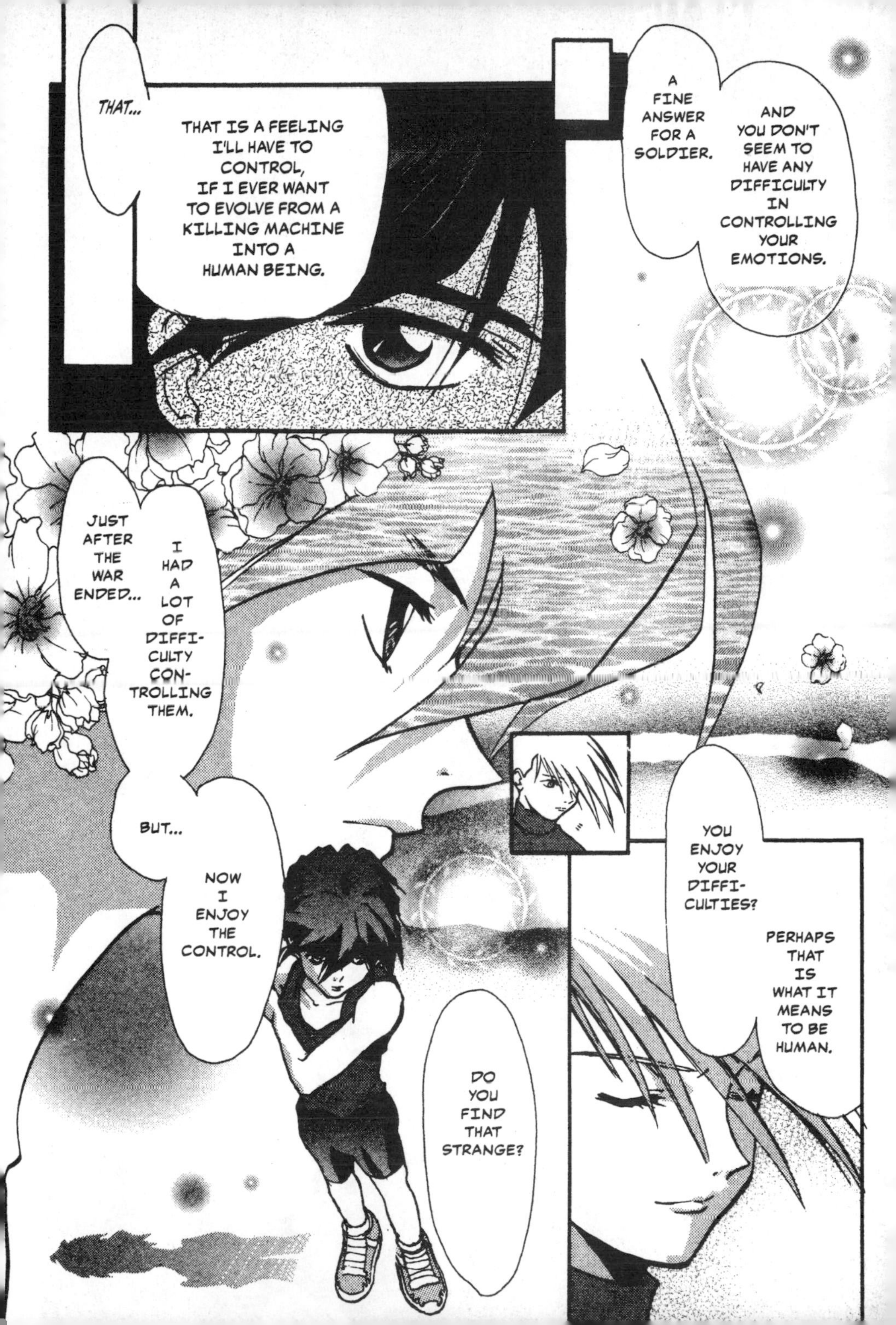
THAT...
THAT IS A FEELING I'LL HAVE TO CONTROL, IF I EVER WANT TO EVOLVE FROM A KILLING MACHINE INTO A HUMAN BEING.
A FINE ANSWER FOR A SOLDIER.
AND YOU DON'T SEEM TO HAVE ANY DIFFICULTY IN CONTROLLING YOUR EMOTIONS.
JUST AFTER THE WAR ENDED...
I HAD A LOT OF DIFFI-CULTY CON-TROLLING THEM.
BUT...
NOW I ENJOY THE CONTROL.
DO YOU FIND THAT STRANGE?
YOU ENJOY YOUR DIFFI-CULTIES?
PERHAPS THAT IS WHAT IT MEANS TO BE HUMAN.

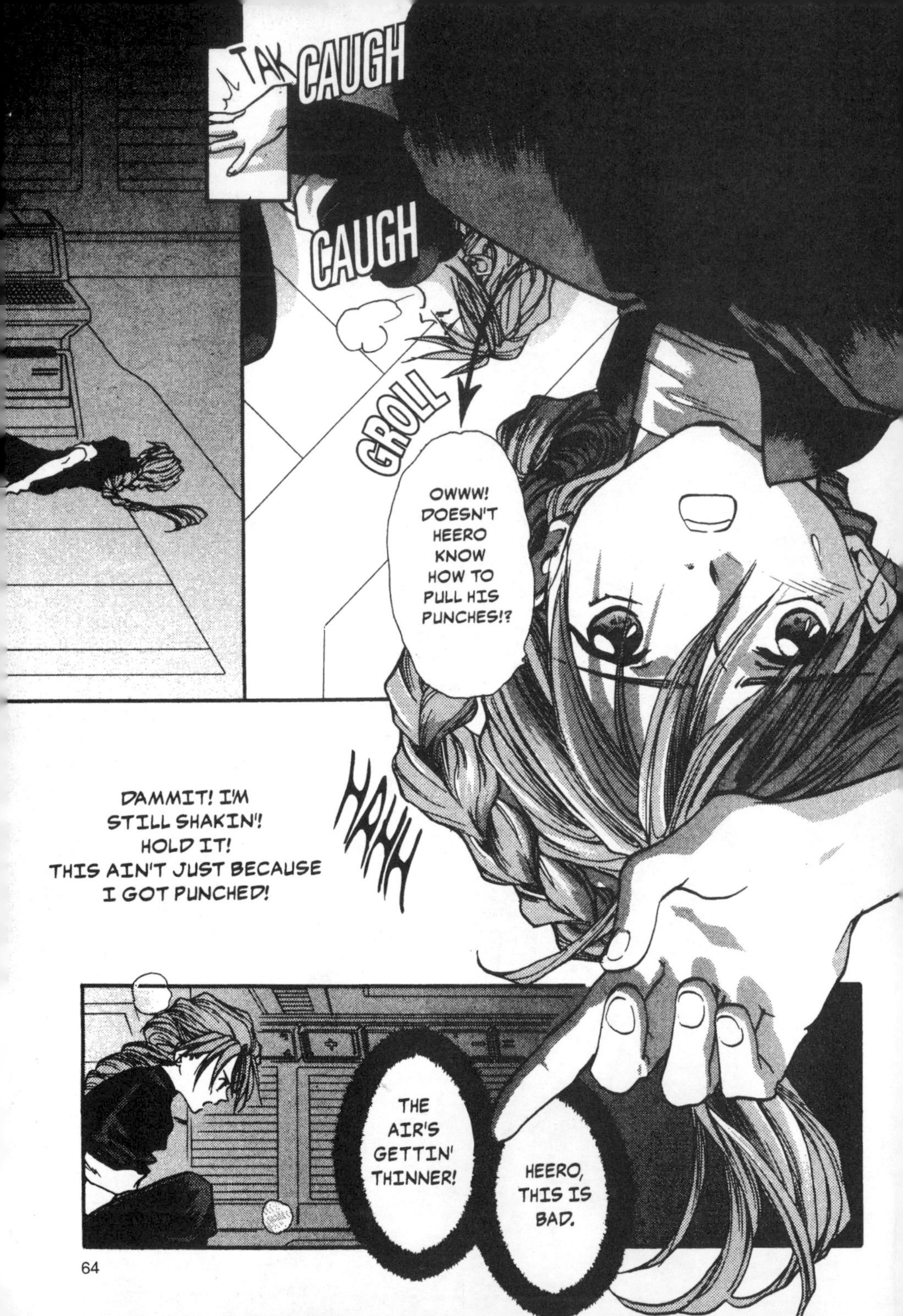
TAK
CAUGH
CAUGH
GROLL
OWWW! DOESN'T HEERO KNOW HOW TO PULL HIS PUNCHES!?
DAMMIT! I'M STILL SHAKIN'! HOLD IT! THIS AIN'T JUST BECAUSE I GOT PUNCHED!
HAHH
THE AIR'S GETTIN' THINNER!
HEERO, THIS IS BAD.

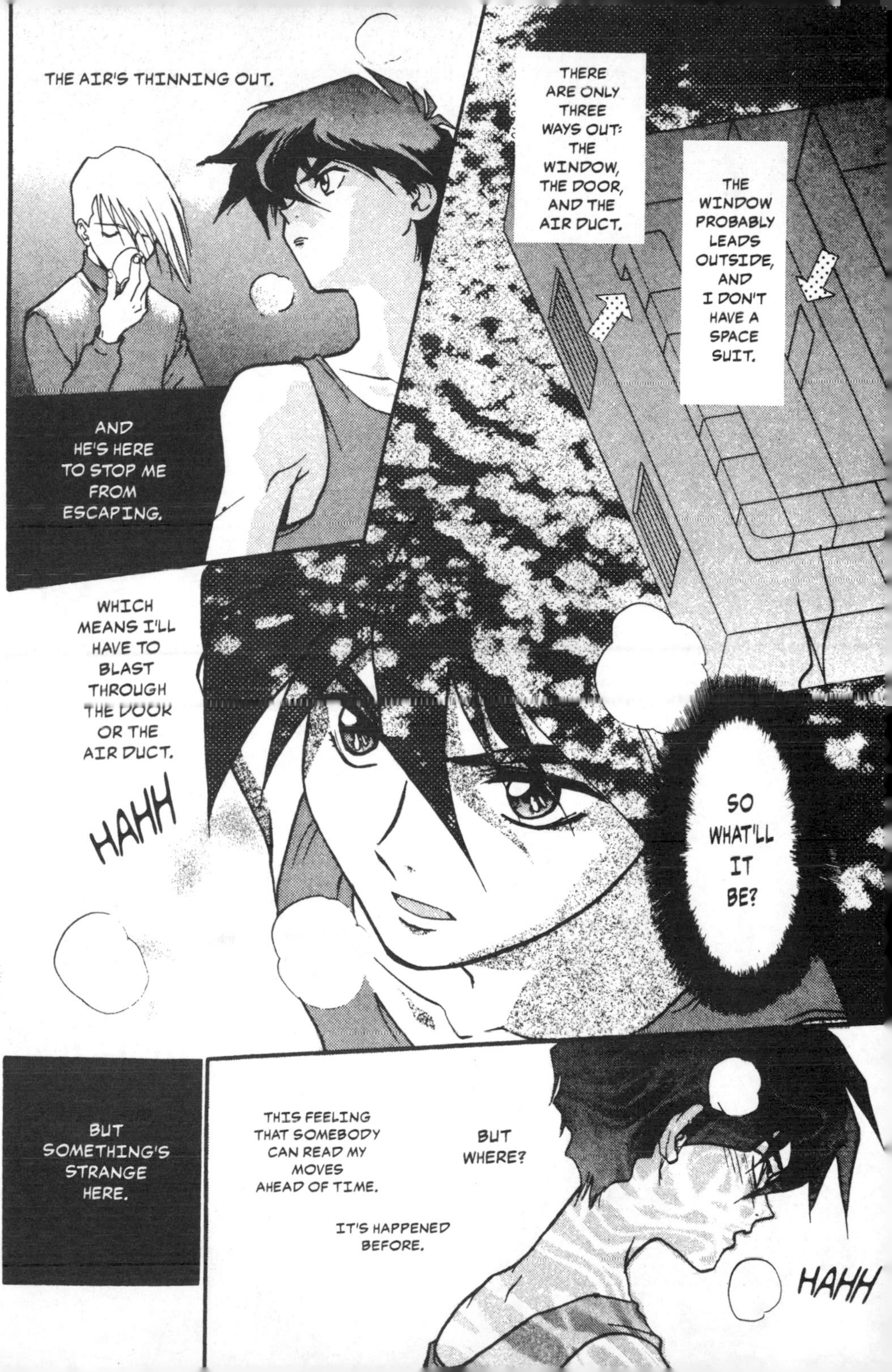
THE AIR'S THINNING OUT.
AND HE'S HERE TO STOP ME FROM ESCAPING.
THERE ARE ONLY THREE WAYS OUT: THE WINDOW, THE DOOR, AND THE AIR DUCT.
THE WINDOW PROBABLY LEADS OUTSIDE, AND I DON'T HAVE A SPACE SUIT.
WHICH MEANS I'LL HAVE TO BLAST THROUGH THE DOOR OR THE AIR DUCT.
HAHH
SO WHAT'LL IT BE?
BUT SOMETHING'S STRANGE HERE.
THIS FEELING THAT SOMEBODY CAN READ MY MOVES AHEAD OF TIME.
BUT WHERE?
IT'S HAPPENED BEFORE.
HAHH

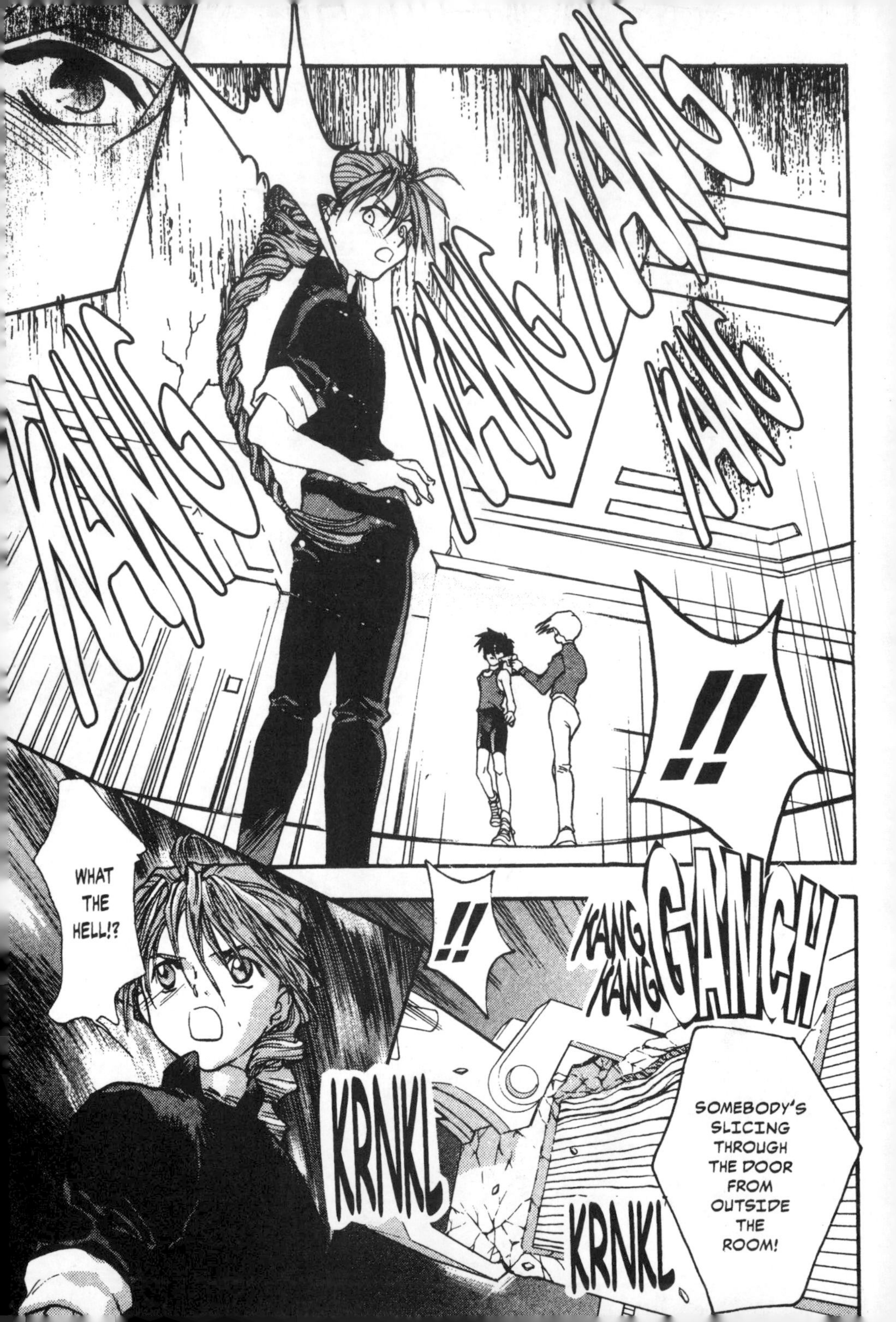
KANG
KANG KANG KANG
KANG
!!
WHAT THE HELL!?
!!
KANG KANG
GANCH
KRNKL
KRNKL
SOMEBODY'S SLICING THROUGH THE DOOR FROM OUTSIDE THE ROOM!

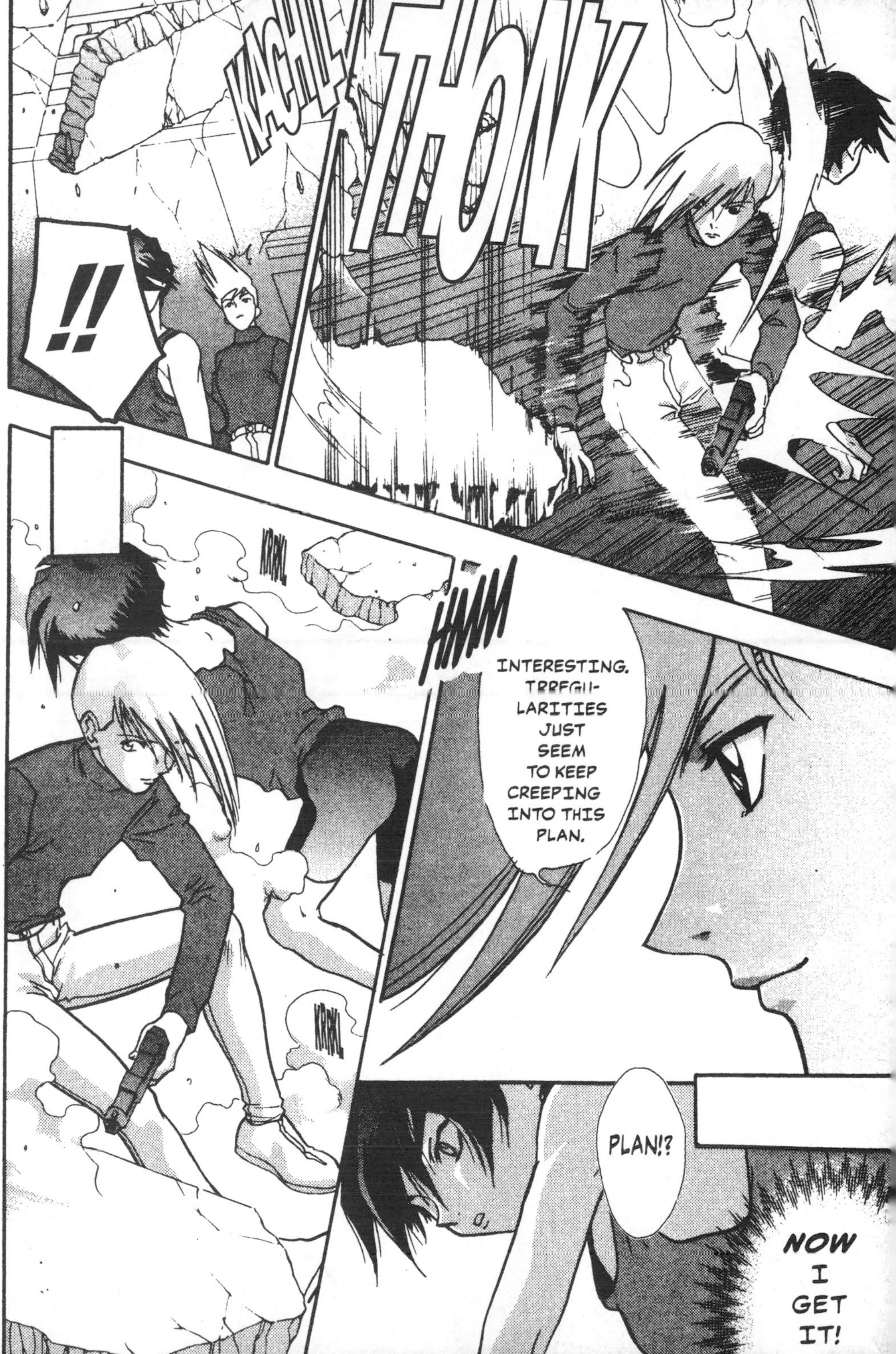
KACHU
THONK
!!
KRRKL
INTERESTING. IRREGU-LARITIES JUST SEEM TO KEEP CREEPING INTO THIS PLAN.
KRRKL
PLAN!?
NOW I GET IT!

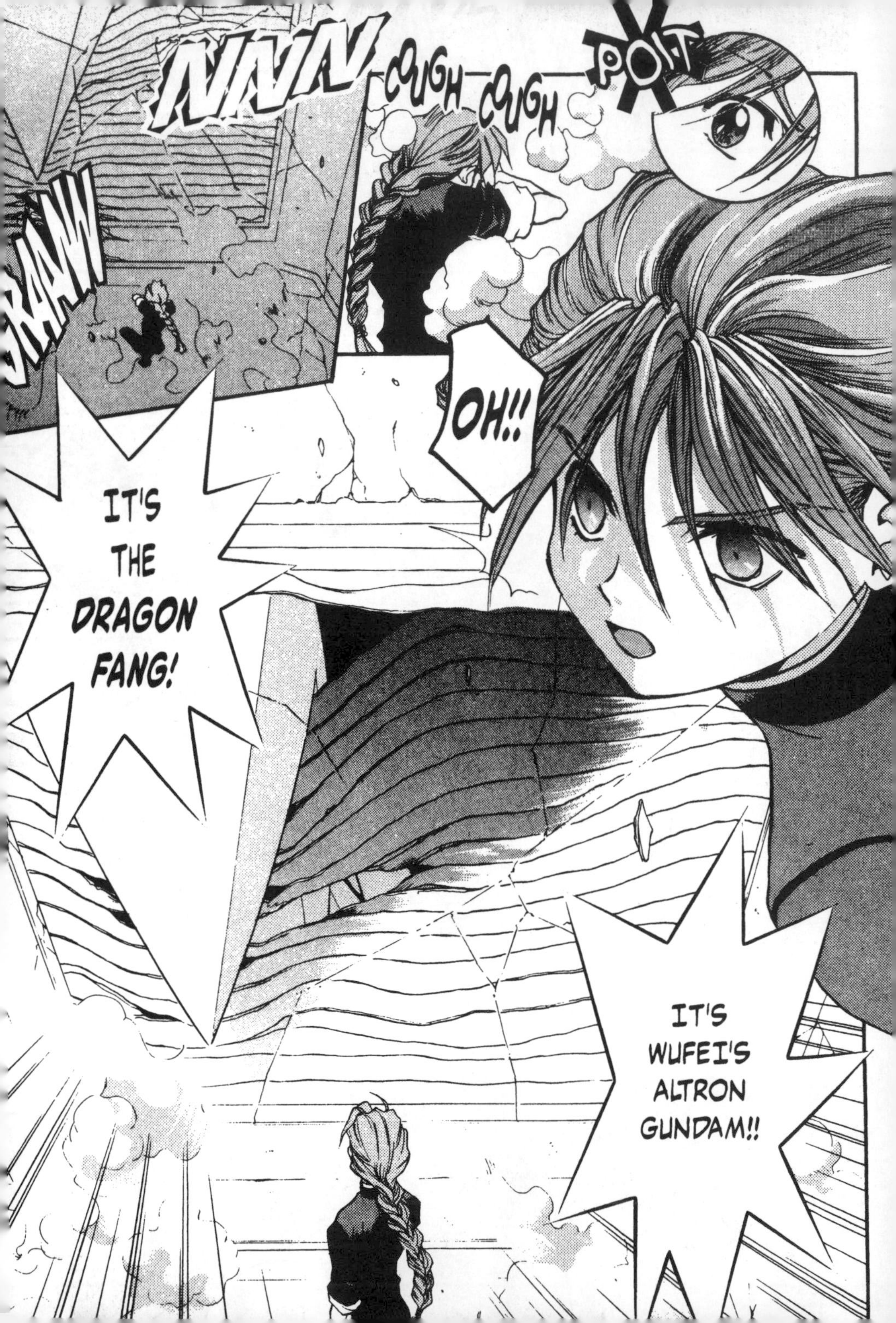

NNN
COUGH COUGH
POI
OH!!
IT'S THE DRAGON FANG!
IT'S WUFEI'S ALTRON GUNDAM!!

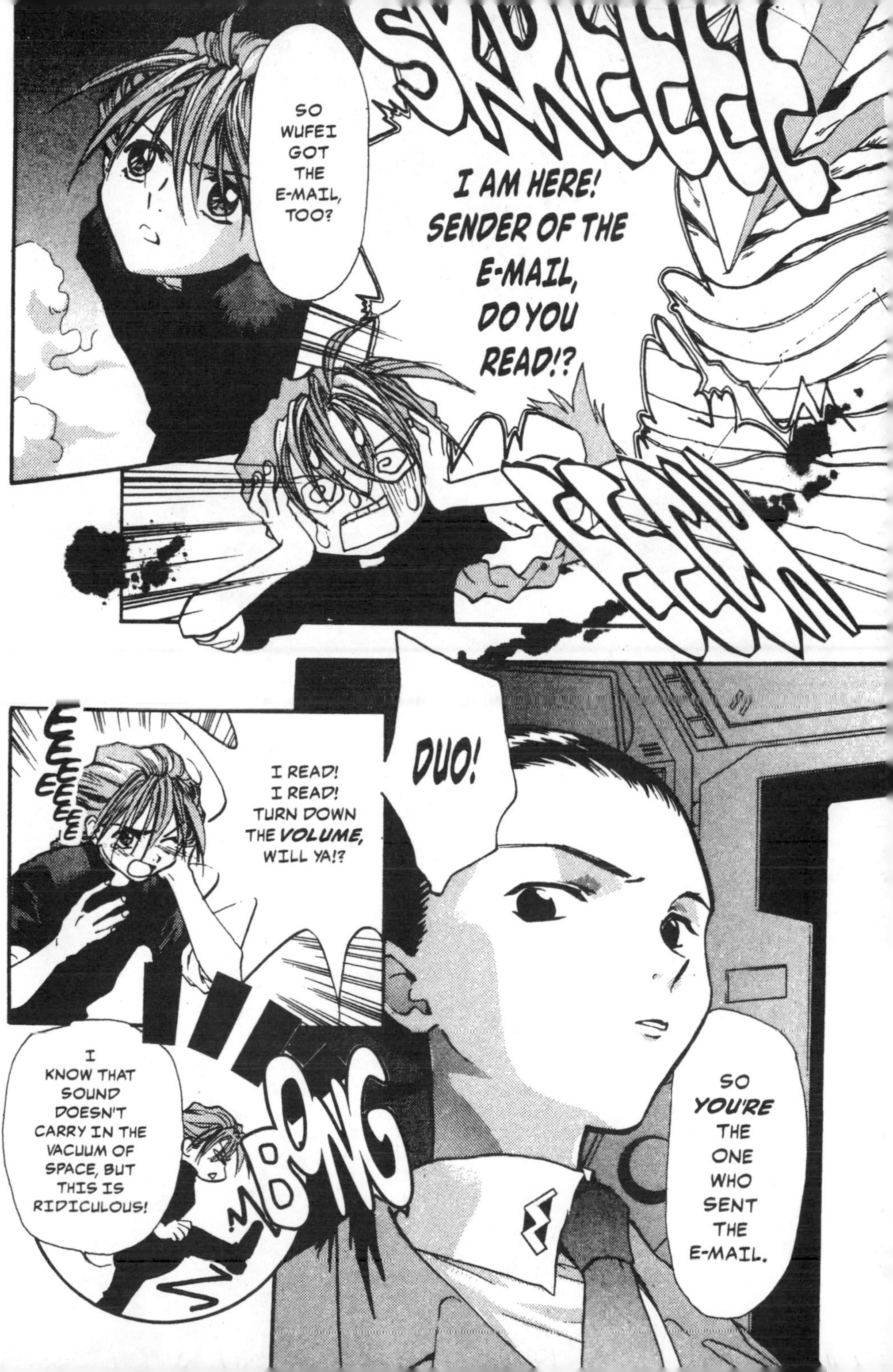
SO WUFEI GOT THE E-MAIL, TOO?
I AM HERE! SENDER OF THE E-MAIL, DO YOU READ!?
I READ! I READ! TURN DOWN THE *VOLUME*, WILL YA!?
I KNOW THAT SOUND DOESN'T CARRY IN THE VACUUM OF SPACE, BUT THIS IS RIDICULOUS!
DUO!
SO *YOU'RE* THE ONE WHO SENT THE E-MAIL.

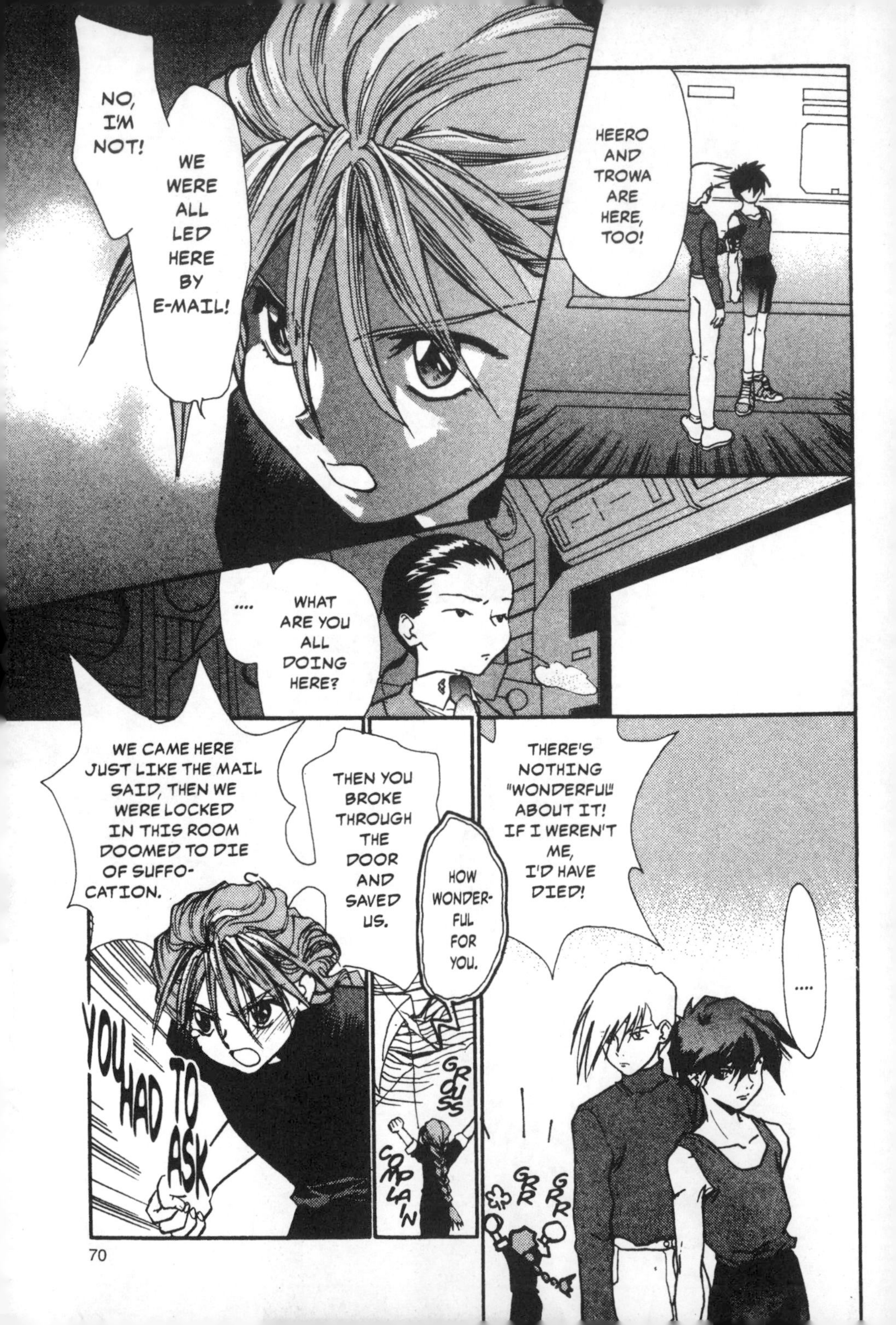
NO, I'M NOT!
WE WERE ALL LED HERE BY E-MAIL!
HEERO AND TROWA ARE HERE, TOO!
....
WHAT ARE YOU ALL DOING HERE?
WE CAME HERE JUST LIKE THE MAIL SAID, THEN WE WERE LOCKED IN THIS ROOM DOOMED TO DIE OF SUFFO-CATION.
YOU HAD TO ASK
THEN YOU BROKE THROUGH THE DOOR AND SAVED US.
HOW WONDER-FUL FOR YOU.
GROUSS
COMPLAIN
THERE'S NOTHING "WONDERFUL" ABOUT IT! IF I WEREN'T ME, I'D HAVE DIED!
....
GRR GRR

ZHIIT

CHANK

SSHT

BY YOUR ACTIONS, IT WOULD SEEM THAT YOU ARE ABOUT TO ATTEMPT ESCAPE USING EXPLOSIVES.

I WOULDN'T IF I WERE YOU.

BOTH THE DOOR AND THE AIR DUCT ARE REINFORCED

IT'S IMPOSSIBLE.

THONK

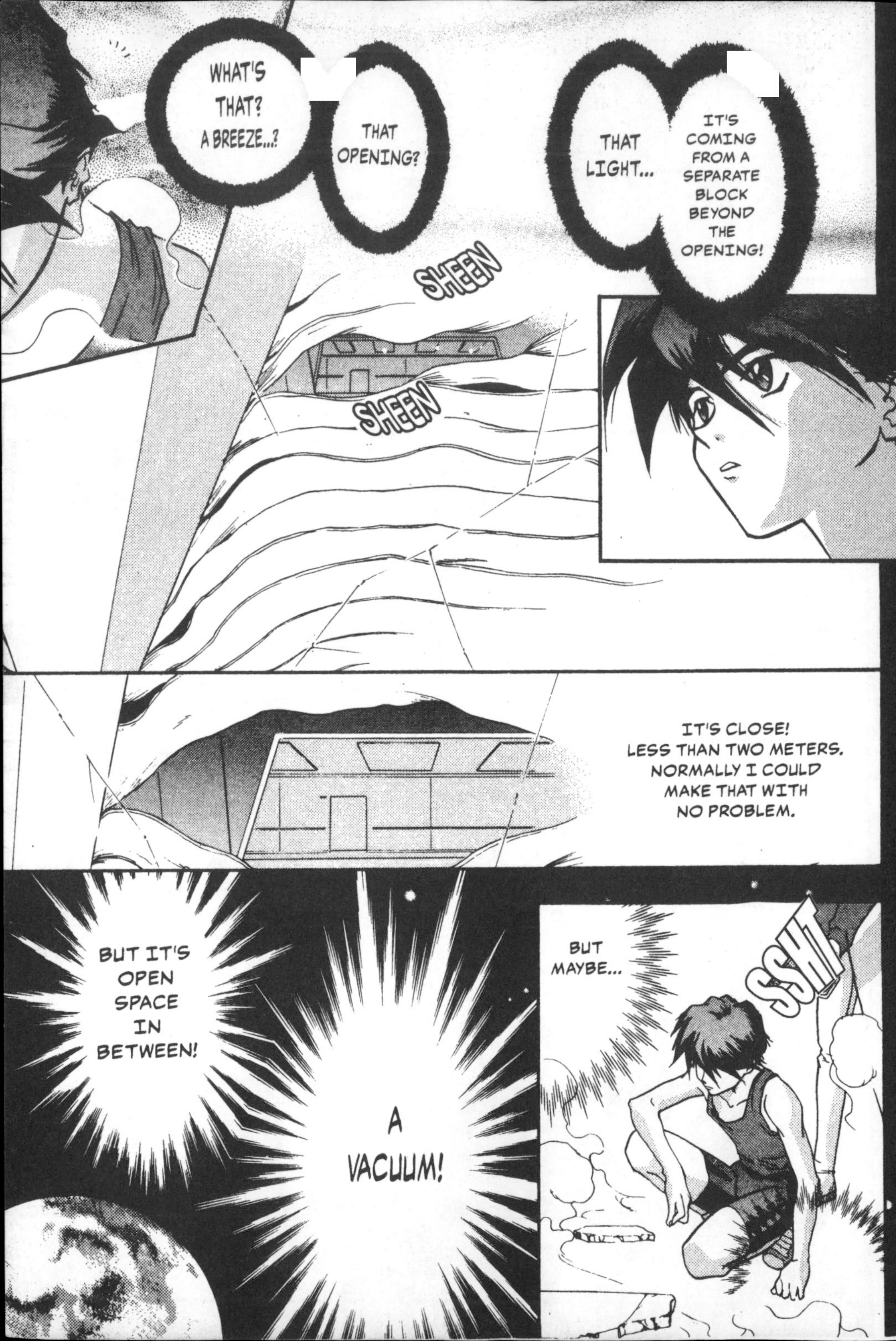
WHAT'S THAT? A BREEZE...?
THAT OPENING?
THAT LIGHT...
IT'S COMING FROM A SEPARATE BLOCK BEYOND THE OPENING!
SHEEN
SHEEN
IT'S CLOSE! LESS THAN TWO METERS. NORMALLY I COULD MAKE THAT WITH NO PROBLEM.
BUT IT'S OPEN SPACE IN BETWEEN!
A VACUUM!
BUT MAYBE...
SSHT

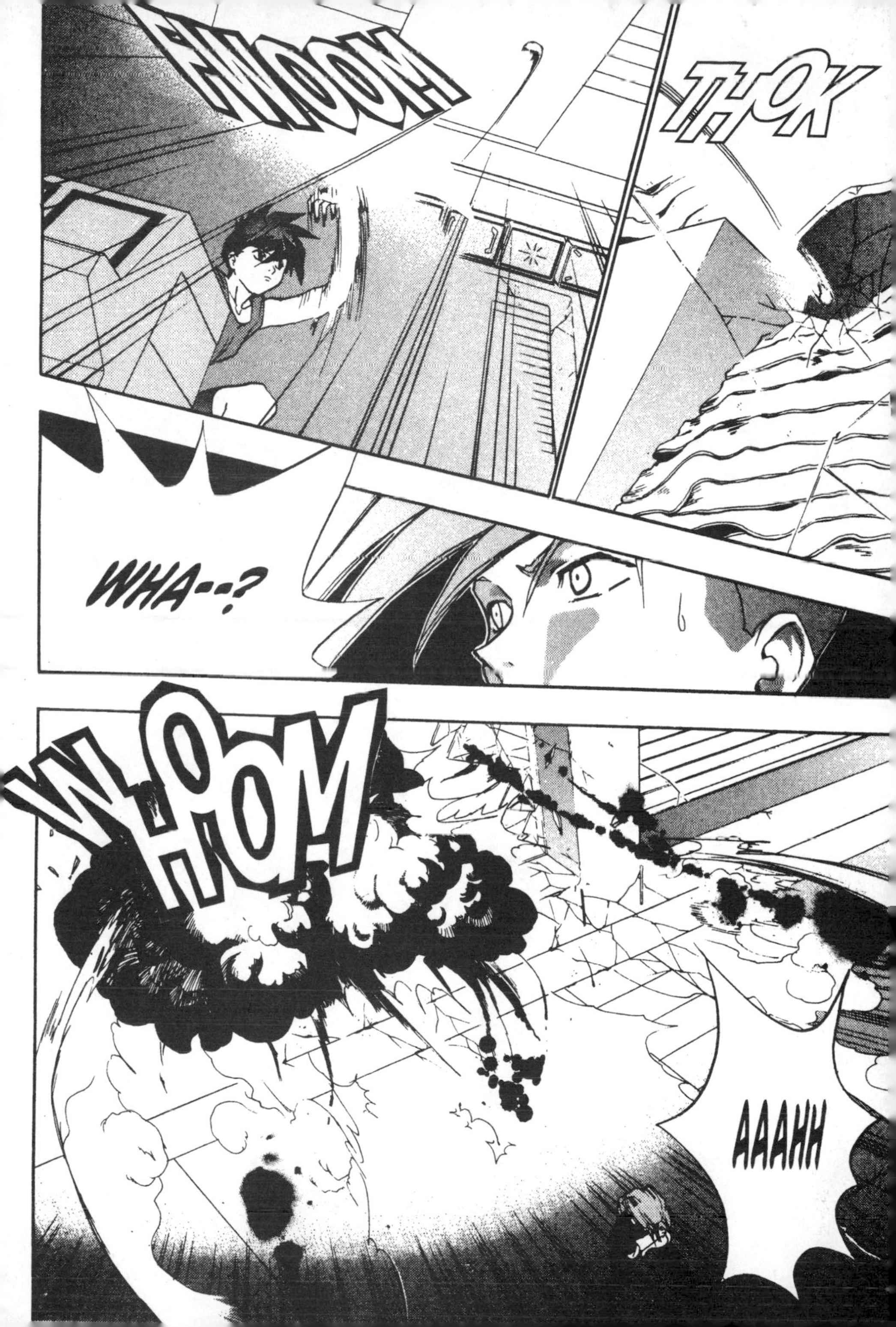
WHOOM
THOK
WHA--?
WHOOM
AAAHH

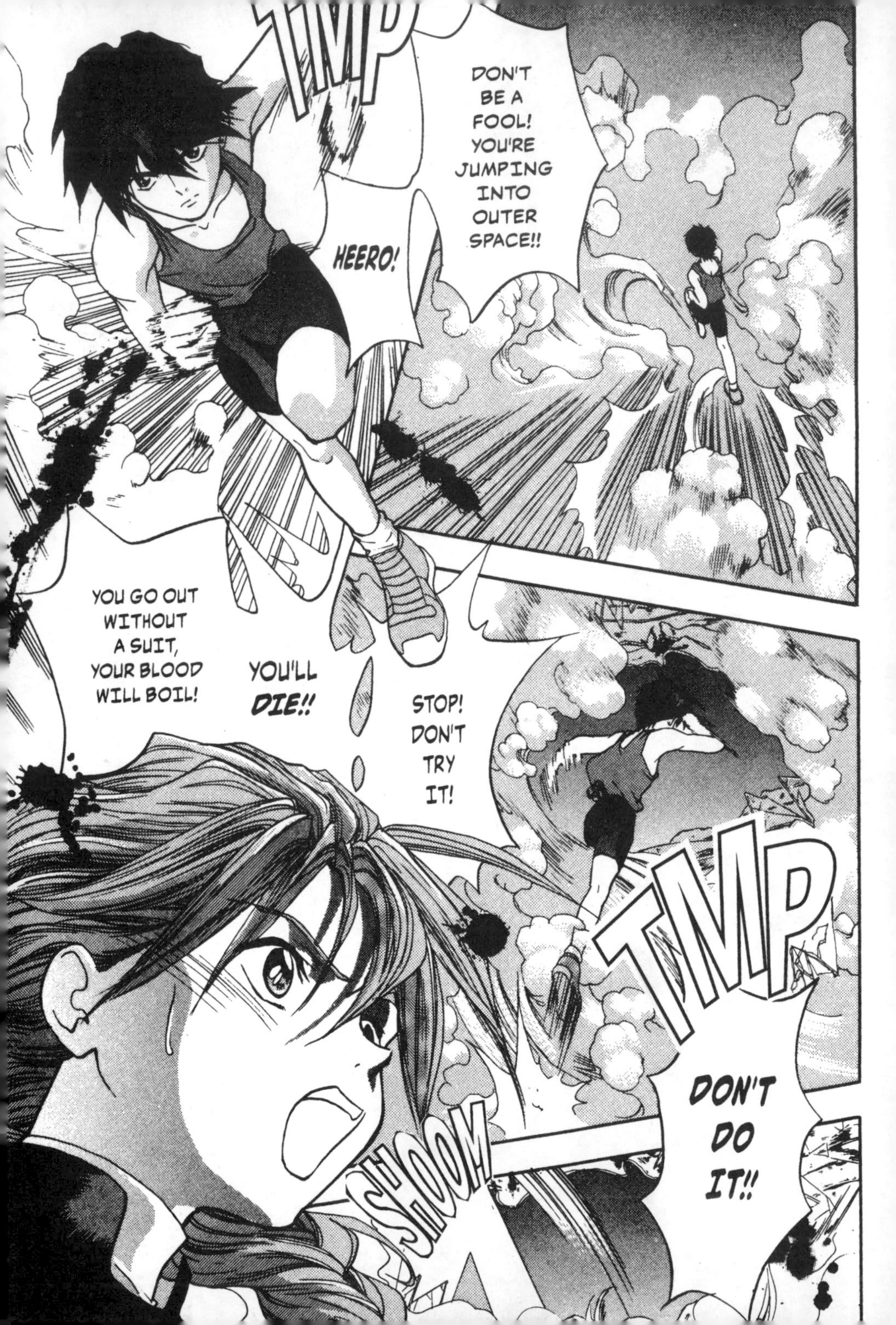
TMP
DON'T BE A FOOL! YOU'RE JUMPING INTO OUTER SPACE!!
HEERO!
YOU GO OUT WITHOUT A SUIT, YOUR BLOOD WILL BOIL!
YOU'LL *DIE!!*
STOP! DON'T TRY IT!
TMP
DON'T DO IT!!
SHOOM

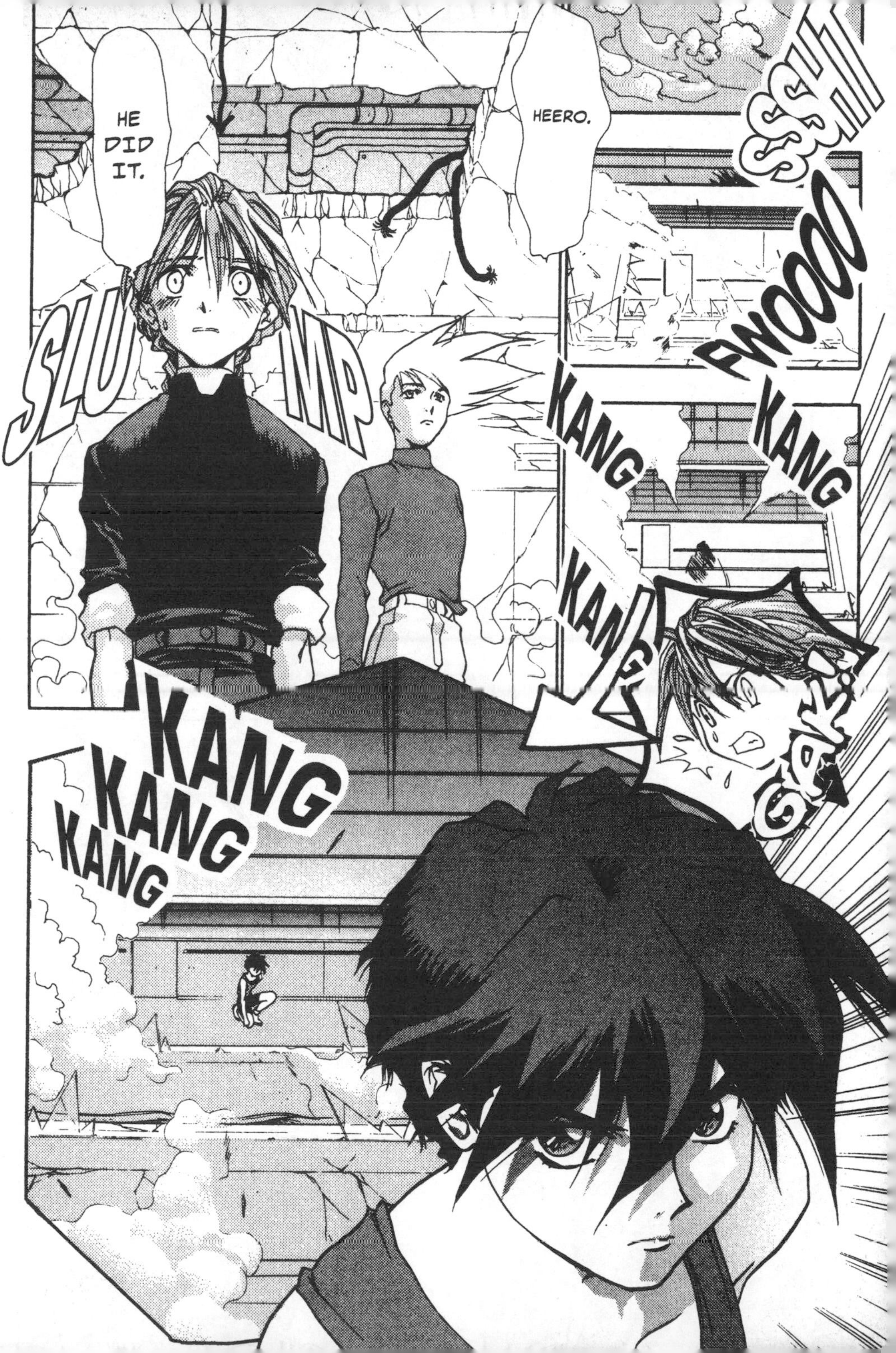
HE DID IT.
SLUMP
HEERO.
SSSHHH
FWOOOO
KANG KANG
KANG KANG
KANG
KANG
KANG
GAK!!

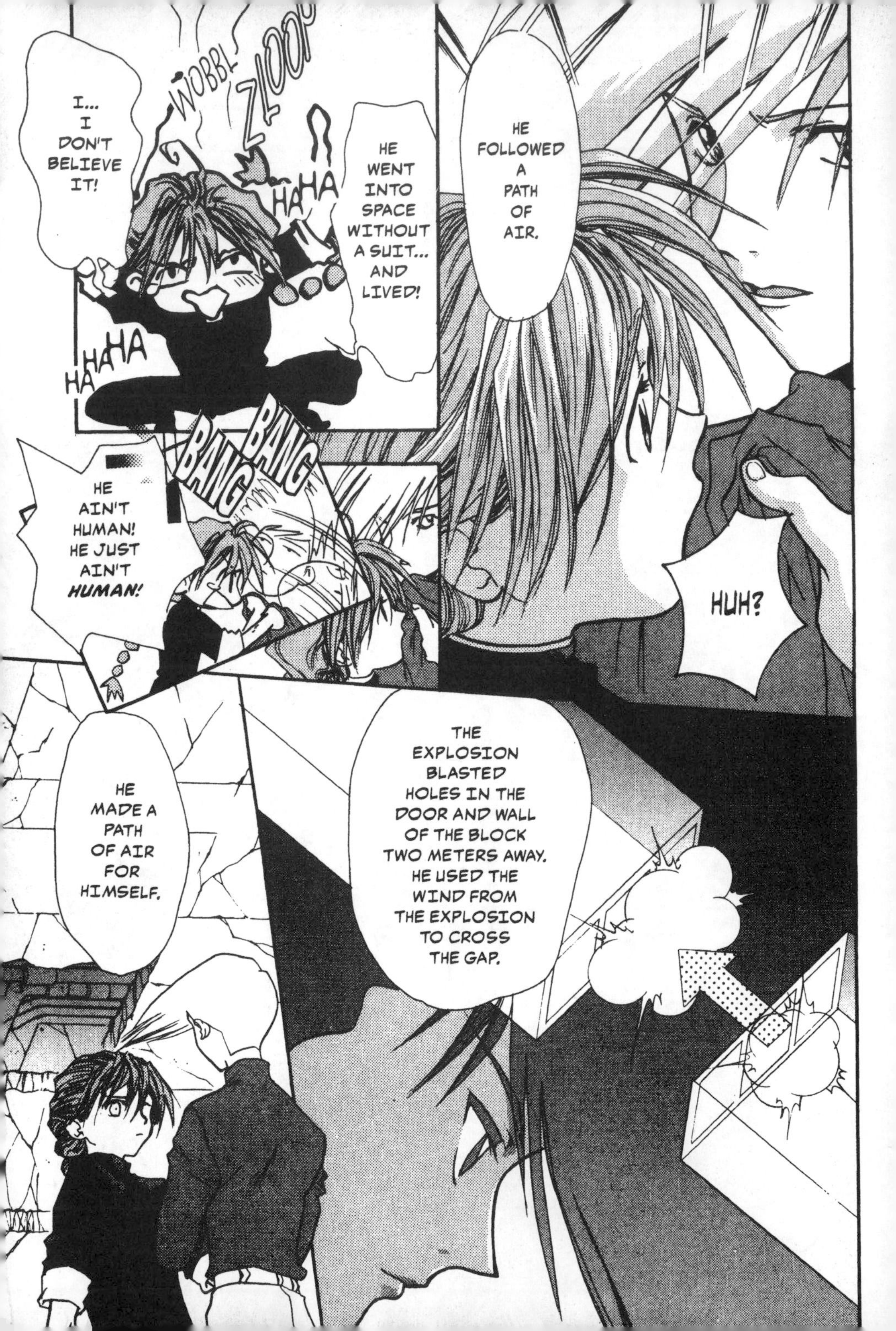
WOBBL
ZLOOP
I... I DON'T BELIEVE IT!
HA HA
HE WENT INTO SPACE WITHOUT A SUIT... AND LIVED!
HA HA HA
BANG BANG
HE AIN'T HUMAN! HE JUST AIN'T ***HUMAN!***
HE FOLLOWED A PATH OF AIR.
HUH?
HE MADE A PATH OF AIR FOR HIMSELF.
THE EXPLOSION BLASTED HOLES IN THE DOOR AND WALL OF THE BLOCK TWO METERS AWAY. HE USED THE WIND FROM THE EXPLOSION TO CROSS THE GAP.

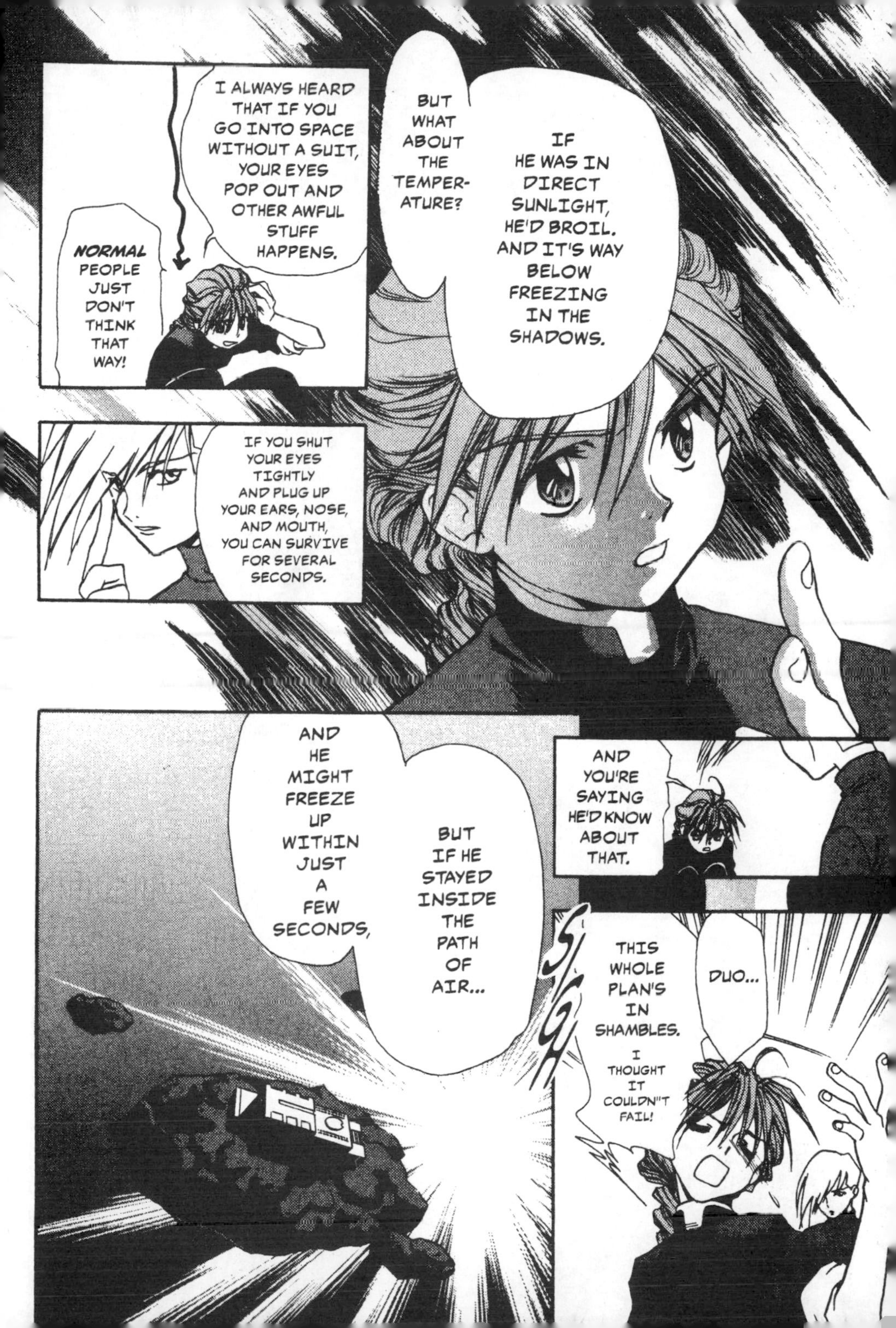
I ALWAYS HEARD THAT IF YOU GO INTO SPACE WITHOUT A SUIT, YOUR EYES POP OUT AND OTHER AWFUL STUFF HAPPENS.
NORMAL PEOPLE JUST DON'T THINK THAT WAY!
IF YOU SHUT YOUR EYES TIGHTLY AND PLUG UP YOUR EARS, NOSE, AND MOUTH, YOU CAN SURVIVE FOR SEVERAL SECONDS.
BUT WHAT ABOUT THE TEMPER-ATURE?
IF HE WAS IN DIRECT SUNLIGHT, HE'D BROIL. AND IT'S WAY BELOW FREEZING IN THE SHADOWS.
AND HE MIGHT FREEZE UP WITHIN JUST A FEW SECONDS,
BUT IF HE STAYED INSIDE THE PATH OF AIR...
AND YOU'RE SAYING HE'D KNOW ABOUT THAT.
SIGH
THIS WHOLE PLAN'S IN SHAMBLES.
DUO...
I THOUGHT IT COULDN'"T FAIL!

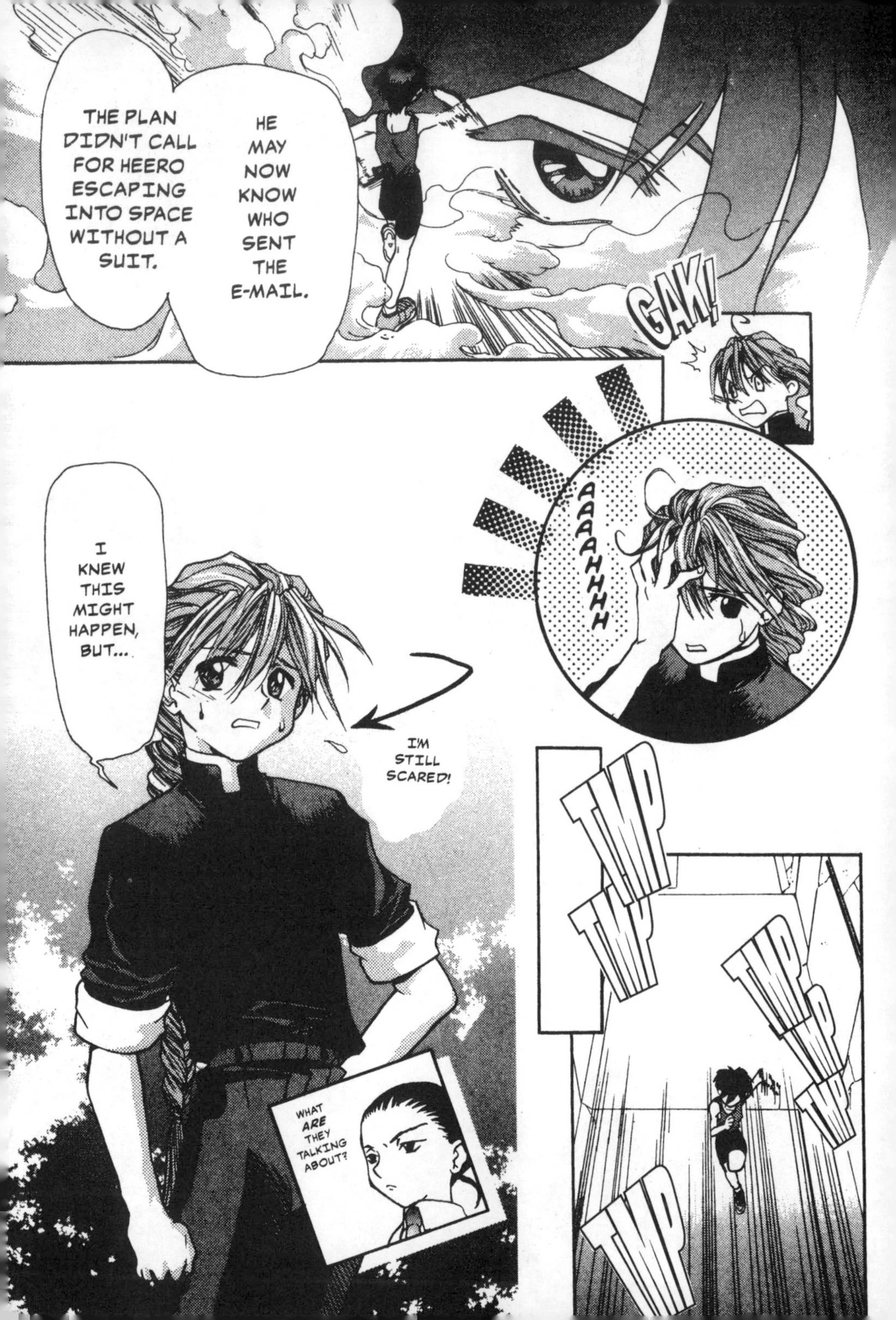
THE PLAN DIDN'T CALL FOR HEERO ESCAPING INTO SPACE WITHOUT A SUIT.
HE MAY NOW KNOW WHO SENT THE E-MAIL.
GAK!
AAAAHHHH
I KNEW THIS MIGHT HAPPEN, BUT...
I'M STILL SCARED!
WHAT *ARE* THEY TALKING ABOUT?
TMP
TMP
TMP
TMP
TMP

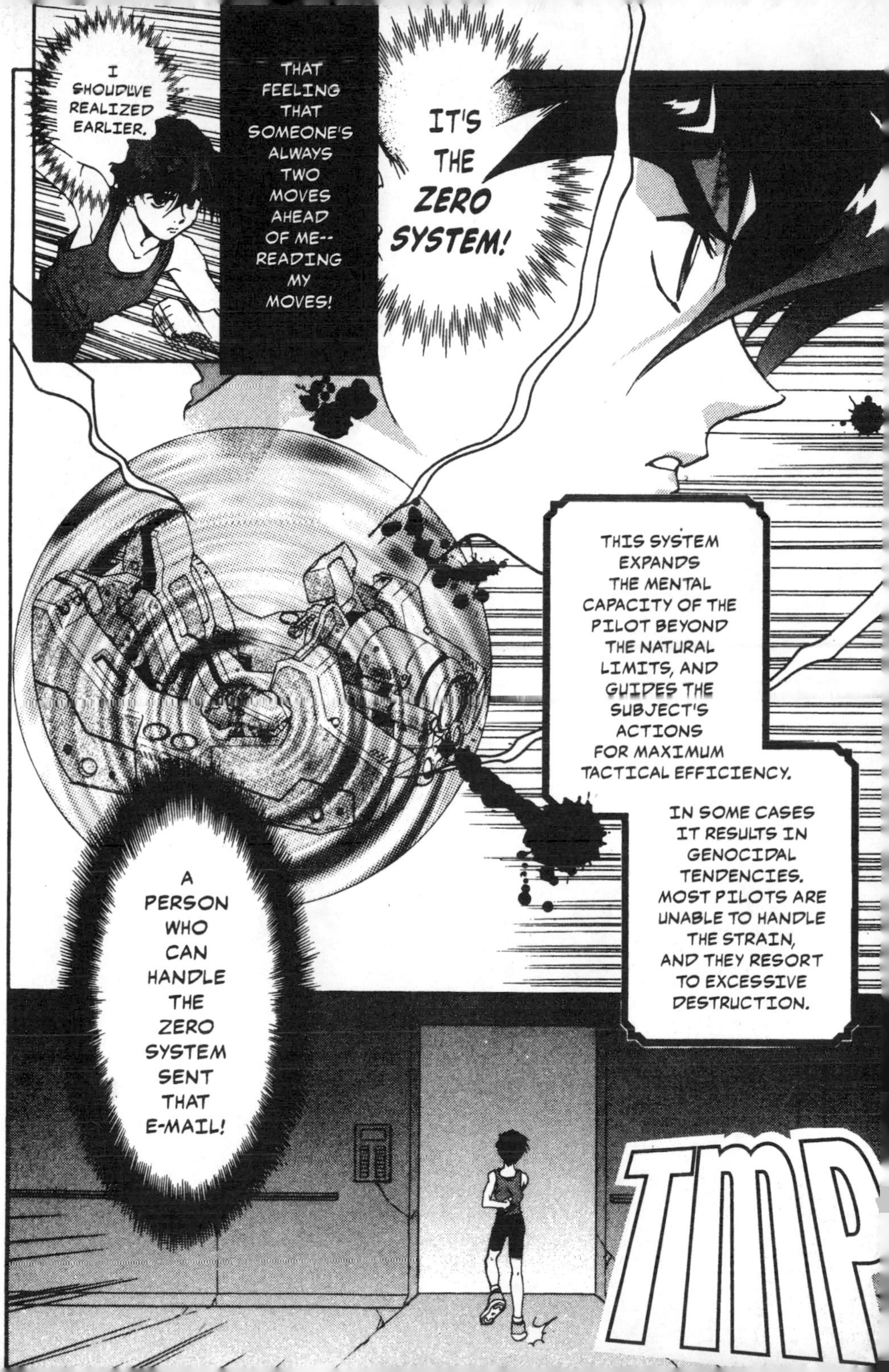
I SHOULD'VE REALIZED EARLIER.
THAT FEELING THAT SOMEONE'S ALWAYS TWO MOVES AHEAD OF ME--READING MY MOVES!
IT'S THE ZERO SYSTEM!
THIS SYSTEM EXPANDS THE MENTAL CAPACITY OF THE PILOT BEYOND THE NATURAL LIMITS, AND GUIDES THE SUBJECT'S ACTIONS FOR MAXIMUM TACTICAL EFFICIENCY.
IN SOME CASES IT RESULTS IN GENOCIDAL TENDENCIES. MOST PILOTS ARE UNABLE TO HANDLE THE STRAIN, AND THEY RESORT TO EXCESSIVE DESTRUCTION.
A PERSON WHO CAN HANDLE THE ZERO SYSTEM SENT THAT E-MAIL!
TMP

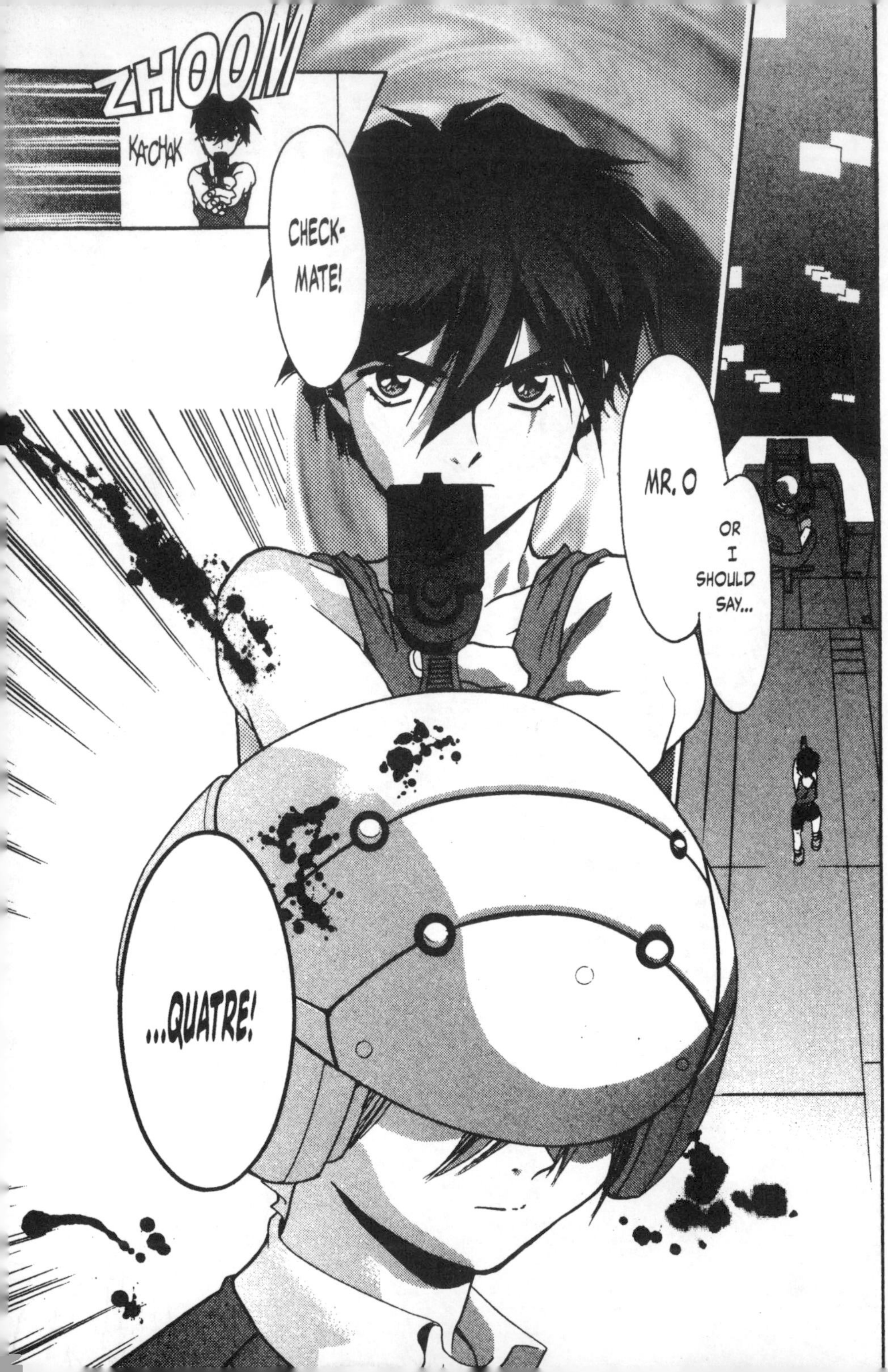
ZHOOM
KA-CHAK
CHECK-MATE!
MR. O
OR I SHOULD SAY...
...QUATRE!

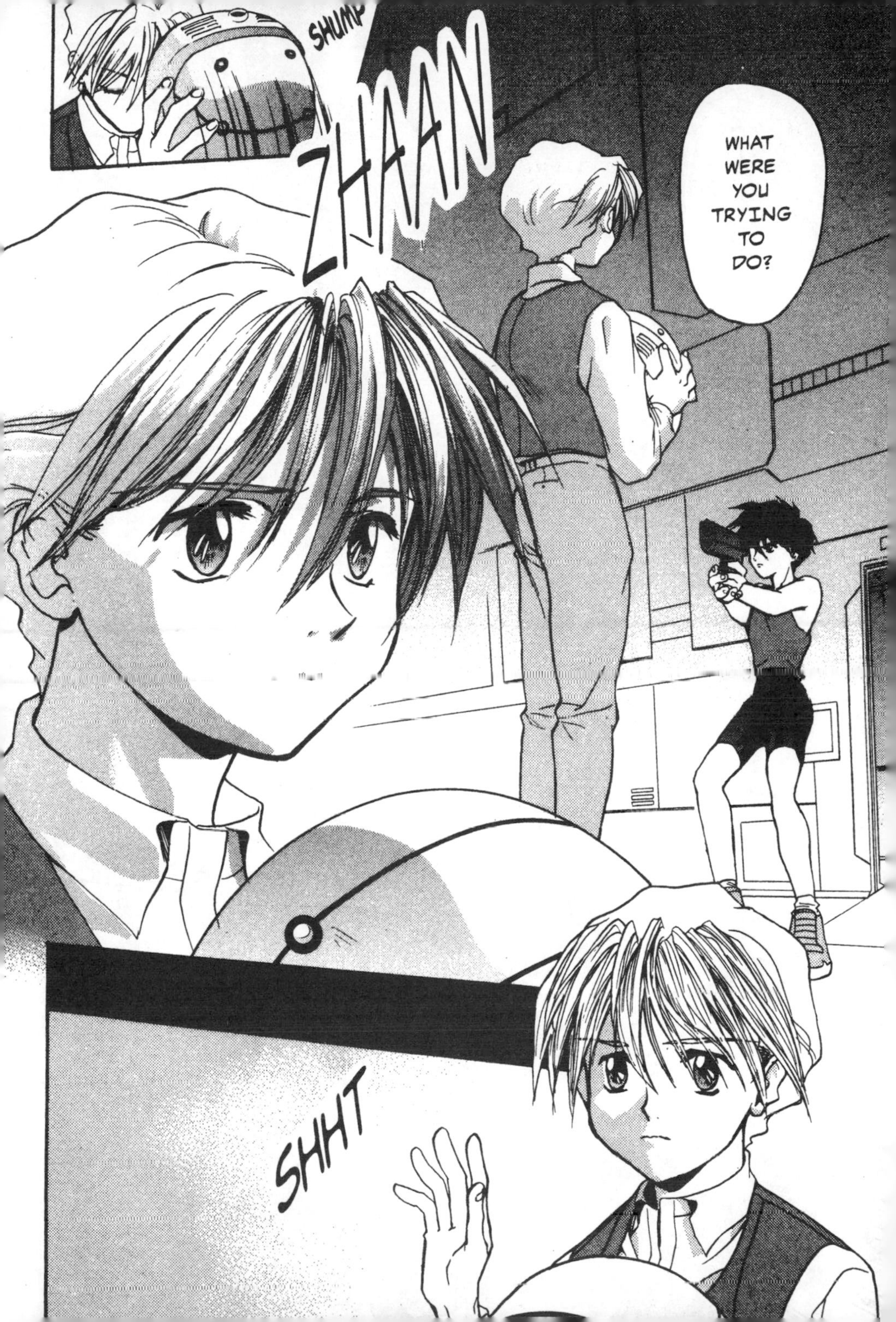
SHUMP
ZHAAN
WHAT WERE YOU TRYING TO DO?
SHHT

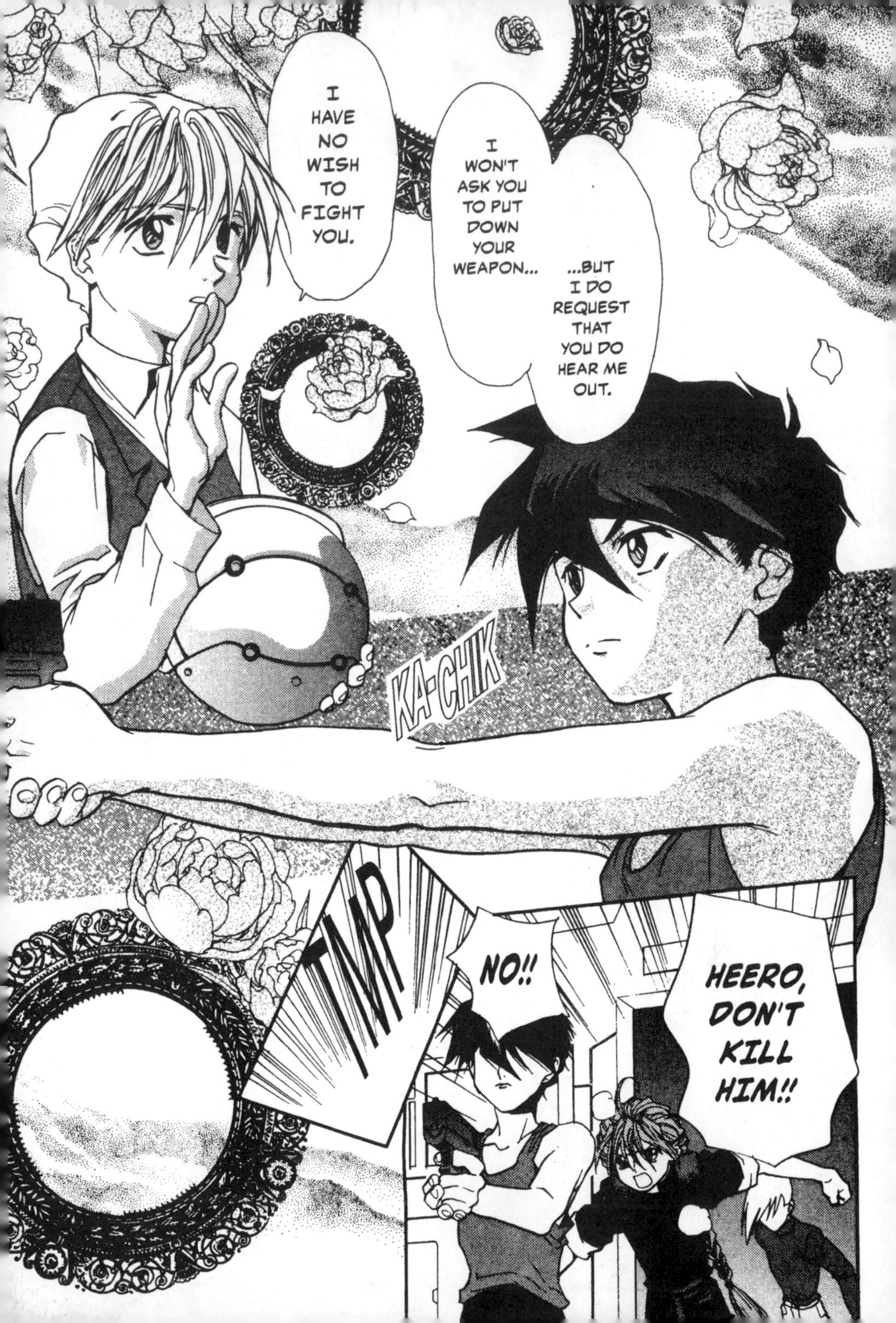
I HAVE NO WISH TO FIGHT YOU.
I WON'T ASK YOU TO PUT DOWN YOUR WEAPON...
...BUT I DO REQUEST THAT YOU DO HEAR ME OUT.
KA-CHIK
TMP
NO!!
HEERO, DON'T KILL HIM!!

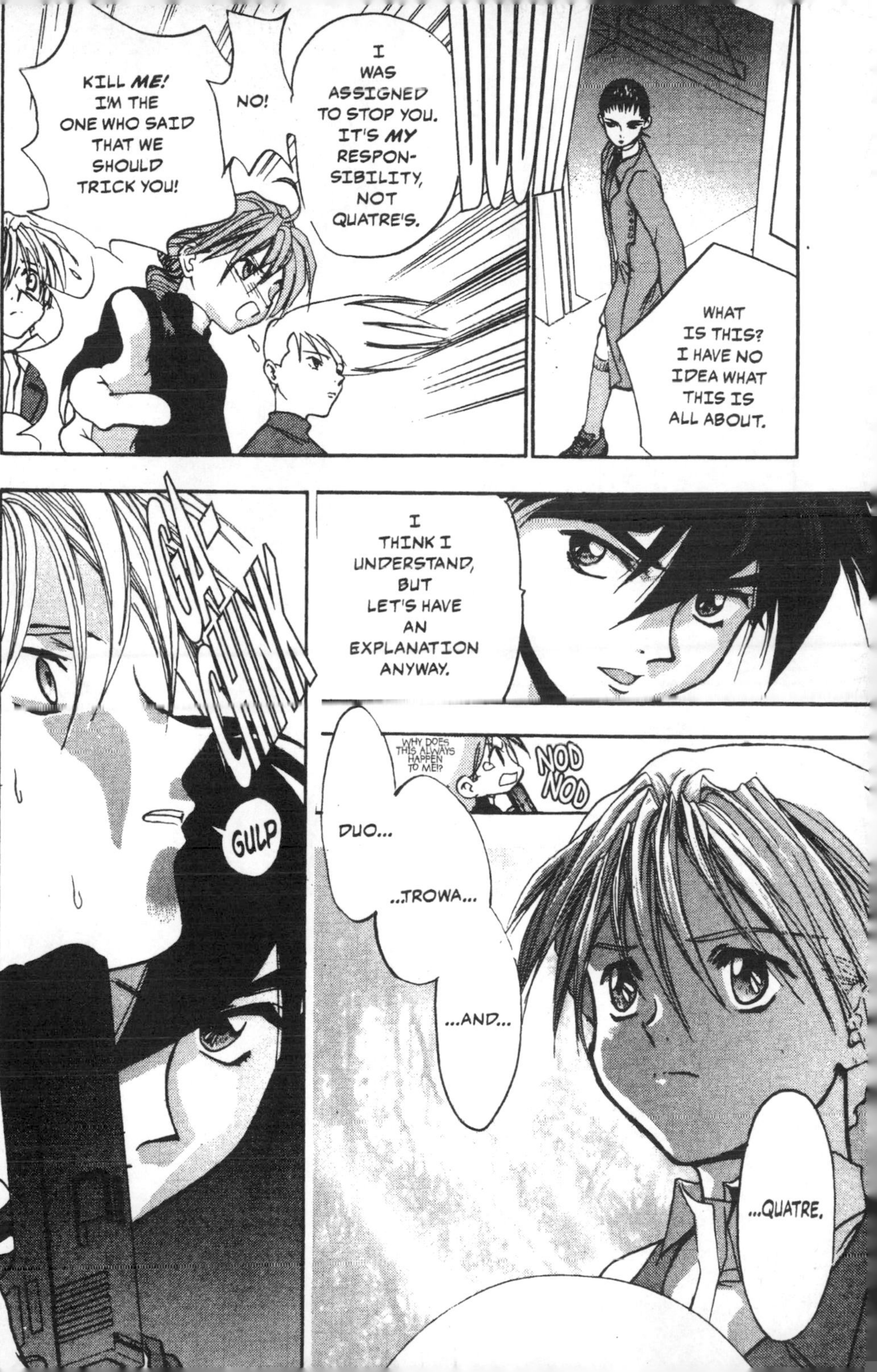
KILL ME! I'M THE ONE WHO SAID THAT WE SHOULD TRICK YOU!
NO!
I WAS ASSIGNED TO STOP YOU. IT'S MY RESPON-SIBILITY, NOT QUATRE'S.
WHAT IS THIS? I HAVE NO IDEA WHAT THIS IS ALL ABOUT.
GA CHINK
GULP
I THINK I UNDERSTAND, BUT LET'S HAVE AN EXPLANATION ANYWAY.
WHY DOES THIS ALWAYS HAPPEN TO ME!?
NOD NOD
DUO...
...TROWA...
...AND...
...QUATRE.

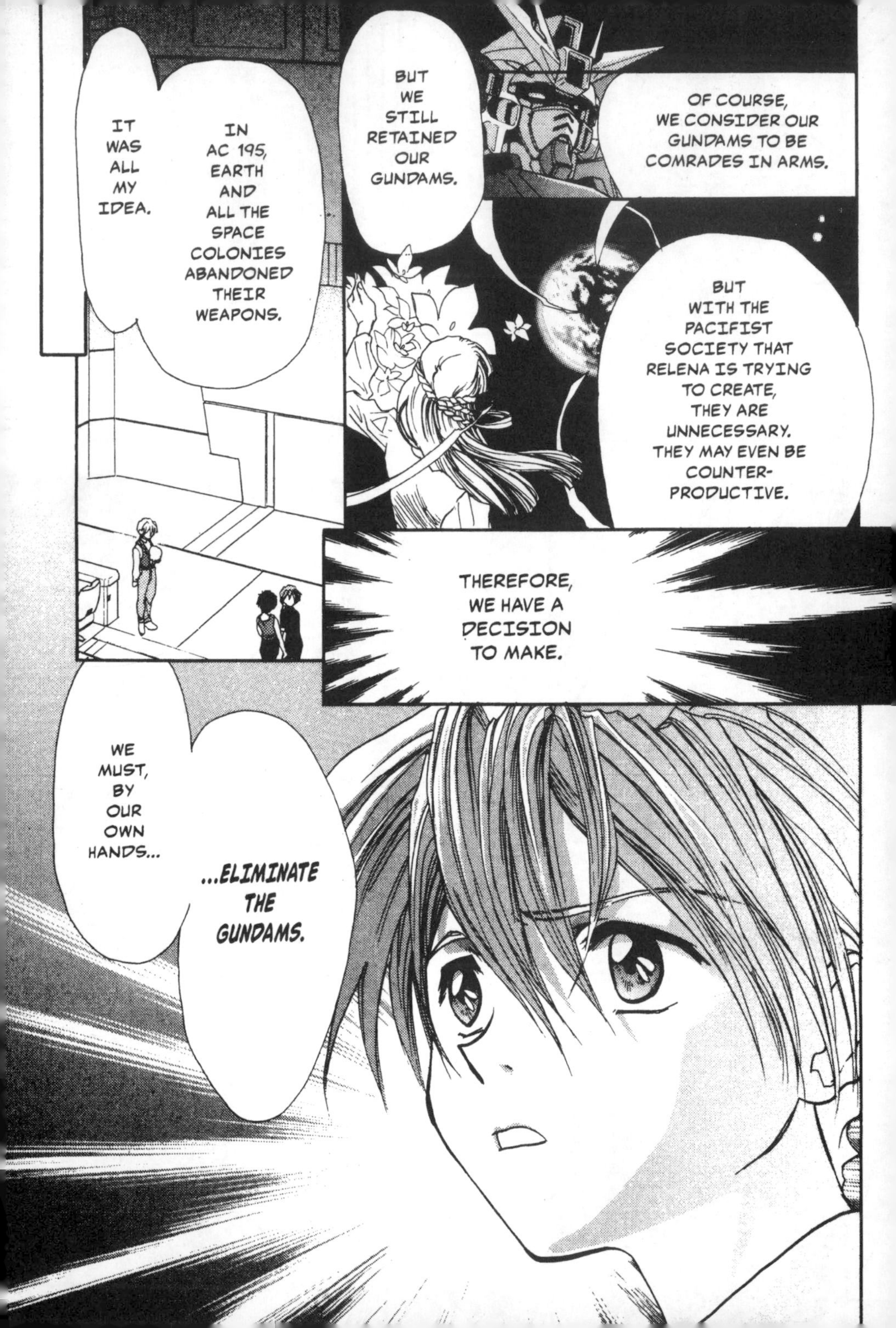
IT WAS ALL MY IDEA.
IN AC 195, EARTH AND ALL THE SPACE COLONIES ABANDONED THEIR WEAPONS.
BUT WE STILL RETAINED OUR GUNDAMS.
OF COURSE, WE CONSIDER OUR GUNDAMS TO BE COMRADES IN ARMS.
BUT WITH THE PACIFIST SOCIETY THAT RELENA IS TRYING TO CREATE, THEY ARE UNNECESSARY. THEY MAY EVEN BE COUNTER-PRODUCTIVE.
THEREFORE, WE HAVE A DECISION TO MAKE.
WE MUST, BY OUR OWN HANDS...
...ELIMINATE THE GUNDAMS.

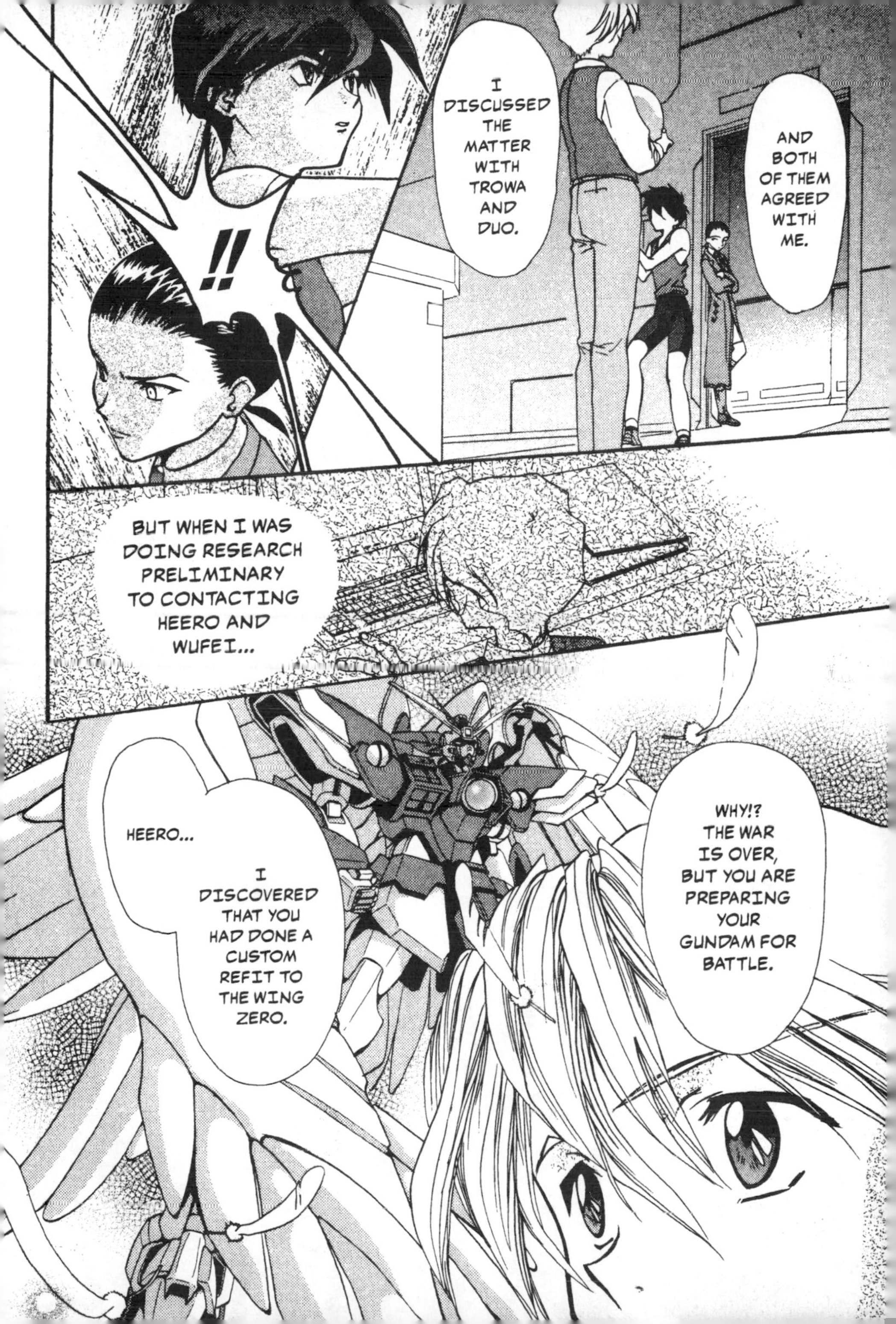
!!
I DISCUSSED THE MATTER WITH TROWA AND DUO.
AND BOTH OF THEM AGREED WITH ME.
BUT WHEN I WAS DOING RESEARCH PRELIMINARY TO CONTACTING HEERO AND WUFEI...
HEERO...
I DISCOVERED THAT YOU HAD DONE A CUSTOM REFIT TO THE WING ZERO.
WHY!? THE WAR IS OVER, BUT YOU ARE PREPARING YOUR GUNDAM FOR BATTLE.

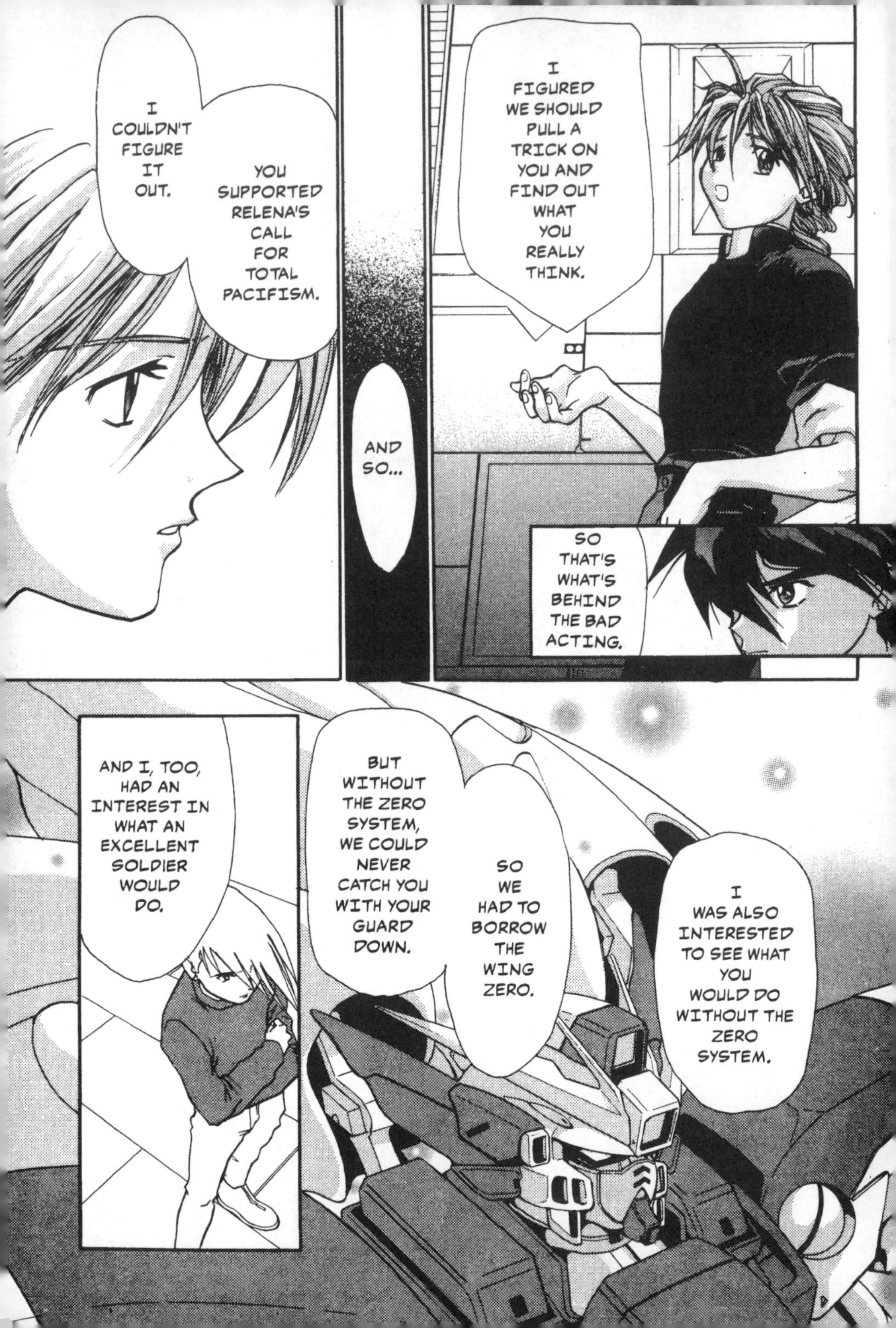
I COULDN'T FIGURE IT OUT.
YOU SUPPORTED RELENA'S CALL FOR TOTAL PACIFISM.
AND SO...
I FIGURED WE SHOULD PULL A TRICK ON YOU AND FIND OUT WHAT YOU REALLY THINK.
SO THAT'S WHAT'S BEHIND THE BAD ACTING.
AND I, TOO, HAD AN INTEREST IN WHAT AN EXCELLENT SOLDIER WOULD DO.
BUT WITHOUT THE ZERO SYSTEM, WE COULD NEVER CATCH YOU WITH YOUR GUARD DOWN.
SO WE HAD TO BORROW THE WING ZERO.
I WAS ALSO INTERESTED TO SEE WHAT YOU WOULD DO WITHOUT THE ZERO SYSTEM.

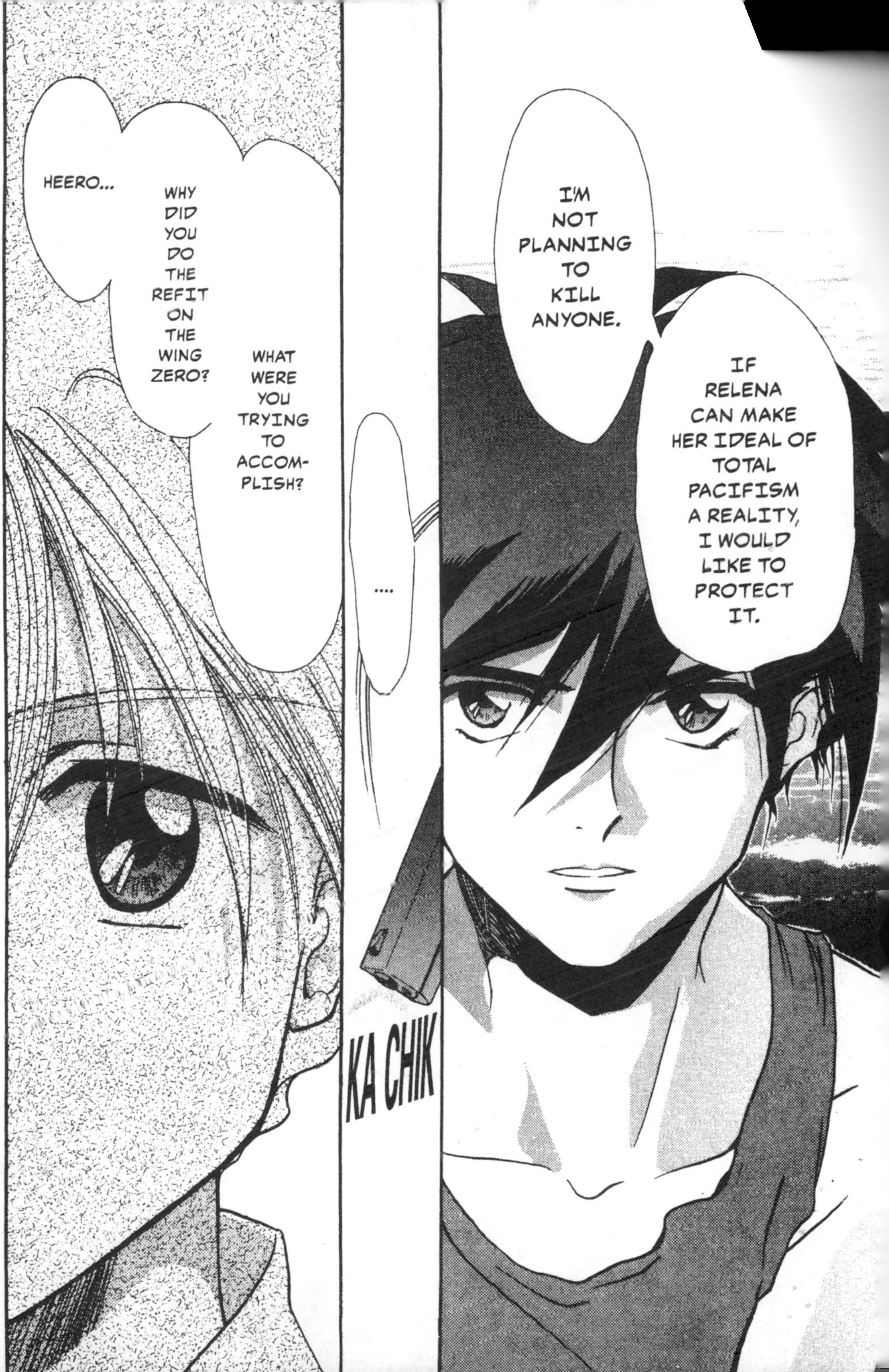
HEERO...
WHY DID YOU DO THE REFIT ON THE WING ZERO?
WHAT WERE YOU TRYING TO ACCOMPLISH?
....
KA CHIK
I'M NOT PLANNING TO KILL ANYONE.
IF RELENA CAN MAKE HER IDEAL OF TOTAL PACIFISM A REALITY, I WOULD LIKE TO PROTECT IT.

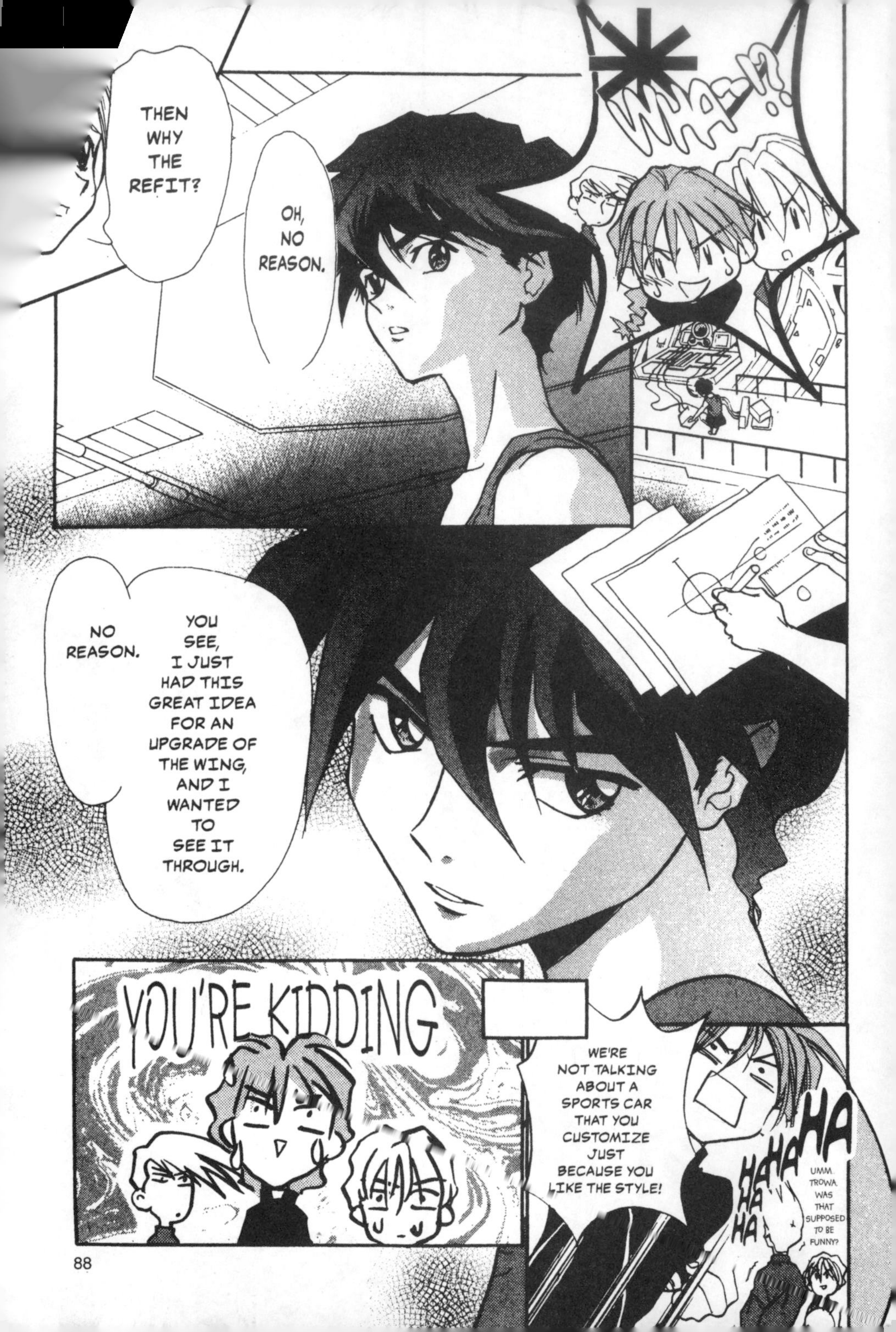
THEN WHY THE REFIT?
OH, NO REASON.
WHA--!?
NO REASON.
YOU SEE, I JUST HAD THIS GREAT IDEA FOR AN UPGRADE OF THE WING, AND I WANTED TO SEE IT THROUGH.
YOU'RE KIDDING
WE'RE NOT TALKING ABOUT A SPORTS CAR THAT YOU CUSTOMIZE JUST BECAUSE YOU LIKE THE STYLE!
HA HA HA HA HA HA HA
UMM.. TROWA, WAS THAT SUPPOSED TO BE FUNNY?

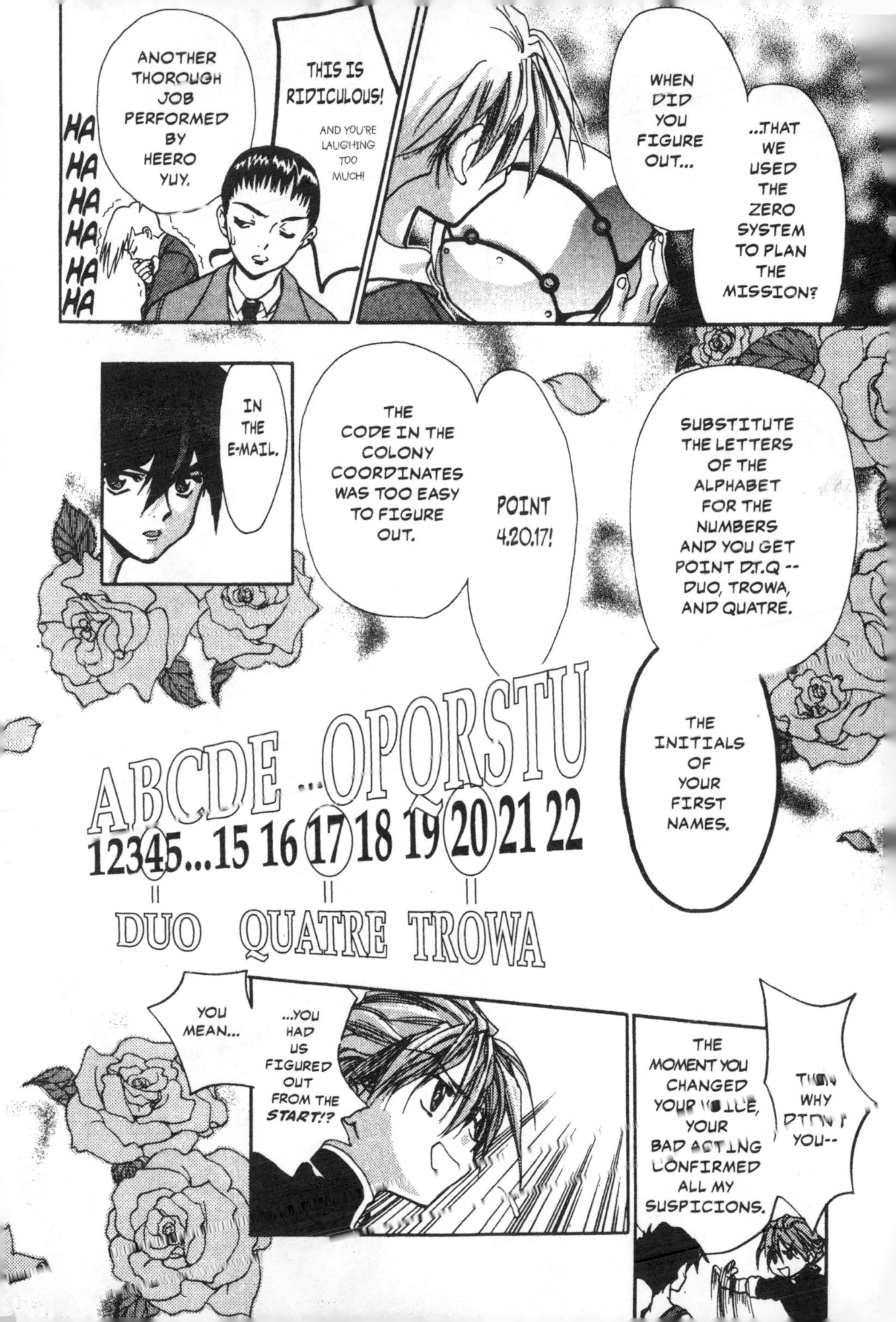
HA HA HA HA HA HA HA
ANOTHER THOROUGH JOB PERFORMED BY HEERO YUY.
THIS IS RIDICULOUS!
AND YOU'RE LAUGHING TOO MUCH!
WHEN DID YOU FIGURE OUT...
...THAT WE USED THE ZERO SYSTEM TO PLAN THE MISSION?
IN THE E-MAIL.
THE CODE IN THE COLONY COORDINATES WAS TOO EASY TO FIGURE OUT.
POINT 4.20.17!
SUBSTITUTE THE LETTERS OF THE ALPHABET FOR THE NUMBERS AND YOU GET POINT D.T.Q -- DUO, TROWA, AND QUATRE.
THE INITIALS OF YOUR FIRST NAMES.
ABCDE ...OPQRSTU
12345...15 16 17 18 19 20 21 22
DUO QUATRE TROWA
YOU MEAN...
...YOU HAD US FIGURED OUT FROM THE START!?
THE MOMENT YOU CHANGED YOUR VOICE, YOUR BAD ACTING CONFIRMED ALL MY SUSPICIONS.
THEN WHY DIDN'T YOU--

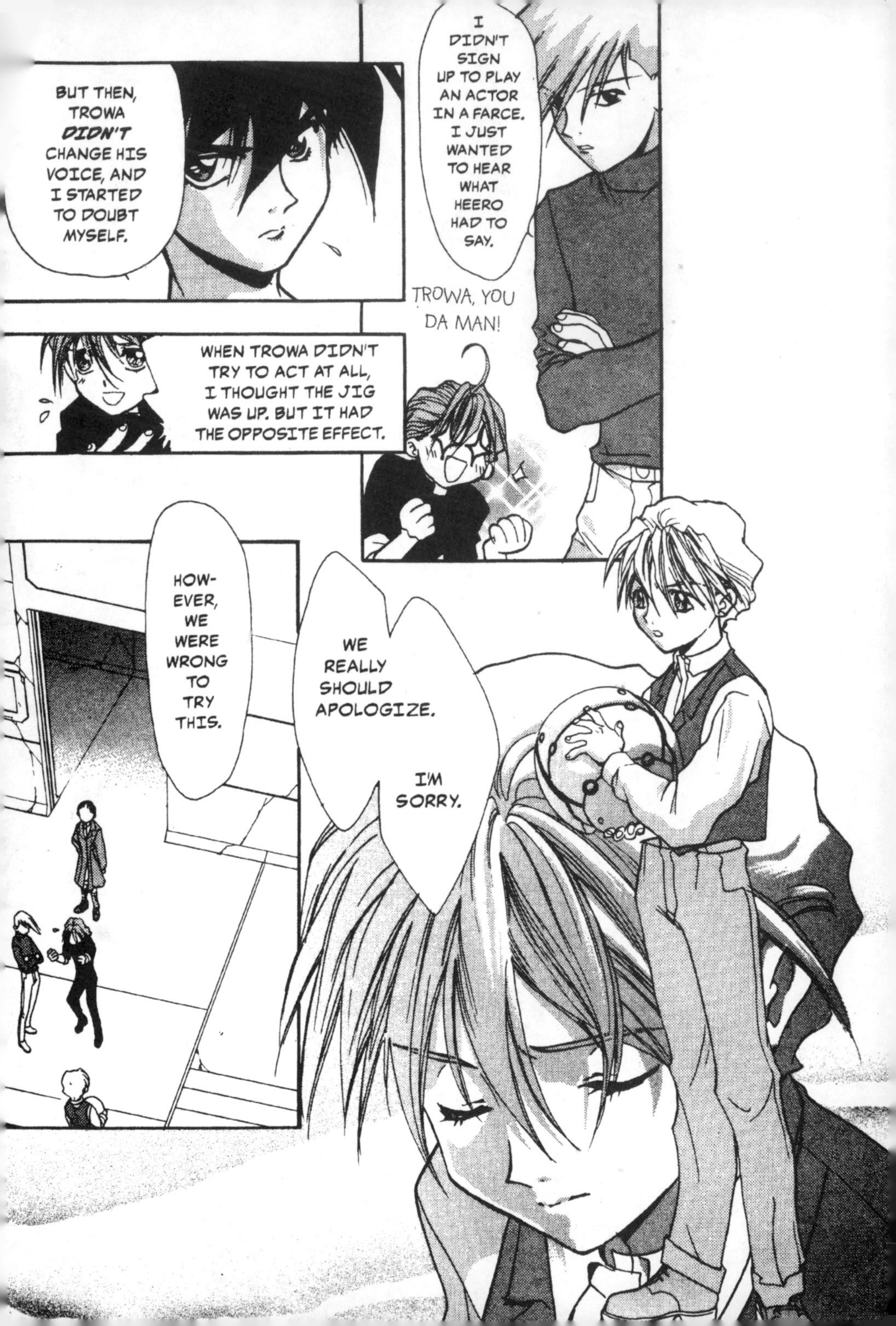
BUT THEN, TROWA *DIDN'T* CHANGE HIS VOICE, AND I STARTED TO DOUBT MYSELF.
WHEN TROWA DIDN'T TRY TO ACT AT ALL, I THOUGHT THE JIG WAS UP. BUT IT HAD THE OPPOSITE EFFECT.
I DIDN'T SIGN UP TO PLAY AN ACTOR IN A FARCE. I JUST WANTED TO HEAR WHAT HEERO HAD TO SAY.
TROWA, YOU DA MAN!
HOW-EVER, WE WERE WRONG TO TRY THIS.
WE REALLY SHOULD APOLOGIZE.
I'M SORRY.

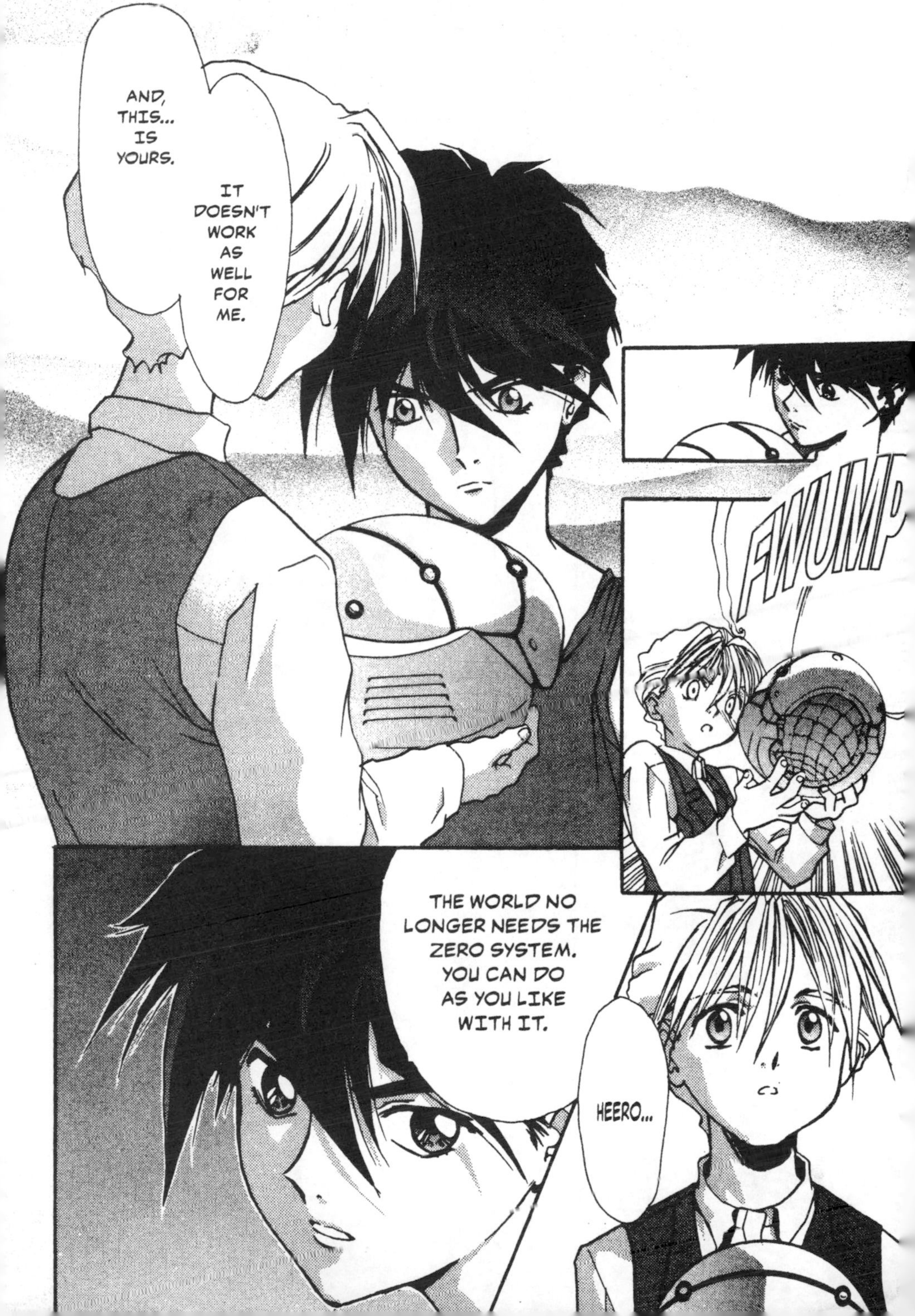
AND, THIS... IS YOURS.
IT DOESN'T WORK AS WELL FOR ME.
FWUMP
THE WORLD NO LONGER NEEDS THE ZERO SYSTEM. YOU CAN DO AS YOU LIKE WITH IT.
HEERO...

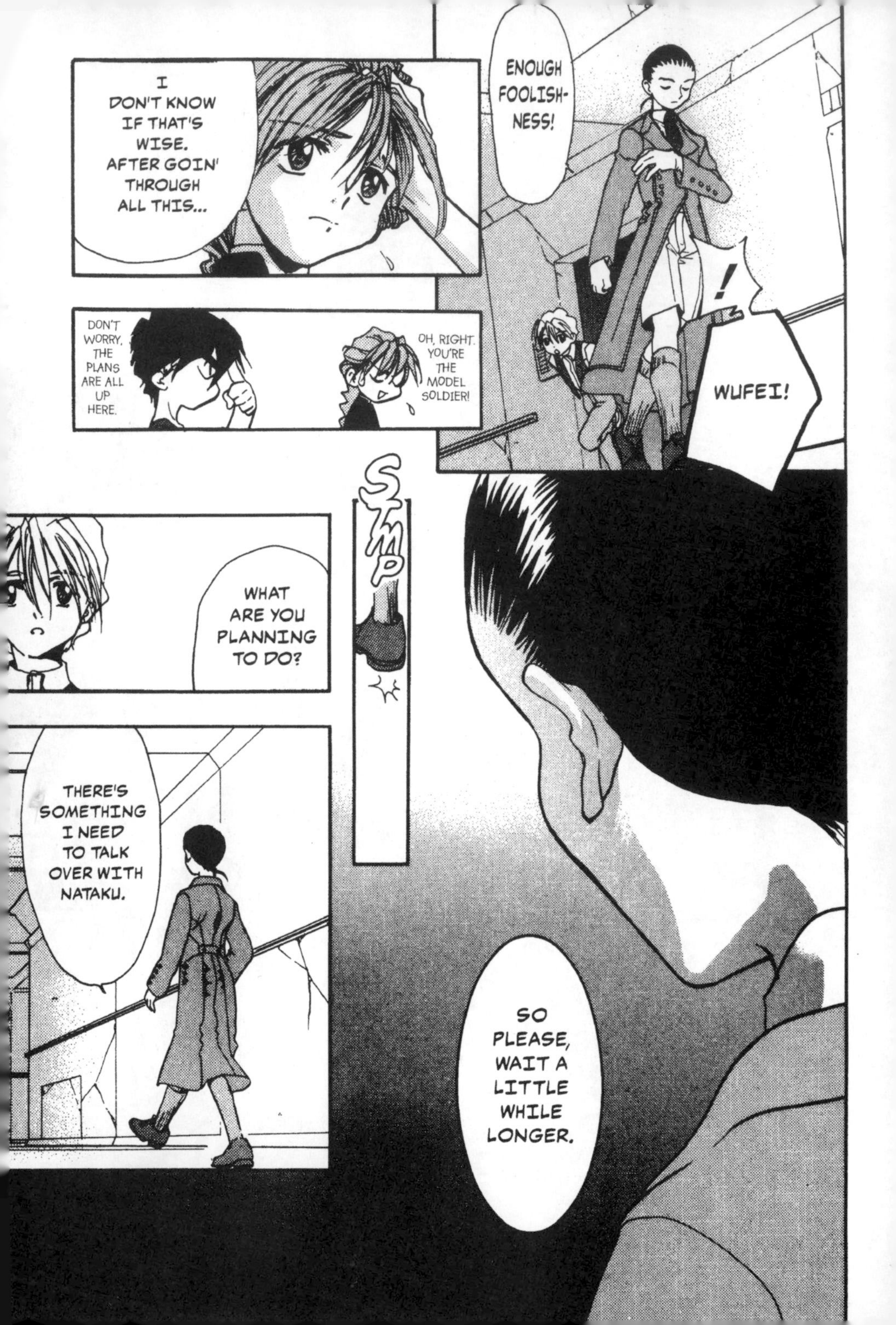
I DON'T KNOW IF THAT'S WISE. AFTER GOIN' THROUGH ALL THIS...
DON'T WORRY, THE PLANS ARE ALL UP HERE.
OH, RIGHT. YOU'RE THE MODEL SOLDIER!
ENOUGH FOOLISH-NESS!
!
WUFEI!
WHAT ARE YOU PLANNING TO DO?
THERE'S SOMETHING I NEED TO TALK OVER WITH NATAKU.
STMP
SO PLEASE, WAIT A LITTLE WHILE LONGER.

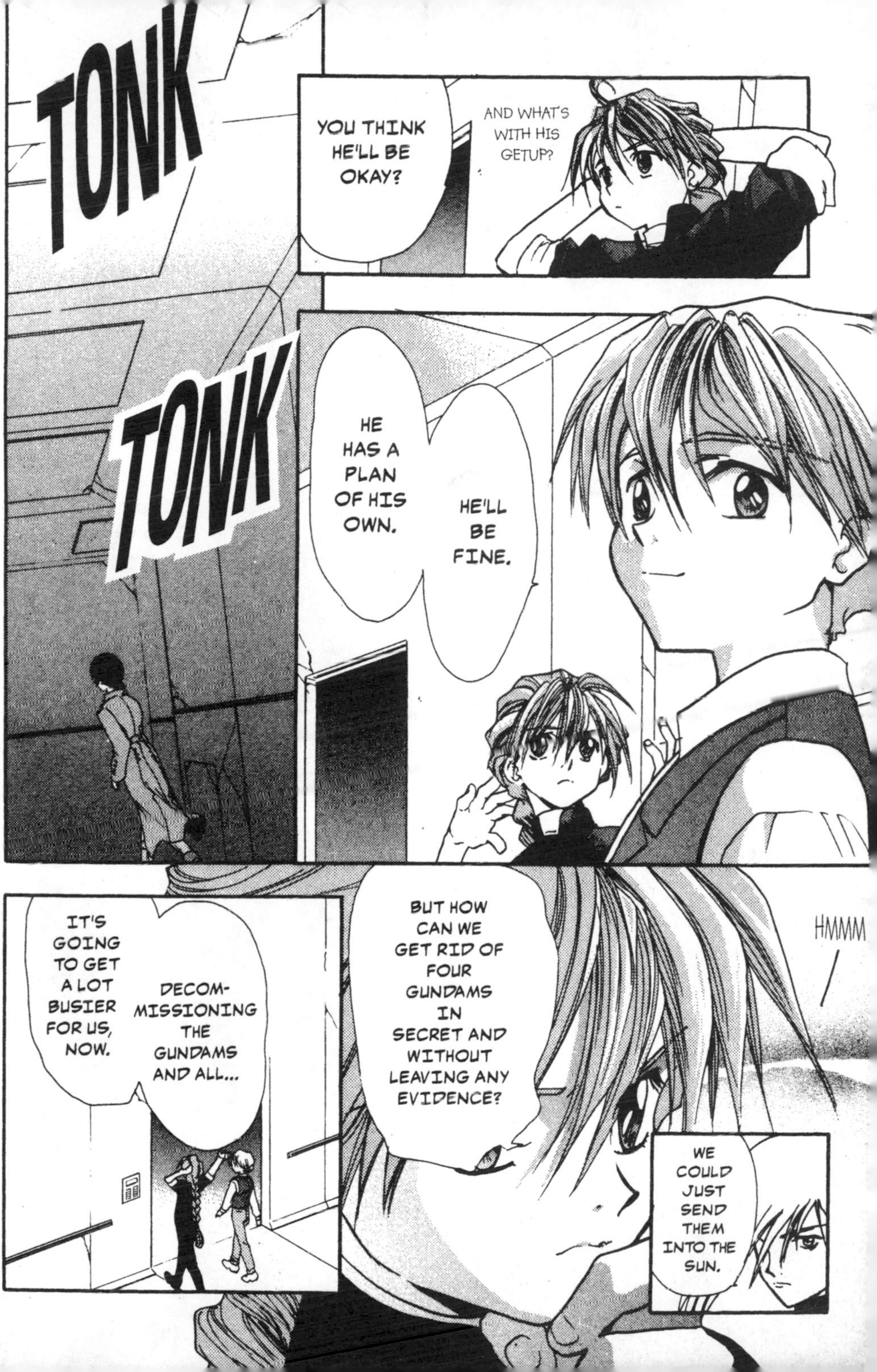
TONK
TONK
YOU THINK HE'LL BE OKAY?
AND WHAT'S WITH HIS GETUP?
HE HAS A PLAN OF HIS OWN.
HE'LL BE FINE.
IT'S GOING TO GET A LOT BUSIER FOR US, NOW.
DECOM-MISSIONING THE GUNDAMS AND ALL...
BUT HOW CAN WE GET RID OF FOUR GUNDAMS IN SECRET AND WITHOUT LEAVING ANY EVIDENCE?
HMMM
WE COULD JUST SEND THEM INTO THE SUN.

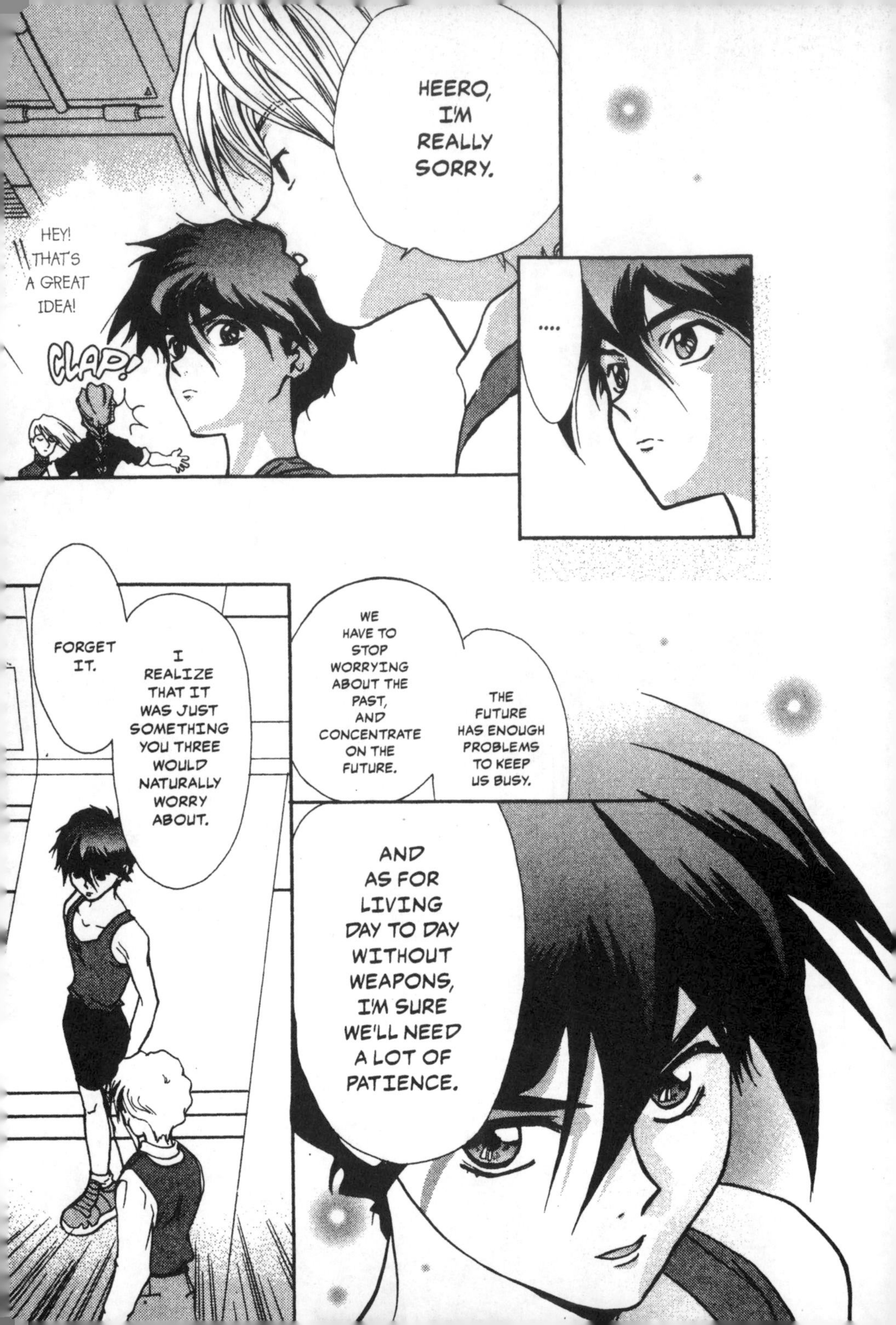
HEY! THAT'S A GREAT IDEA!
CLAP!
HEERO, I'M REALLY SORRY.
....
FORGET IT.
I REALIZE THAT IT WAS JUST SOMETHING YOU THREE WOULD NATURALLY WORRY ABOUT.
WE HAVE TO STOP WORRYING ABOUT THE PAST, AND CONCENTRATE ON THE FUTURE.
THE FUTURE HAS ENOUGH PROBLEMS TO KEEP US BUSY.
AND AS FOR LIVING DAY TO DAY WITHOUT WEAPONS, I'M SURE WE'LL NEED A LOT OF PATIENCE.

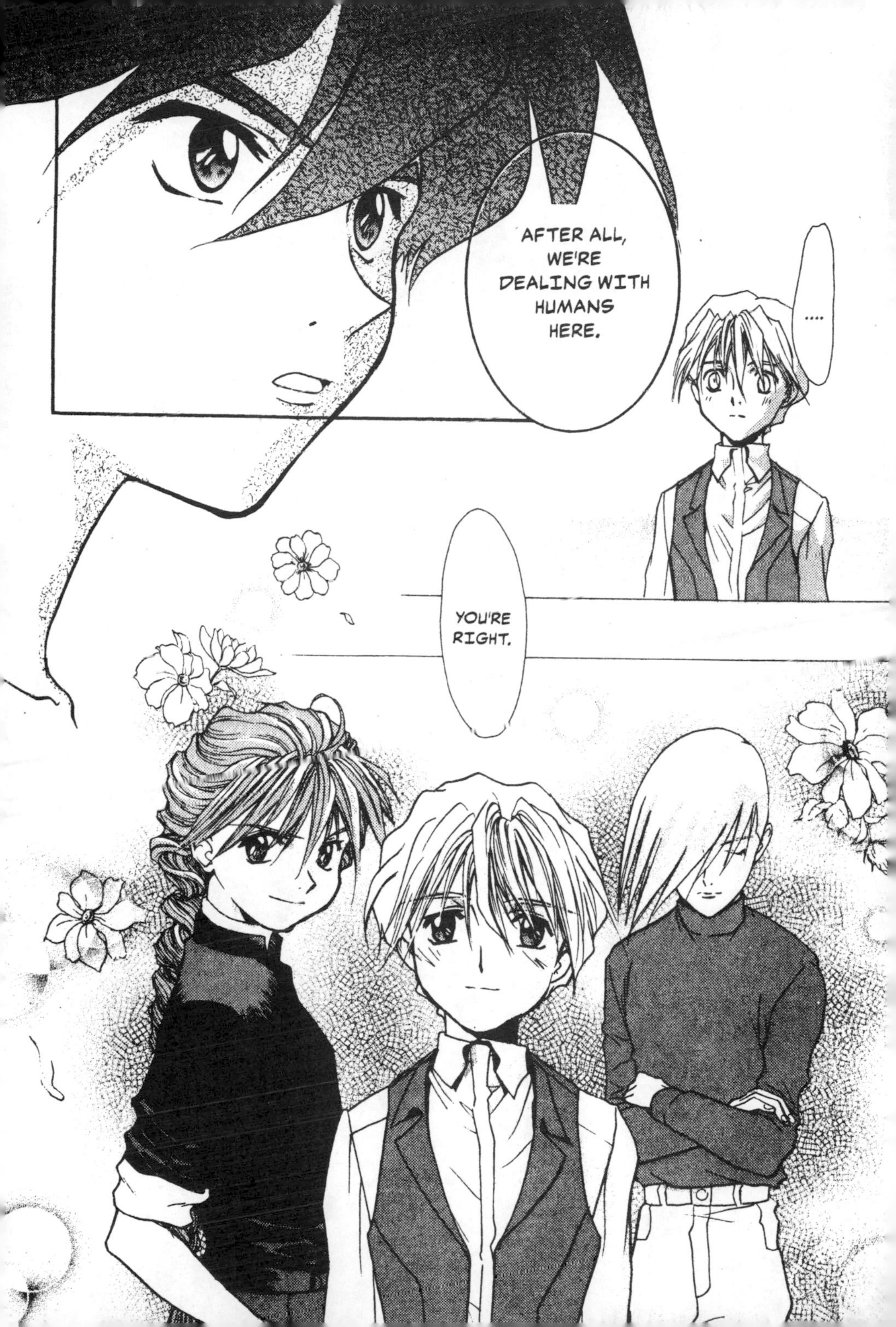
AFTER ALL, WE'RE DEALING WITH HUMANS HERE.
....
YOU'RE RIGHT.

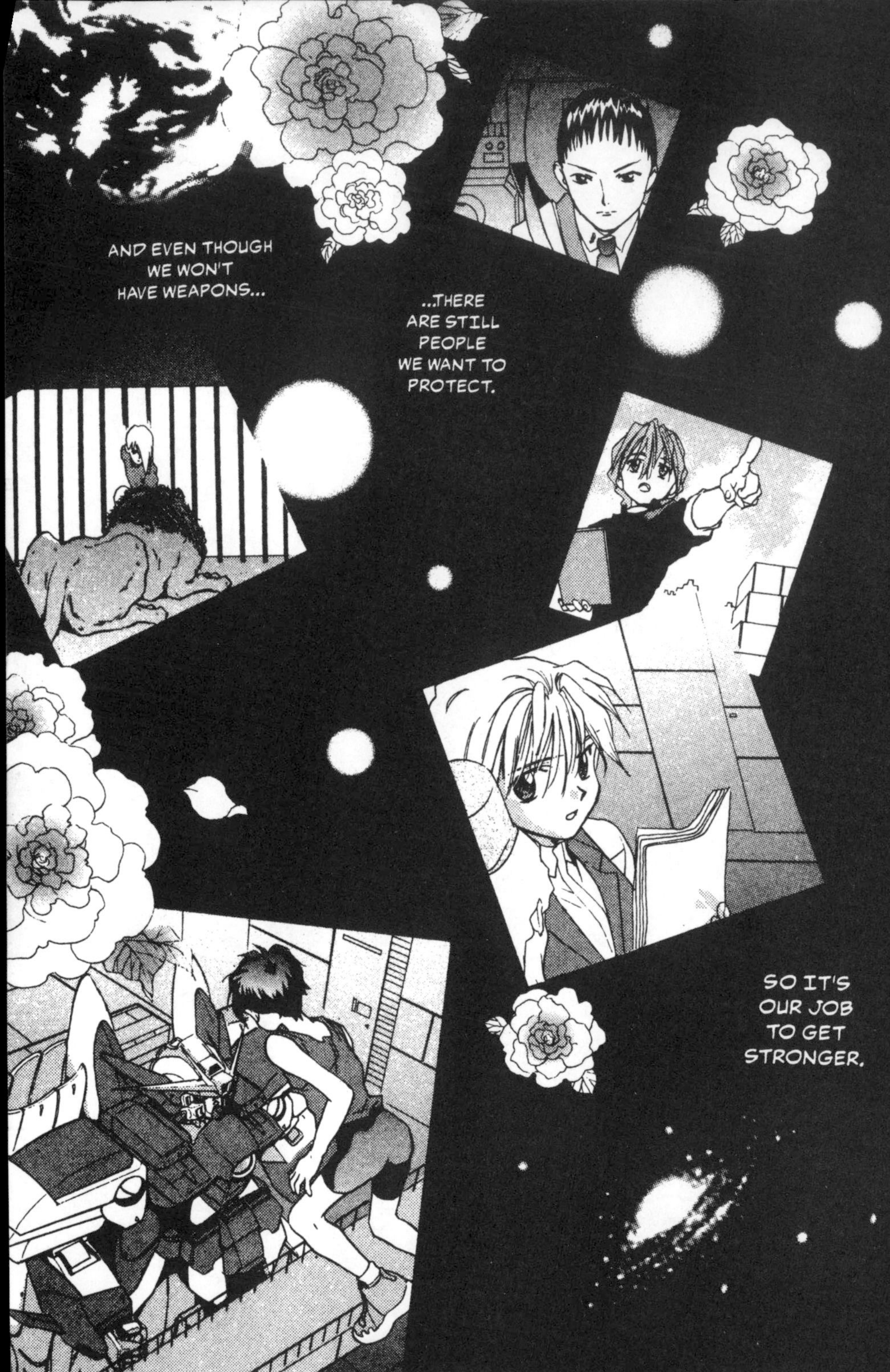
AND EVEN THOUGH WE WON'T HAVE WEAPONS...
...THERE ARE STILL PEOPLE WE WANT TO PROTECT.
SO IT'S OUR JOB TO GET STRONGER.

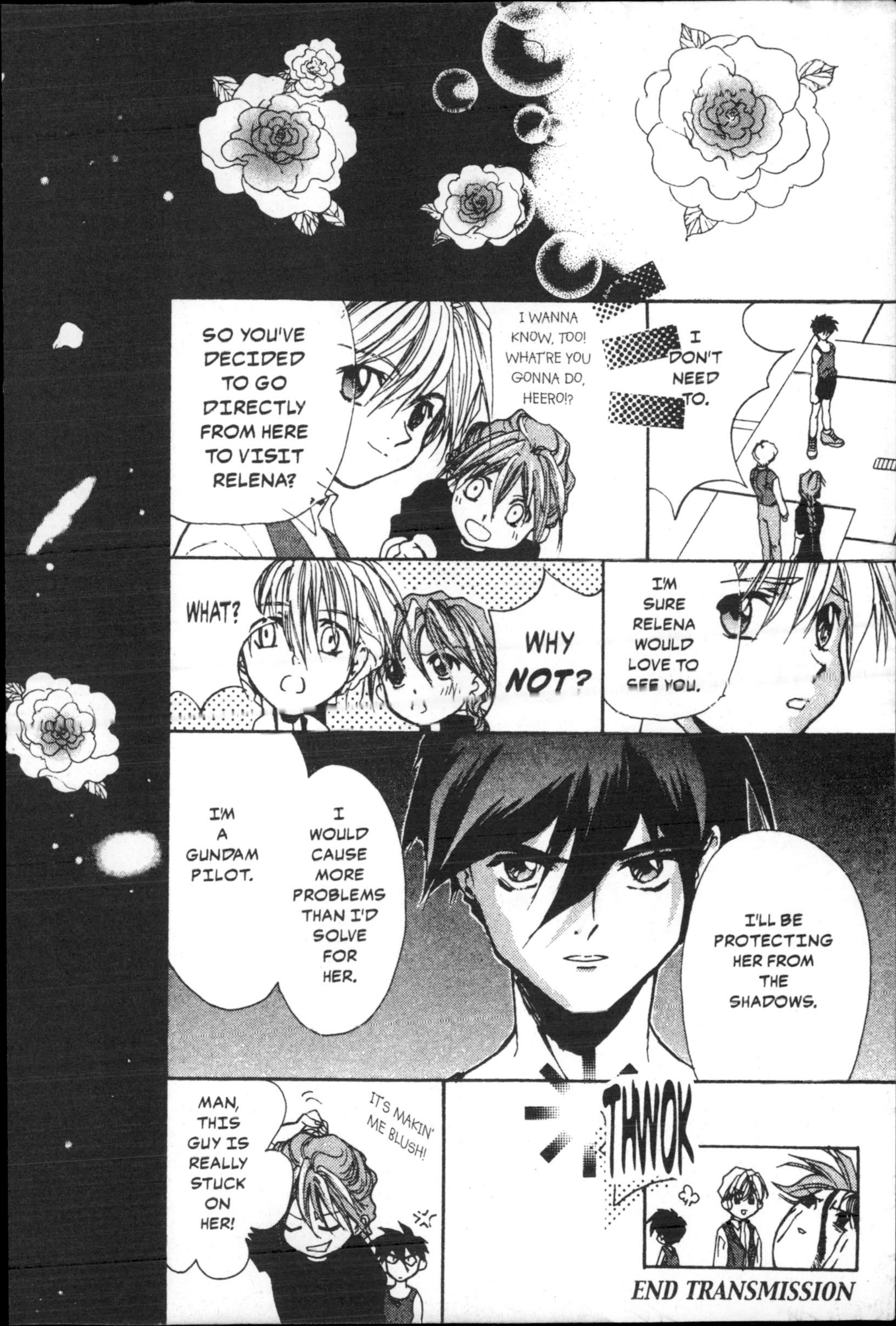
SO YOU'VE DECIDED TO GO DIRECTLY FROM HERE TO VISIT RELENA?
I WANNA KNOW, TOO! WHAT'RE YOU GONNA DO, HEERO!?
I DON'T NEED TO.
WHAT?
WHY NOT?
I'M SURE RELENA WOULD LOVE TO SEE YOU.
I'M A GUNDAM PILOT.
I WOULD CAUSE MORE PROBLEMS THAN I'D SOLVE FOR HER.
I'LL BE PROTECTING HER FROM THE SHADOWS.
MAN, THIS GUY IS REALLY STUCK ON HER!
IT'S MAKIN' ME BLUSH!
THWOK
END TRANSMISSION

CHAPTER THREE

イン・ローザ

IN·ROSE

Perhaps you see roses blooming on dark, deep wooden skin.

From the same stalk that strikes lingering agony;

Now, life bursts forth a blaze of serene red; And rushes higher, scattering brilliant light. The crucifix no longer signifies the grave. The fragrance that rushes to greet you is the perfume of rebirth.

—Friedrich Lienhard

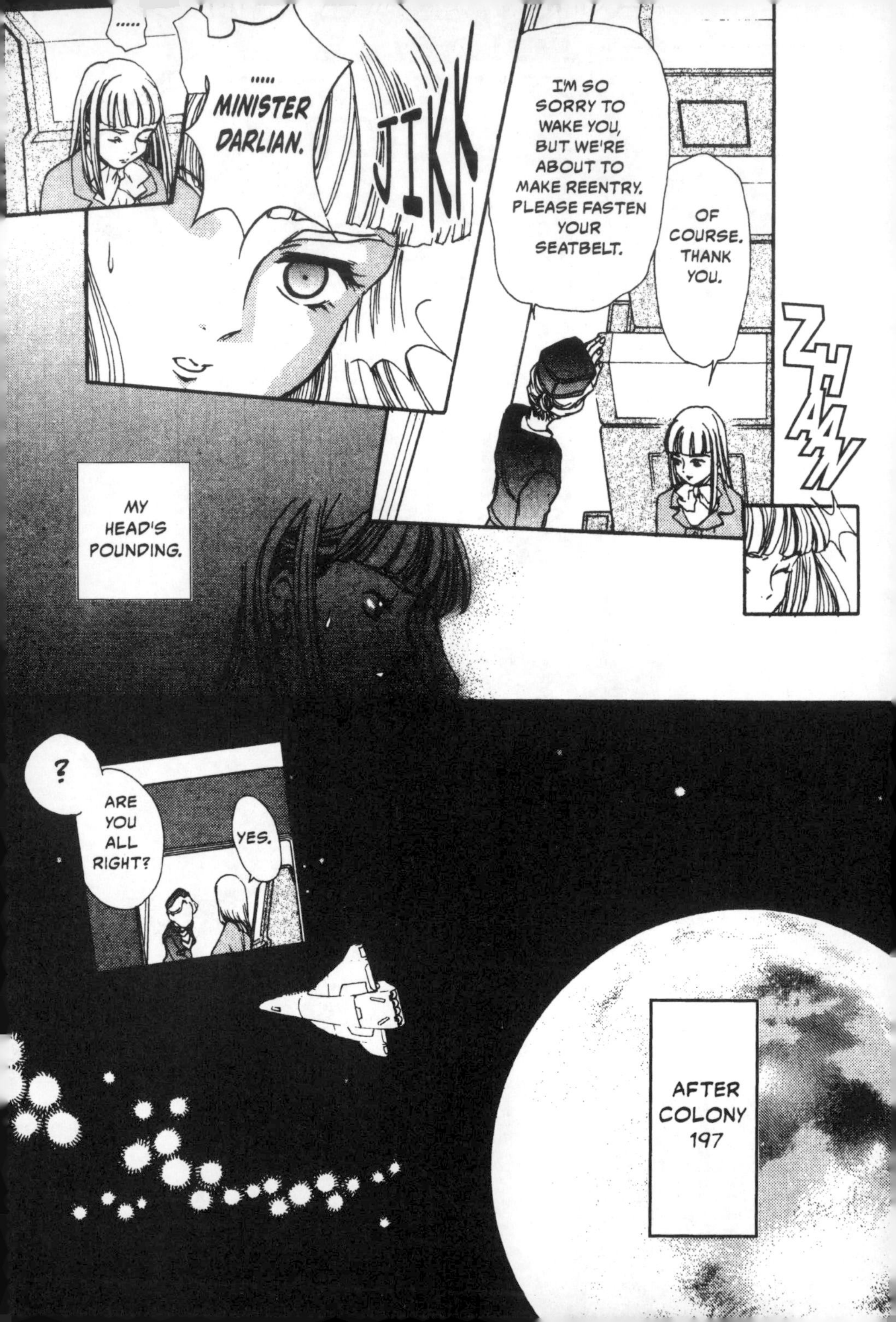
......
...... MINISTER DARLIAN.
JIKK
I'M SO SORRY TO WAKE YOU, BUT WE'RE ABOUT TO MAKE REENTRY. PLEASE FASTEN YOUR SEATBELT.
OF COURSE. THANK YOU.
ZHAAAN
MY HEAD'S POUNDING.
?
ARE YOU ALL RIGHT?
YES.
AFTER COLONY 197

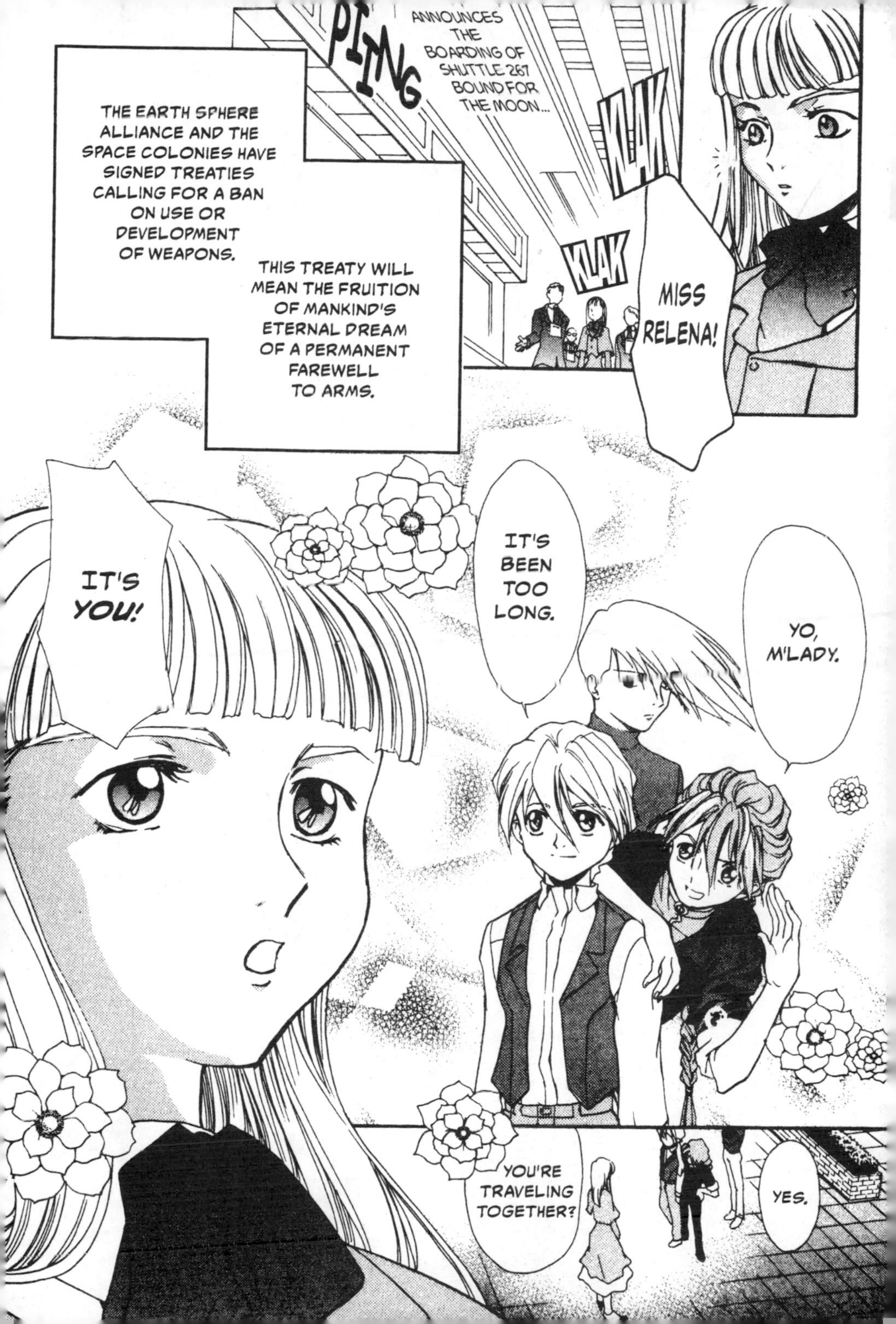
THE EARTH SPHERE ALLIANCE AND THE SPACE COLONIES HAVE SIGNED TREATIES CALLING FOR A BAN ON USE OR DEVELOPMENT OF WEAPONS.
THIS TREATY WILL MEAN THE FRUITION OF MANKIND'S ETERNAL DREAM OF A PERMANENT FAREWELL TO ARMS.
PITING
ANNOUNCES THE BOARDING OF SHUTTLE 267 BOUND FOR THE MOON...
KLAK
KLAK
MISS RELENA!
IT'S YOU!
IT'S BEEN TOO LONG.
YO, M'LADY.
YOU'RE TRAVELING TOGETHER?
YES.

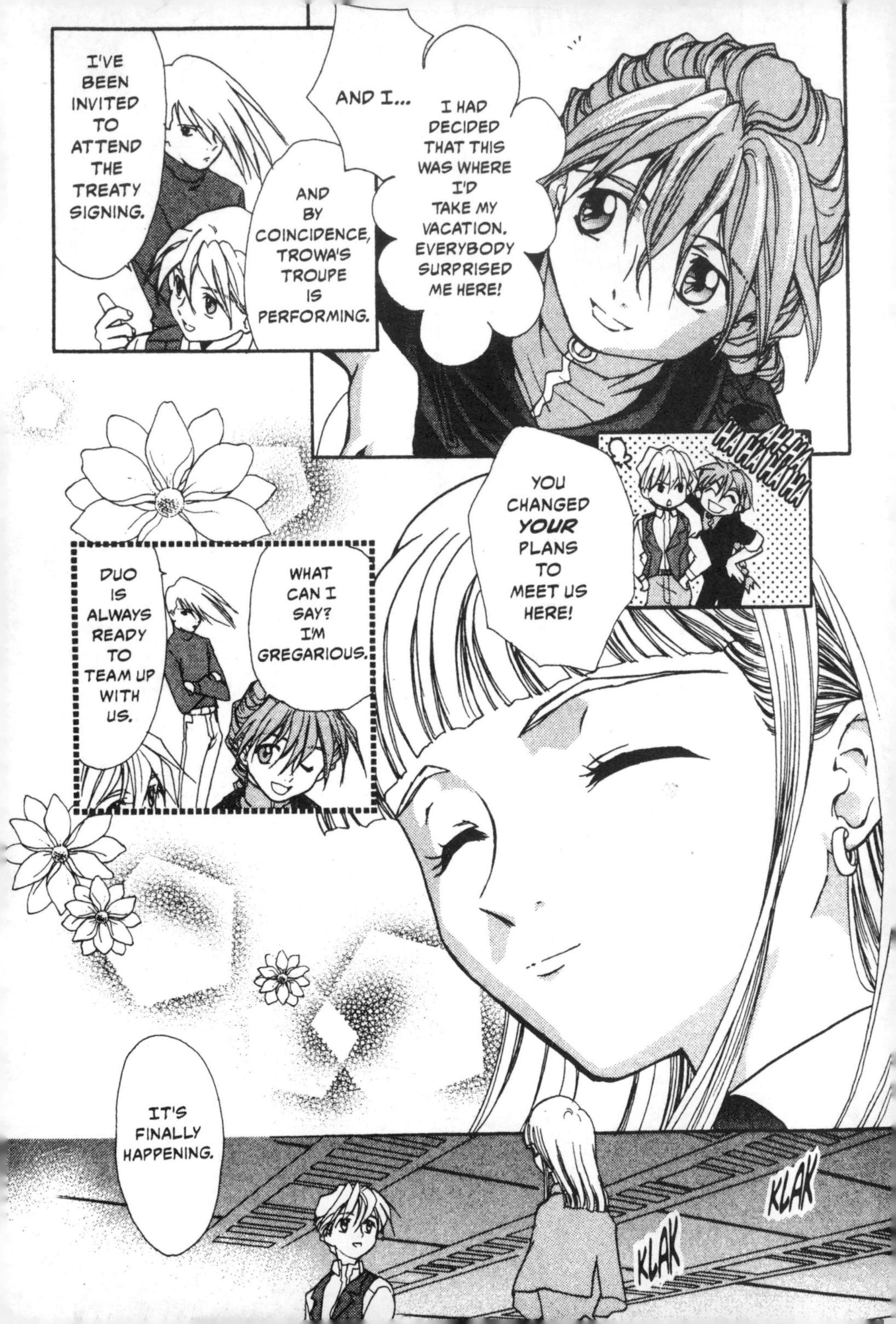
I'VE BEEN INVITED TO ATTEND THE TREATY SIGNING.
AND BY COINCIDENCE, TROWA'S TROUPE IS PERFORMING.
AND I...
I HAD DECIDED THAT THIS WAS WHERE I'D TAKE MY VACATION. EVERYBODY SURPRISED ME HERE!
DUO IS ALWAYS READY TO TEAM UP WITH US.
WHAT CAN I SAY? I'M GREGARIOUS.
YOU CHANGED ***YOUR*** PLANS TO MEET US HERE!
AH-HA
HA HA HA HA HA
IT'S FINALLY HAPPENING.
KLAK
KLAK

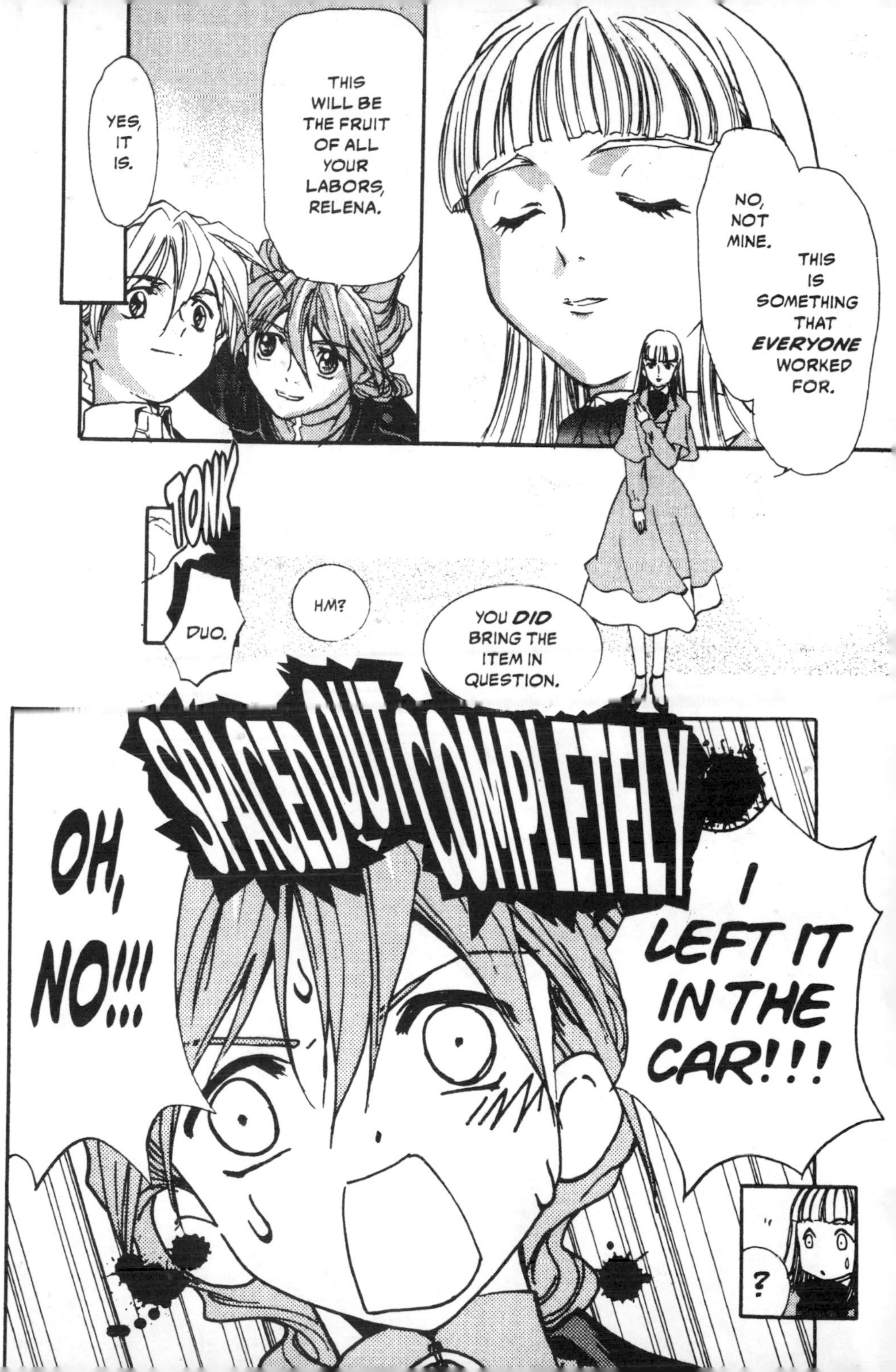

YES, IT IS.
THIS WILL BE THE FRUIT OF ALL YOUR LABORS, RELENA.
NO, NOT MINE.
THIS IS SOMETHING THAT *EVERYONE* WORKED FOR.
TONK
DUO.
HM?
YOU *DID* BRING THE ITEM IN QUESTION.
SPACED OUT COMPLETELY
OH, NO!!!
I LEFT IT IN THE CAR!!!
?

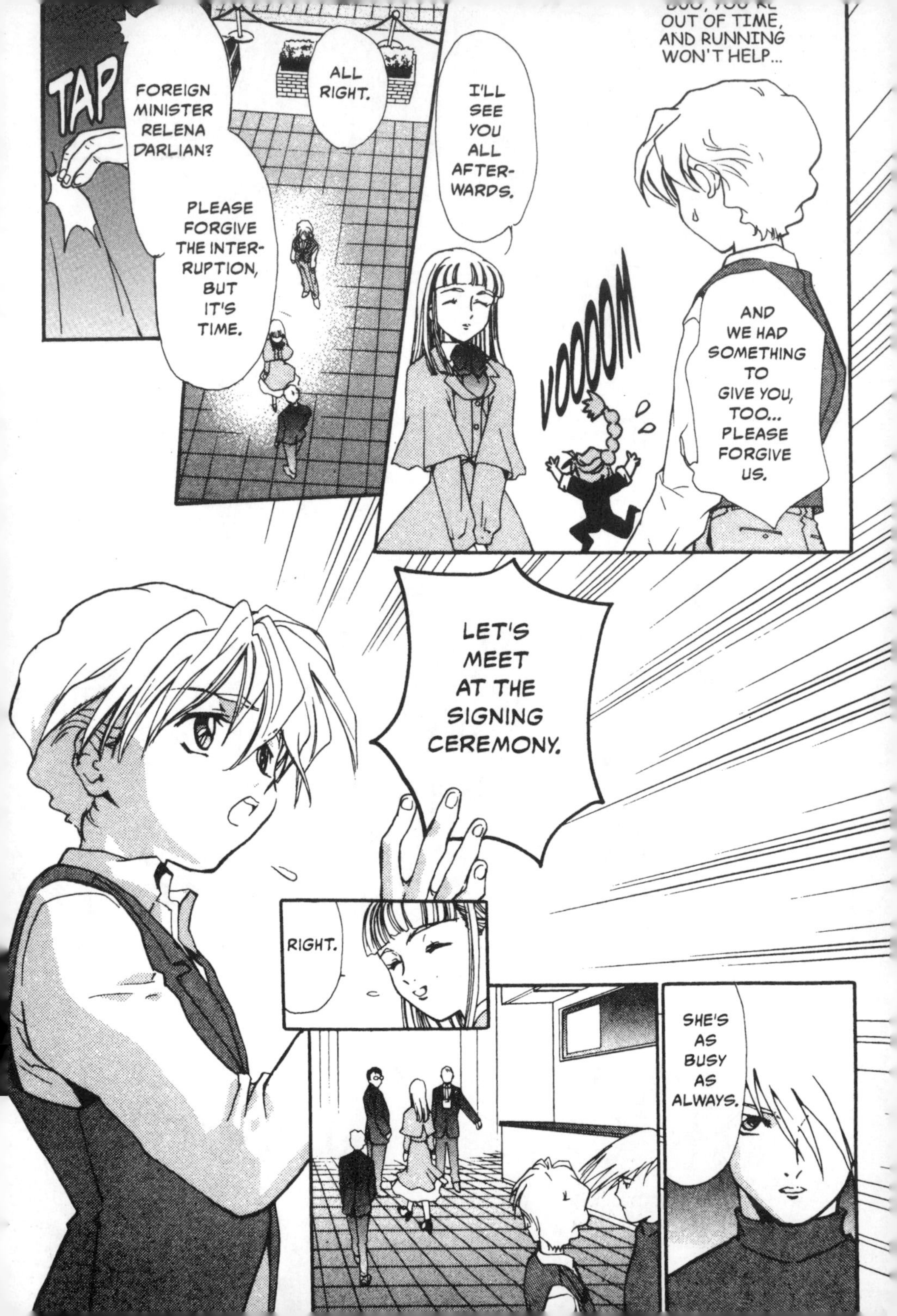
TAP
FOREIGN MINISTER RELENA DARLIAN?
PLEASE FORGIVE THE INTERRUPTION, BUT IT'S TIME.
ALL RIGHT.
I'LL SEE YOU ALL AFTERWARDS.
OUT OF TIME, AND RUNNING WON'T HELP...
VOOOOM
AND WE HAD SOMETHING TO GIVE YOU, TOO... PLEASE FORGIVE US.
LET'S MEET AT THE SIGNING CEREMONY.
RIGHT.
SHE'S AS BUSY AS ALWAYS.

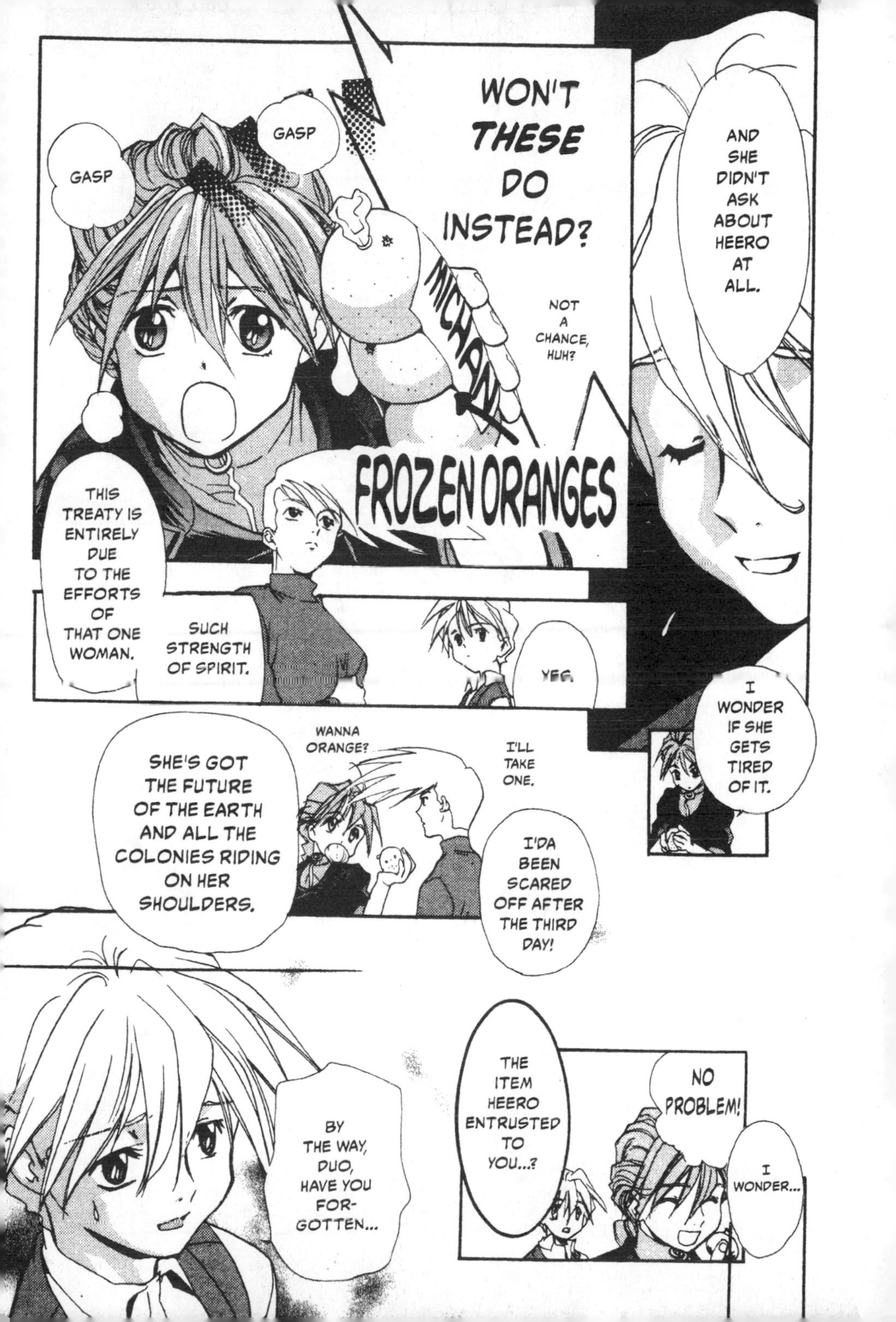
GASP
GASP
WON'T THESE DO INSTEAD?
MICHAN!
NOT A CHANCE, HUH?
FROZEN ORANGES
THIS TREATY IS ENTIRELY DUE TO THE EFFORTS OF THAT ONE WOMAN.
SUCH STRENGTH OF SPIRIT.
YES.
AND SHE DIDN'T ASK ABOUT HEERO AT ALL.
SHE'S GOT THE FUTURE OF THE EARTH AND ALL THE COLONIES RIDING ON HER SHOULDERS.
WANNA ORANGE?
I'LL TAKE ONE.
I'DA BEEN SCARED OFF AFTER THE THIRD DAY!
I WONDER IF SHE GETS TIRED OF IT.
BY THE WAY, DUO, HAVE YOU FOR-GOTTEN...
THE ITEM HEERO ENTRUSTED TO YOU...?
NO PROBLEM!
I WONDER...

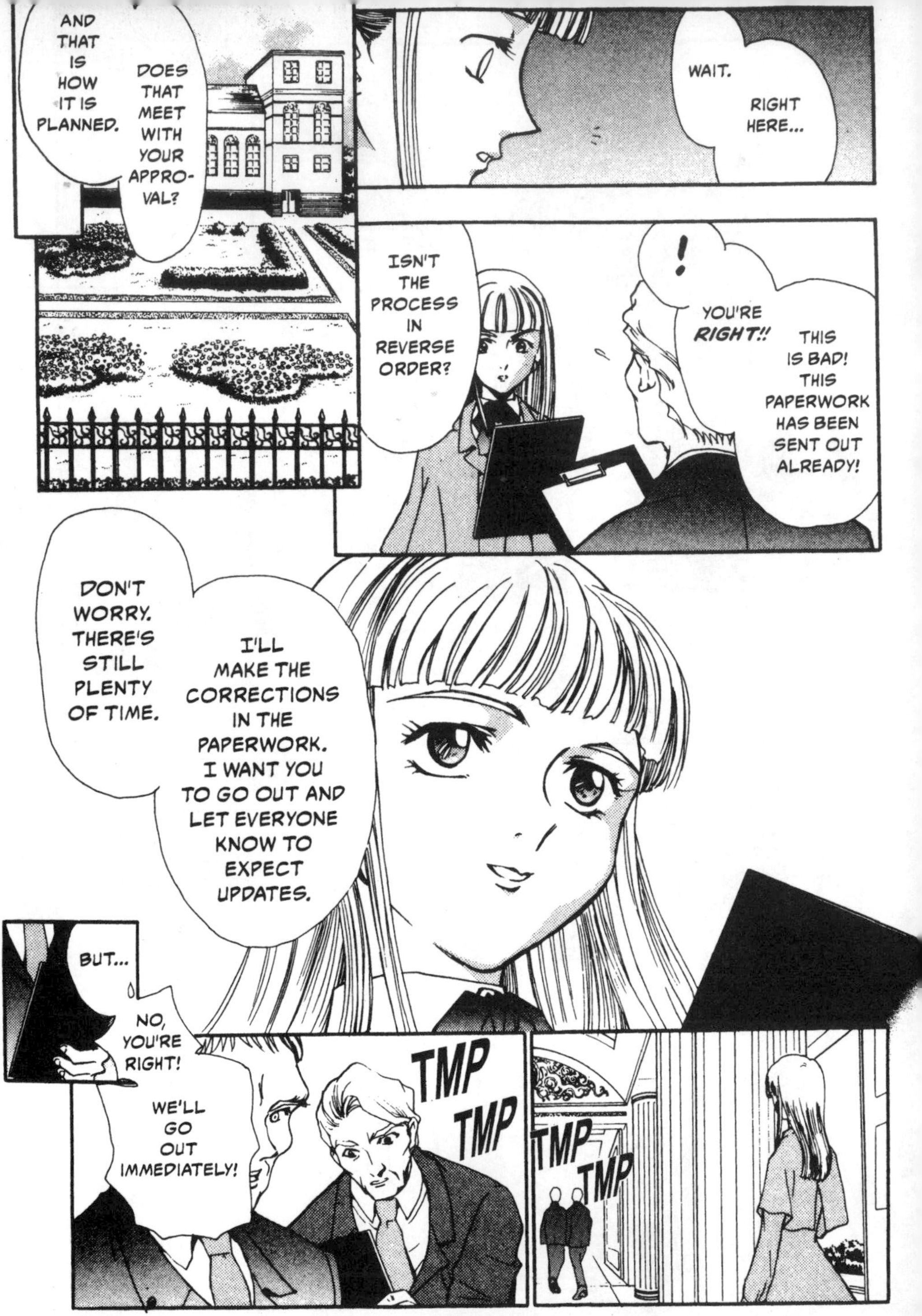

AND THAT IS HOW IT IS PLANNED.
DOES THAT MEET WITH YOUR APPROVAL?
WAIT.
RIGHT HERE...
ISN'T THE PROCESS IN REVERSE ORDER?
!
YOU'RE **RIGHT!!**
THIS IS BAD! THIS PAPERWORK HAS BEEN SENT OUT ALREADY!
DON'T WORRY. THERE'S STILL PLENTY OF TIME.
I'LL MAKE THE CORRECTIONS IN THE PAPERWORK. I WANT YOU TO GO OUT AND LET EVERYONE KNOW TO EXPECT UPDATES.
BUT...
NO, YOU'RE RIGHT!
WE'LL GO OUT IMMEDIATELY!
TMP TMP
TMP TMP

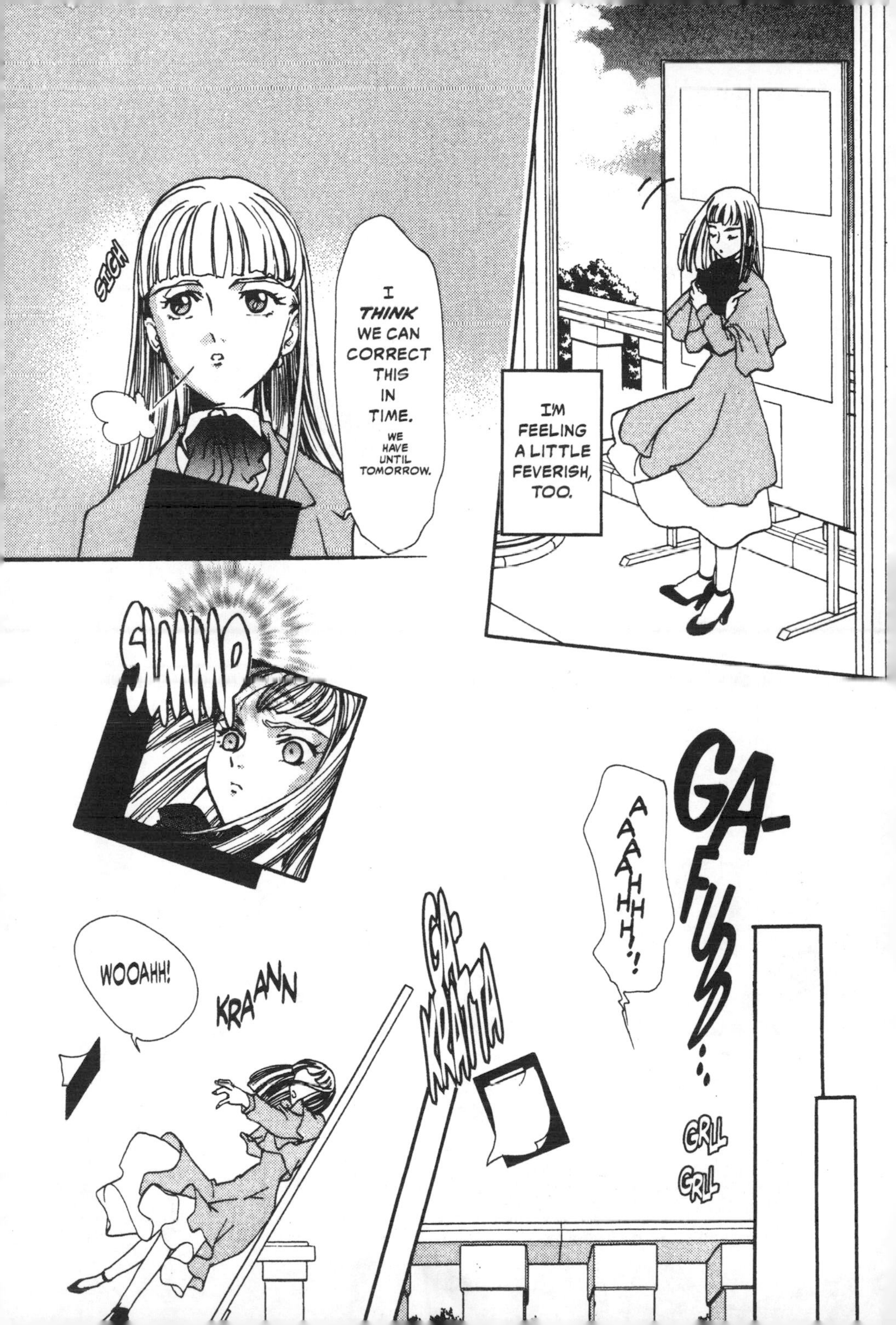
SIGH
I *THINK* WE CAN CORRECT THIS IN TIME.
WE HAVE UNTIL TOMORROW.
I'M FEELING A LITTLE FEVERISH, TOO.
SLAMMP
WOOAHH!
KRAANN
GA-KRATTA
AAAHHH?!
GA-FUSS...
GRLL
GRLL

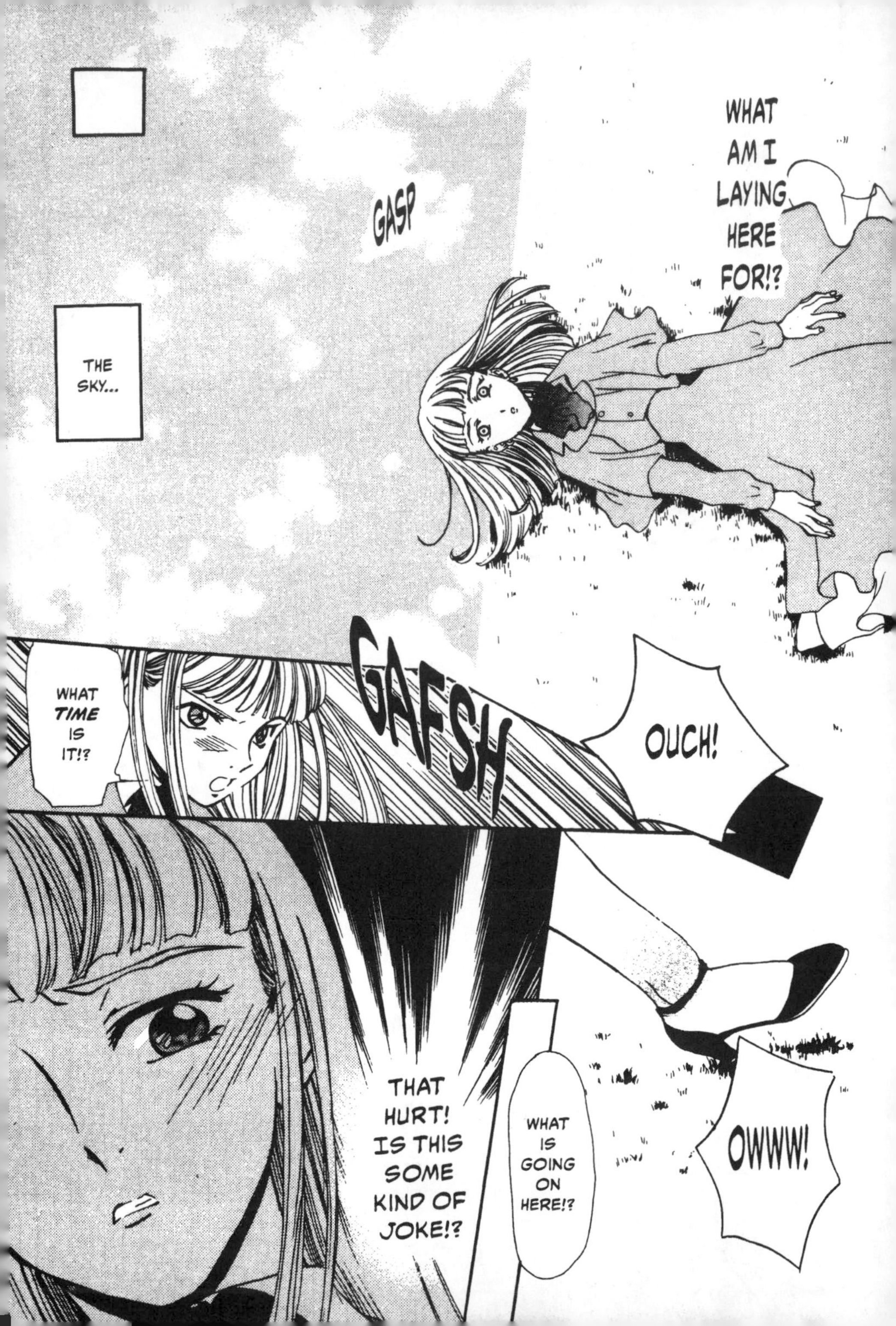
THE SKY...
GASP
WHAT AM I LAYING HERE FOR!?
WHAT *TIME* IS IT!?
GAFSH
OUCH!
THAT HURT! IS THIS SOME KIND OF JOKE!?
WHAT IS GOING ON HERE!?
OWWW!

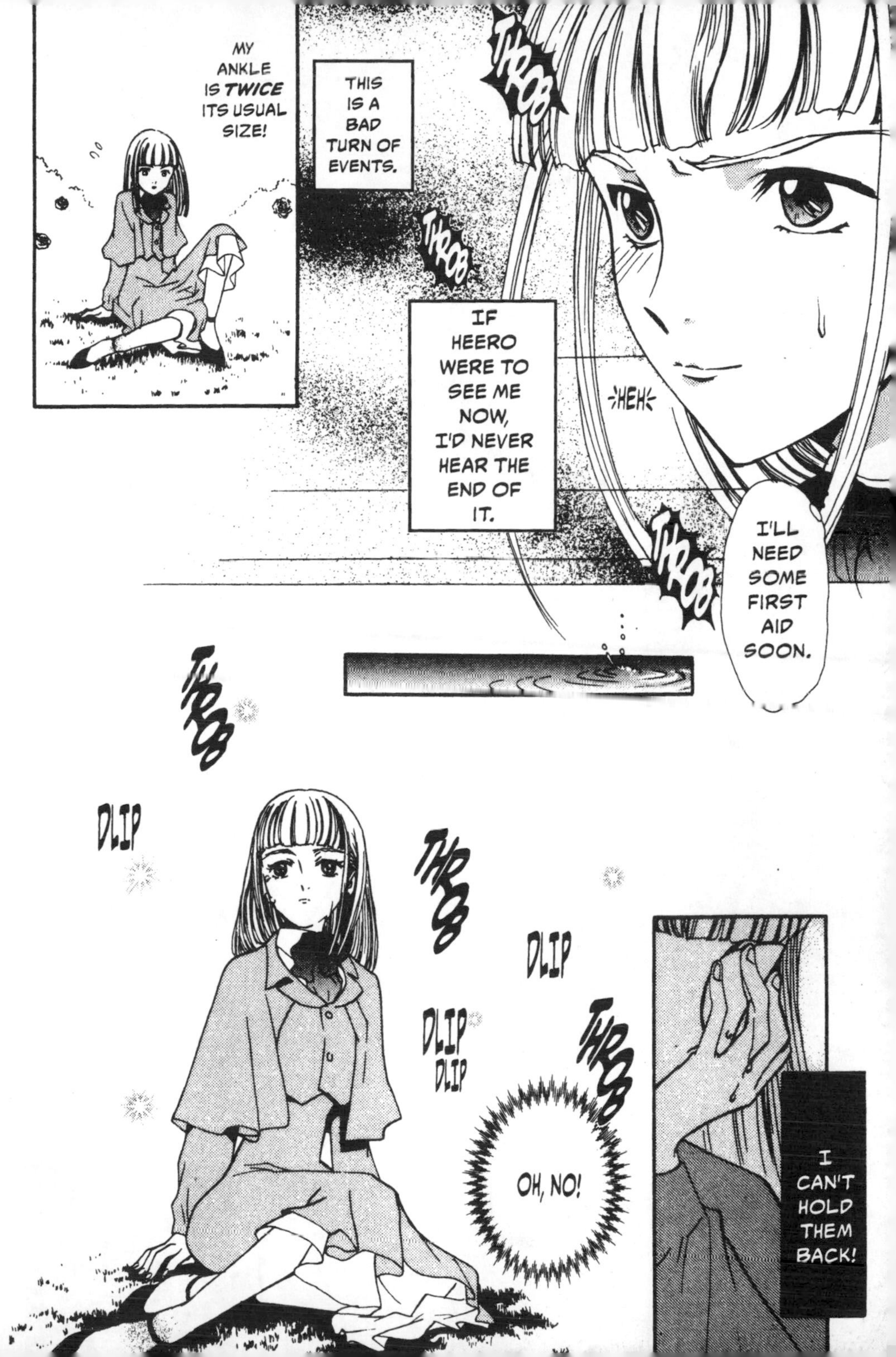
MY ANKLE IS *TWICE* ITS USUAL SIZE!
THIS IS A BAD TURN OF EVENTS.
THROB
THROB
IF HEERO WERE TO SEE ME NOW, I'D NEVER HEAR THE END OF IT.
HEH
THROB
I'LL NEED SOME FIRST AID SOON.
THROB
DLIP
THROB
DLIP
DLIP DLIP
THROB
OH, NO!
I CAN'T HOLD THEM BACK!

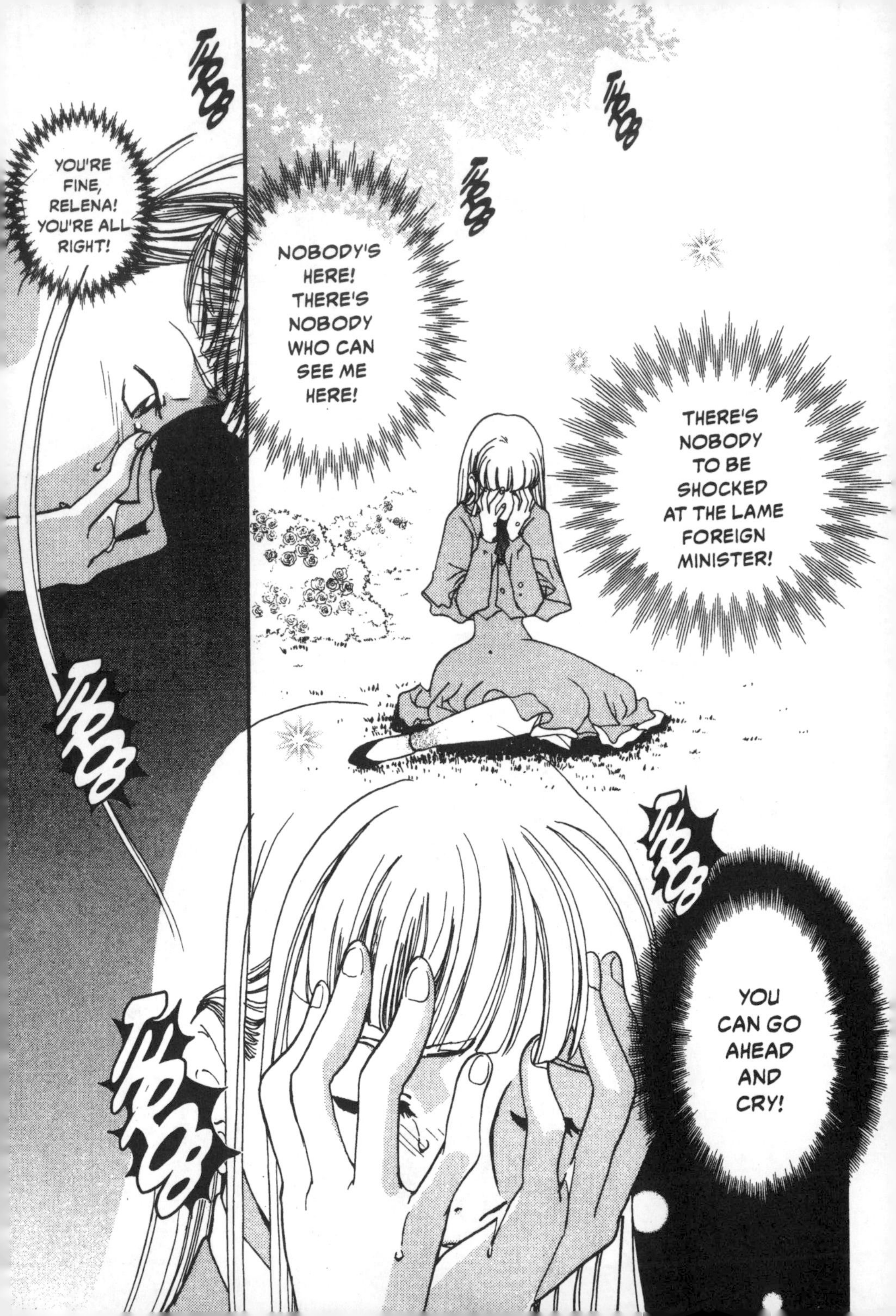
YOU'RE FINE, RELENA! YOU'RE ALL RIGHT!
NOBODY'S HERE! THERE'S NOBODY WHO CAN SEE ME HERE!
THERE'S NOBODY TO BE SHOCKED AT THE LAME FOREIGN MINISTER!
YOU CAN GO AHEAD AND CRY!

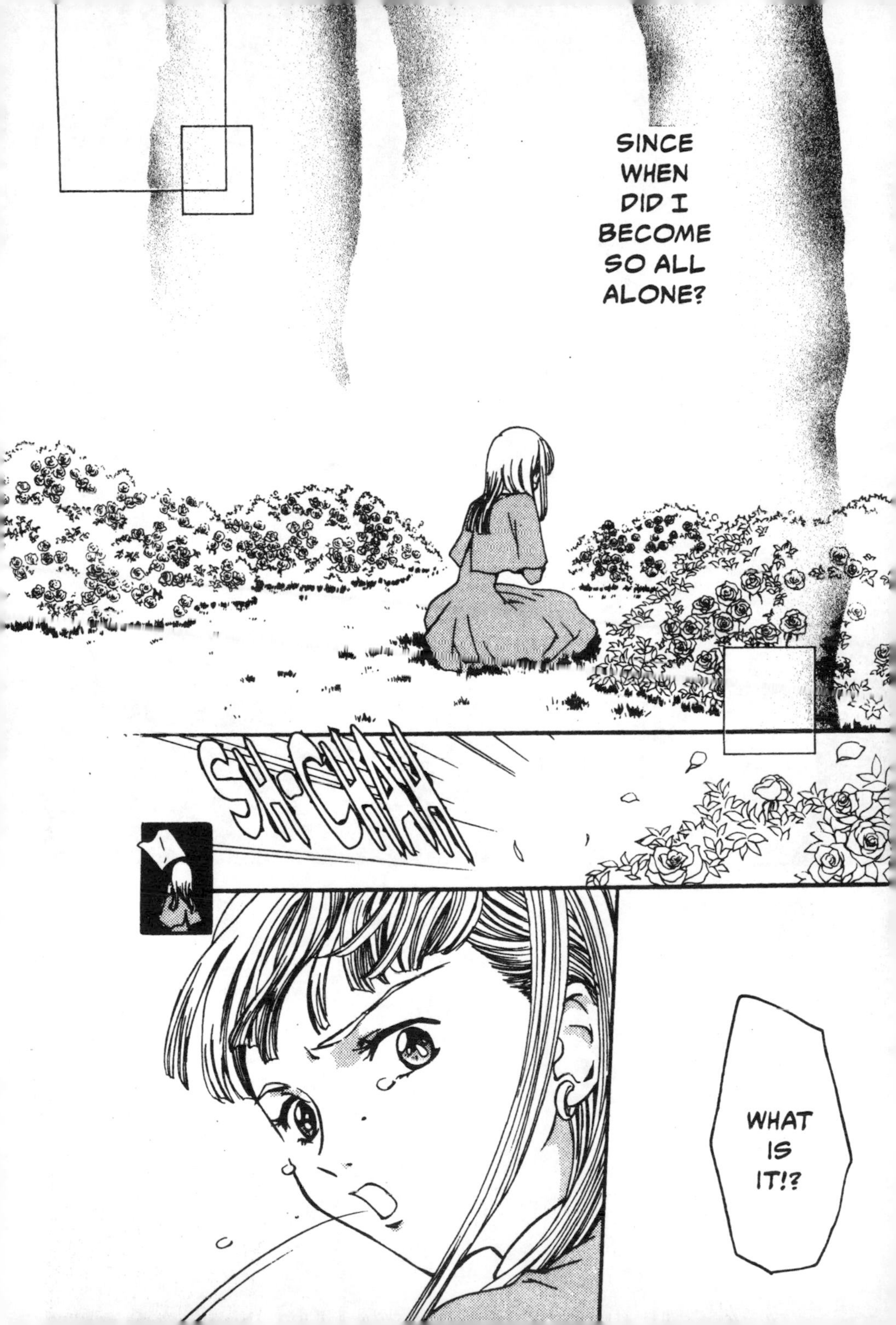
SINCE WHEN DID I BECOME SO ALL ALONE?
SHCHAH
WHAT IS IT!?

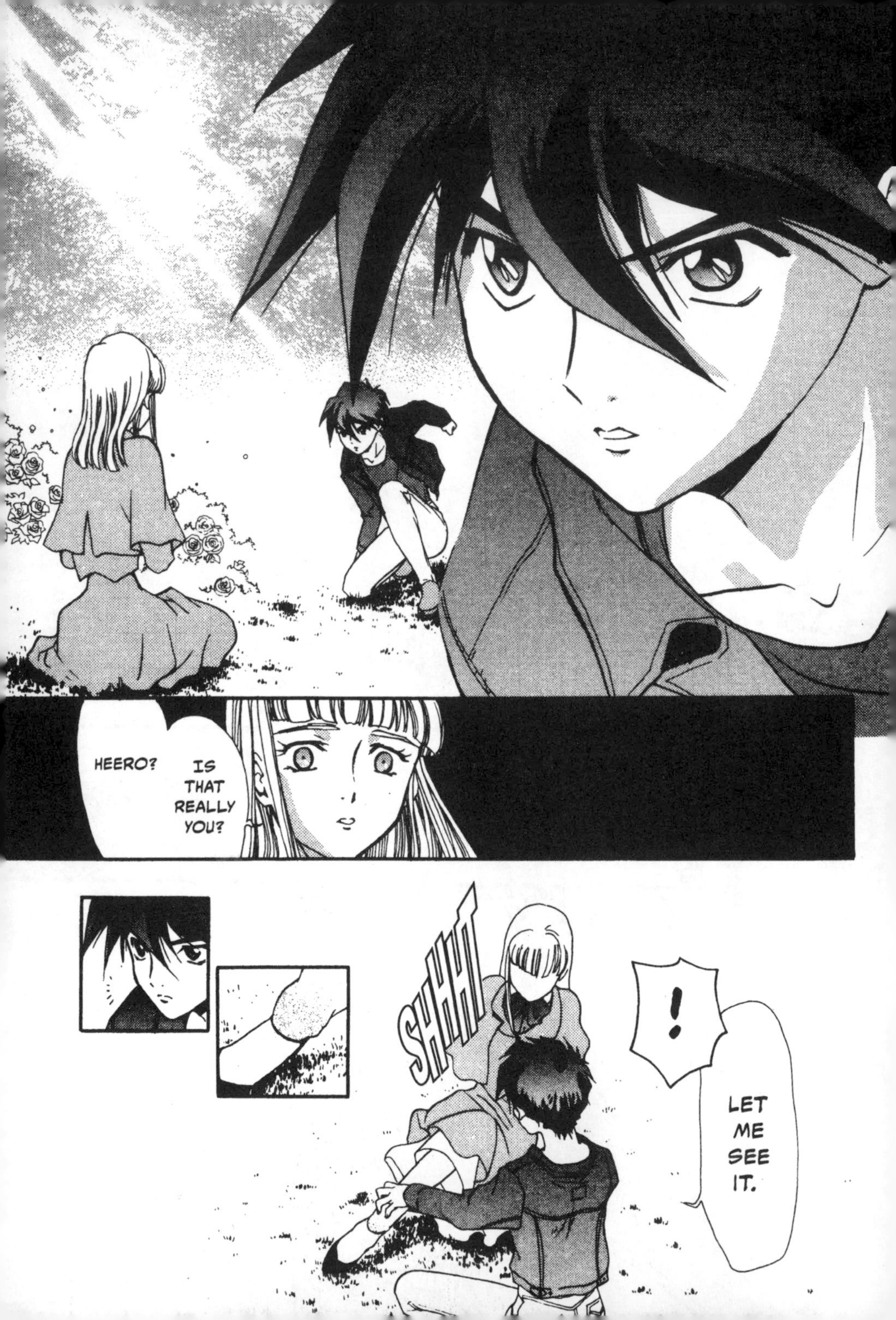
HEERO?
IS THAT REALLY YOU?
SHHHT
!
LET ME SEE IT.

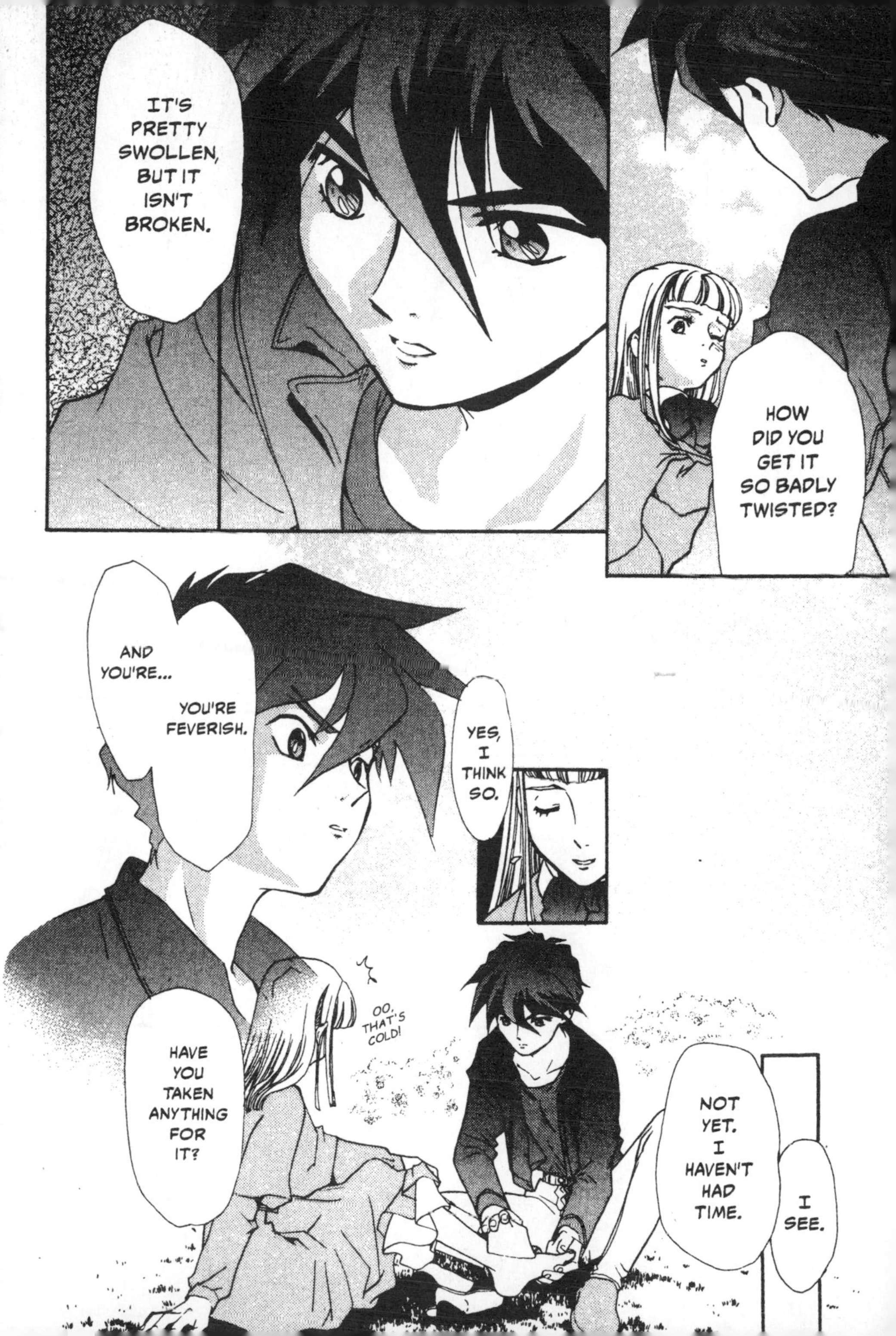
IT'S PRETTY SWOLLEN, BUT IT ISN'T BROKEN.
HOW DID YOU GET IT SO BADLY TWISTED?
AND YOU'RE...
YOU'RE FEVERISH.
YES, I THINK SO.
HAVE YOU TAKEN ANYTHING FOR IT?
OO, THAT'S COLD!
NOT YET. I HAVEN'T HAD TIME.
I SEE.

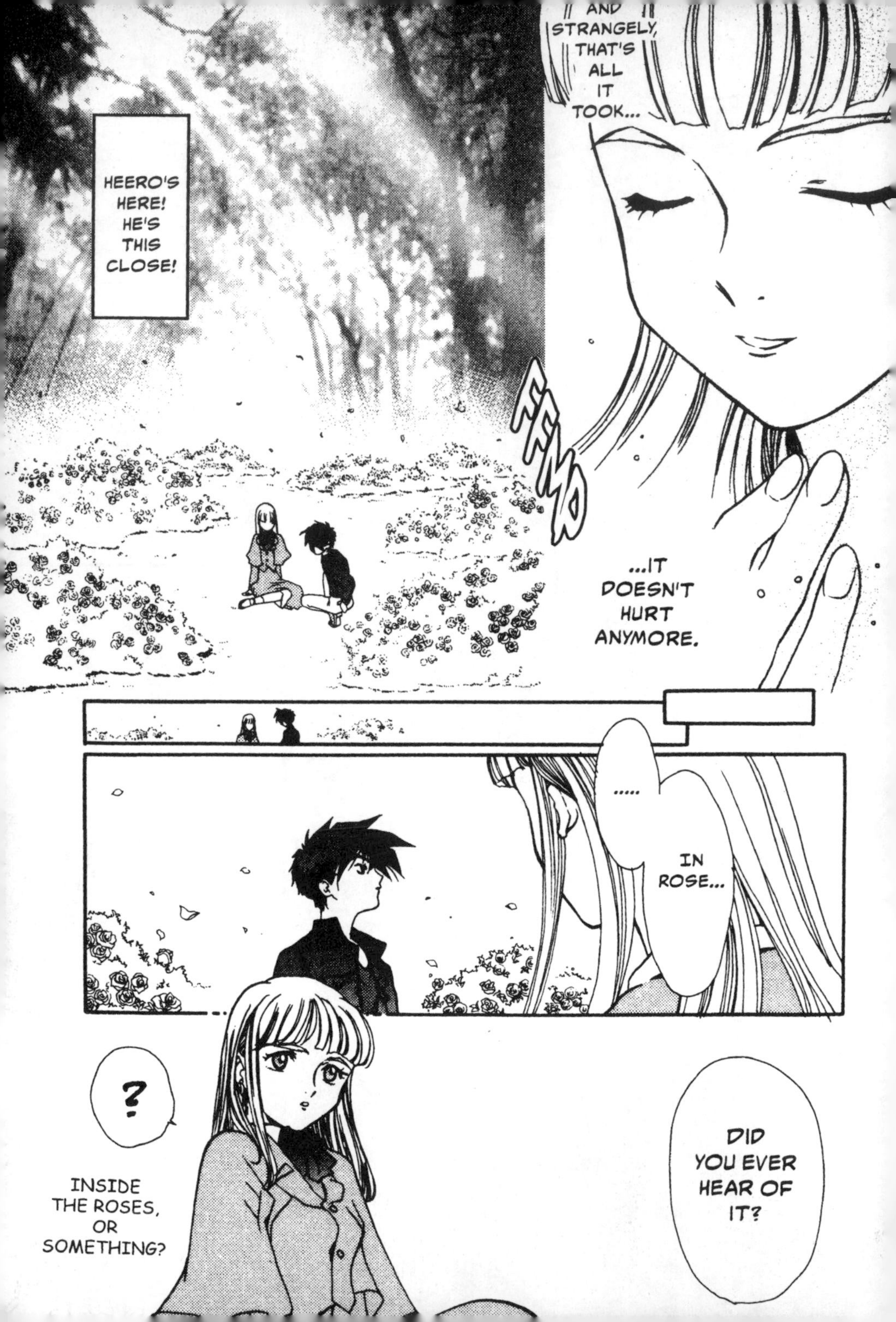
HEERO'S HERE! HE'S THIS CLOSE!
AND STRANGELY, THAT'S ALL IT TOOK...
...IT DOESN'T HURT ANYMORE.
.....
IN ROSE...
?
INSIDE THE ROSES, OR SOMETHING?
DID YOU EVER HEAR OF IT?

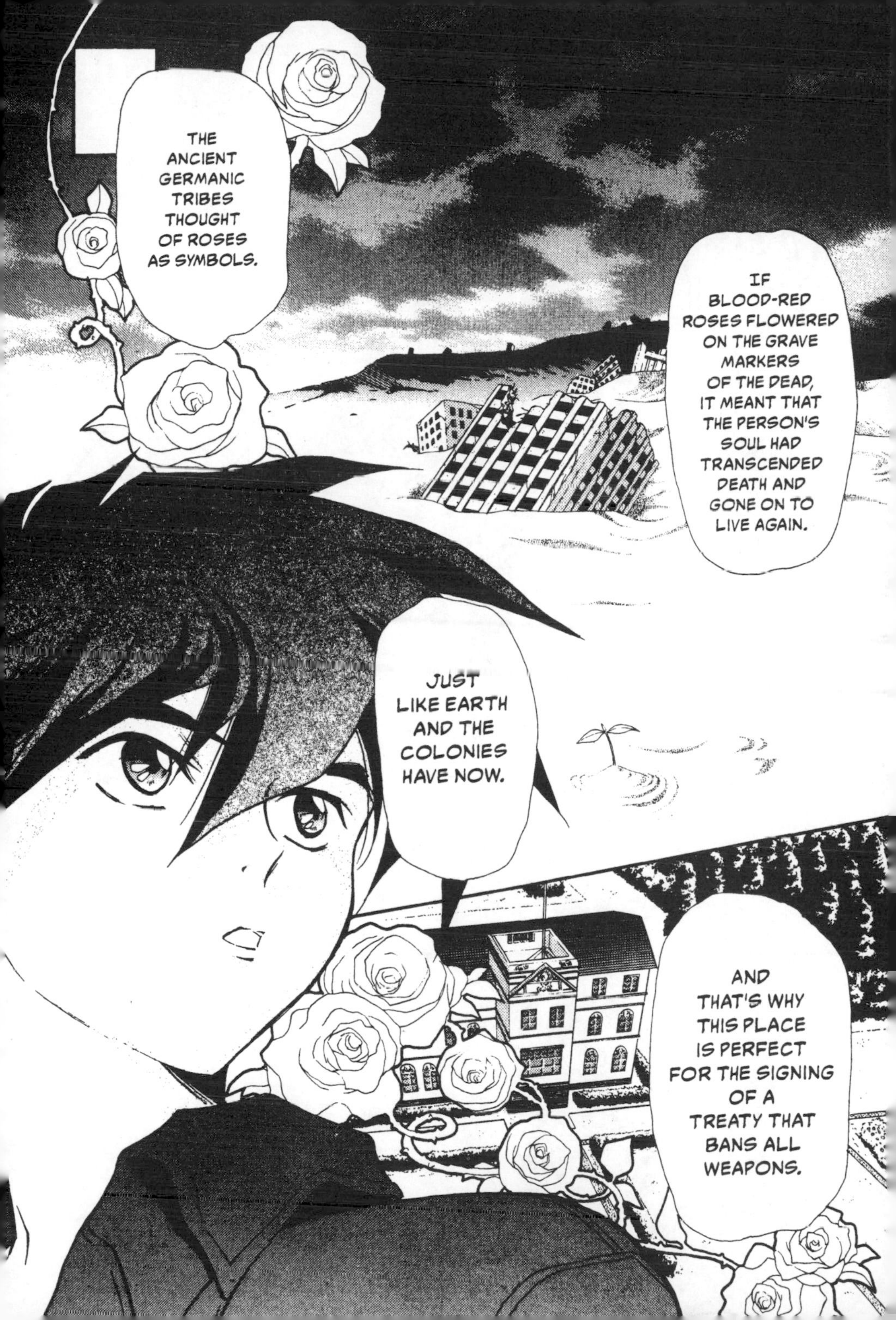
THE ANCIENT GERMANIC TRIBES THOUGHT OF ROSES AS SYMBOLS.
IF BLOOD-RED ROSES FLOWERED ON THE GRAVE MARKERS OF THE DEAD, IT MEANT THAT THE PERSON'S SOUL HAD TRANSCENDED DEATH AND GONE ON TO LIVE AGAIN.
JUST LIKE EARTH AND THE COLONIES HAVE NOW.
AND THAT'S WHY THIS PLACE IS PERFECT FOR THE SIGNING OF A TREATY THAT BANS ALL WEAPONS.

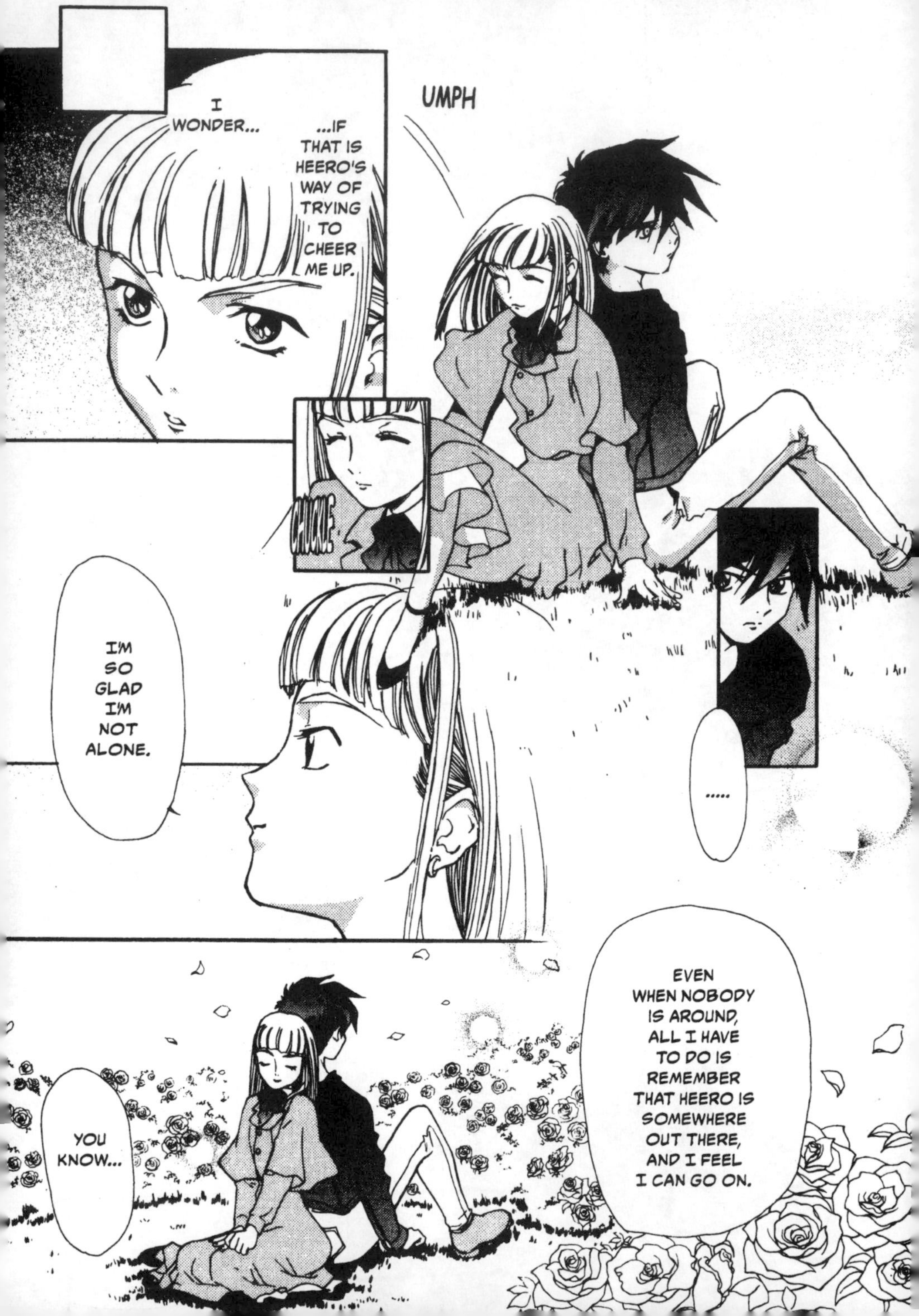
I WONDER...
...IF THAT IS HEERO'S WAY OF TRYING TO CHEER ME UP.
UMPH
CHUCKLE
I'M SO GLAD I'M NOT ALONE.
.....
YOU KNOW...
EVEN WHEN NOBODY IS AROUND, ALL I HAVE TO DO IS REMEMBER THAT HEERO IS SOMEWHERE OUT THERE, AND I FEEL I CAN GO ON.

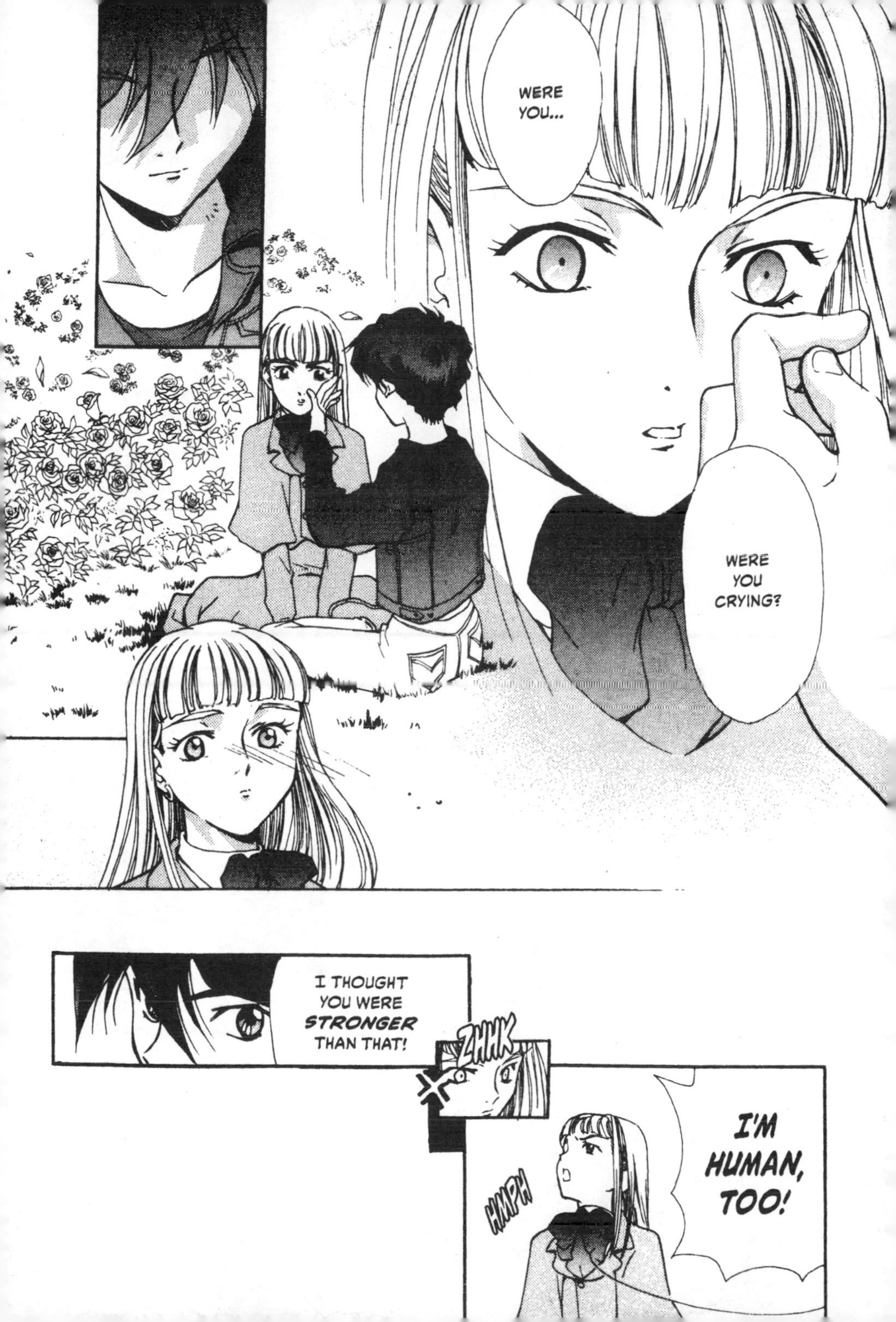

WERE YOU...
WERE YOU CRYING?
I THOUGHT YOU WERE **STRONGER** THAN THAT!
ZHHK
HMPH
I'M HUMAN, TOO!

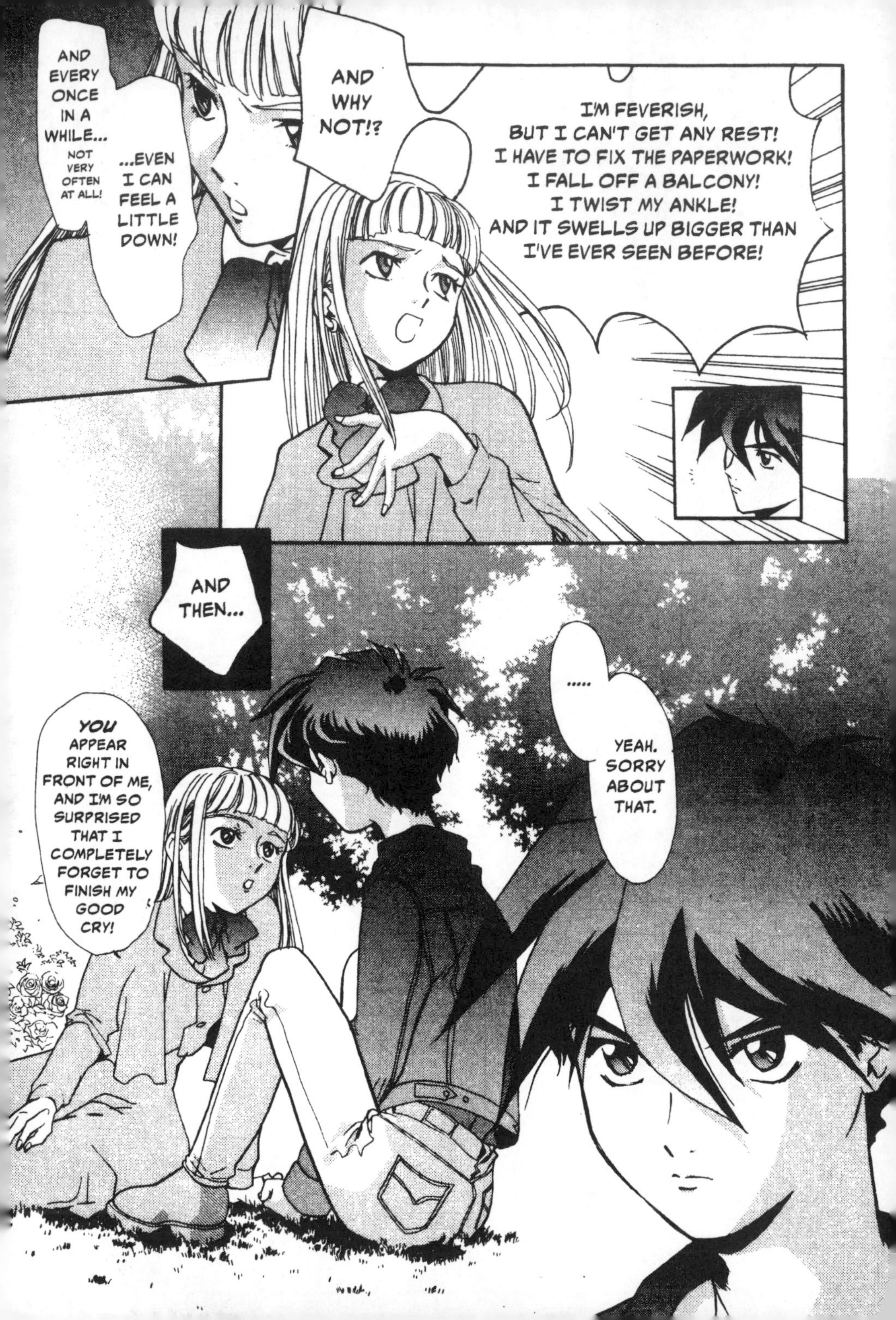
AND EVERY ONCE IN A WHILE...
NOT VERY OFTEN AT ALL!
...EVEN I CAN FEEL A LITTLE DOWN!
AND WHY NOT!?
I'M FEVERISH, BUT I CAN'T GET ANY REST! I HAVE TO FIX THE PAPERWORK! I FALL OFF A BALCONY! I TWIST MY ANKLE! AND IT SWELLS UP BIGGER THAN I'VE EVER SEEN BEFORE!
AND THEN...
YOU APPEAR RIGHT IN FRONT OF ME, AND I'M SO SURPRISED THAT I COMPLETELY FORGET TO FINISH MY GOOD CRY!
.....
YEAH. SORRY ABOUT THAT.

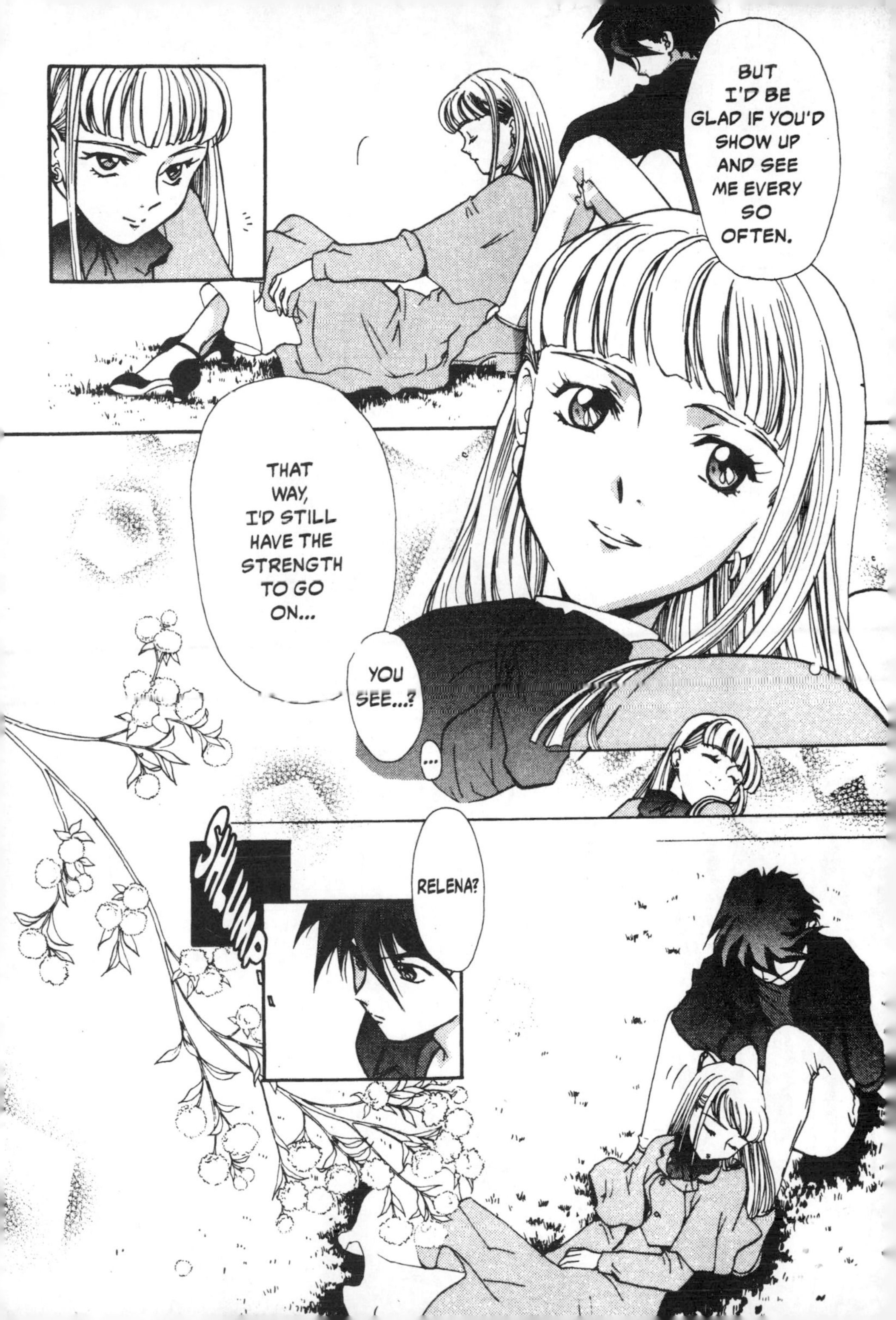
BUT I'D BE GLAD IF YOU'D SHOW UP AND SEE ME EVERY SO OFTEN.
THAT WAY, I'D STILL HAVE THE STRENGTH TO GO ON...
YOU SEE...?
...
SHLUMP
RELENA?

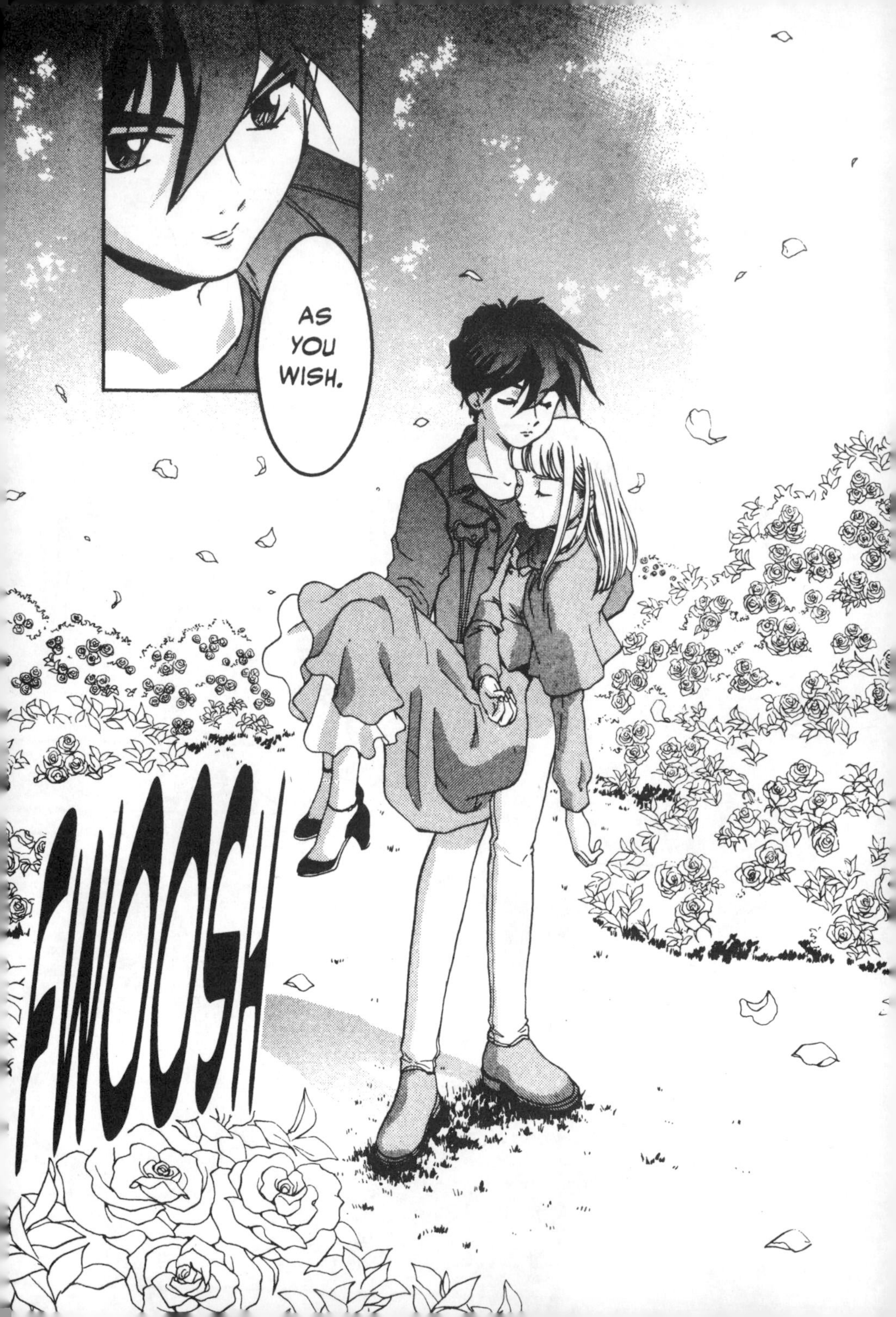
AS YOU WISH.
FWOOSH

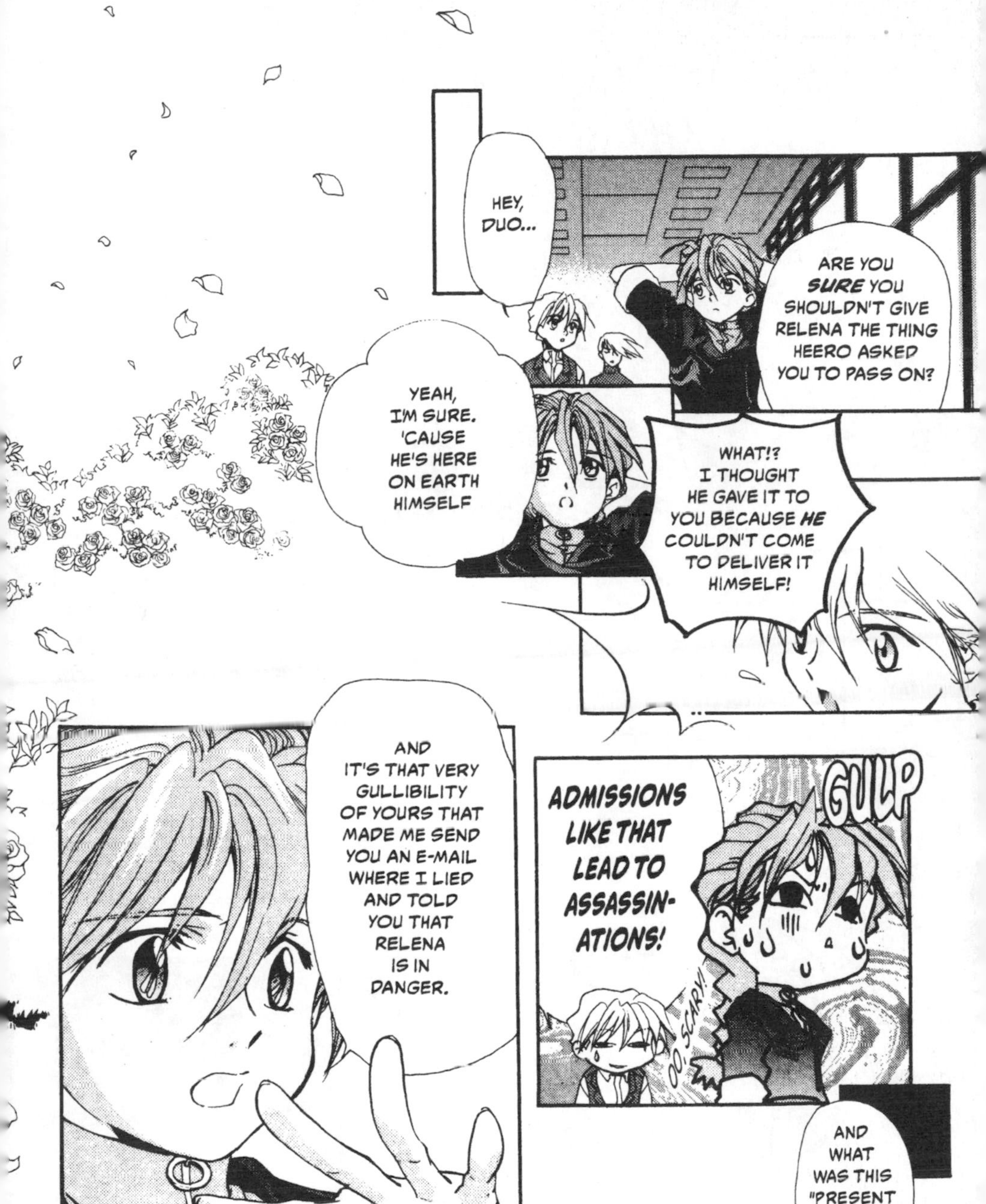
HEY, DUO...
ARE YOU SURE YOU SHOULDN'T GIVE RELENA THE THING HEERO ASKED YOU TO PASS ON?
YEAH, I'M SURE. 'CAUSE HE'S HERE ON EARTH HIMSELF
WHAT!? I THOUGHT HE GAVE IT TO YOU BECAUSE HE COULDN'T COME TO DELIVER IT HIMSELF!
...
AND IT'S THAT VERY GULLIBILITY OF YOURS THAT MADE ME SEND YOU AN E-MAIL WHERE I LIED AND TOLD YOU THAT RELENA IS IN DANGER.
ADMISSIONS LIKE THAT LEAD TO ASSASSIN-ATIONS!
GULP
OO, SCARY!
AND WHAT WAS THIS "PRESENT FOR RELENA"?

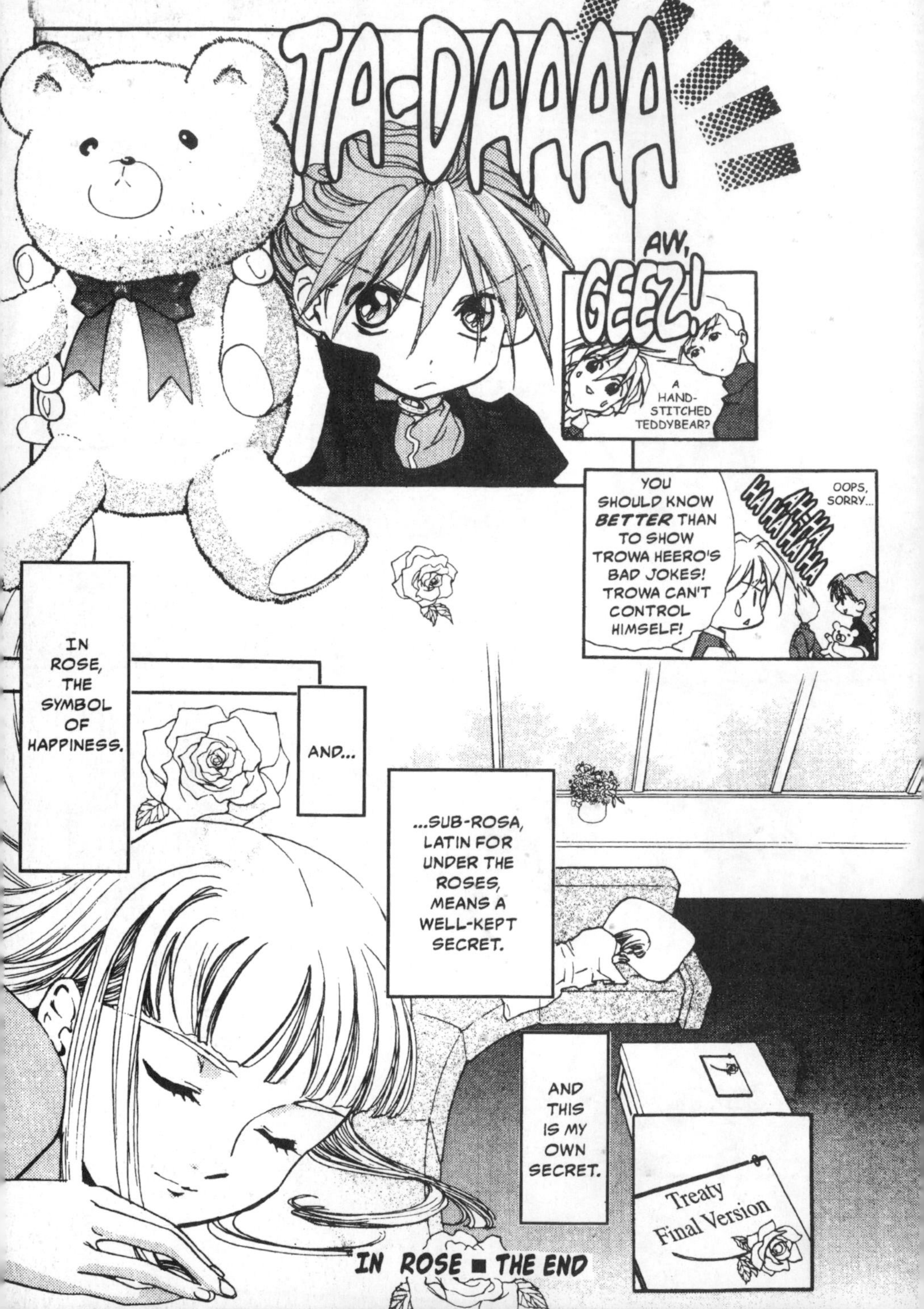
TA-DAAAA
AW, GEEZ!
A HAND-STITCHED TEDDYBEAR?
YOU SHOULD KNOW **BETTER** THAN TO SHOW TROWA HEERO'S BAD JOKES! TROWA CAN'T CONTROL HIMSELF!
AH-HA HA HA HA HA
OOPS, SORRY...
IN ROSE, THE SYMBOL OF HAPPINESS.
AND...
...SUB-ROSA, LATIN FOR UNDER THE ROSES, MEANS A WELL-KEPT SECRET.
AND THIS IS MY OWN SECRET.
Treaty
Final Version
IN ROSE ■ THE END

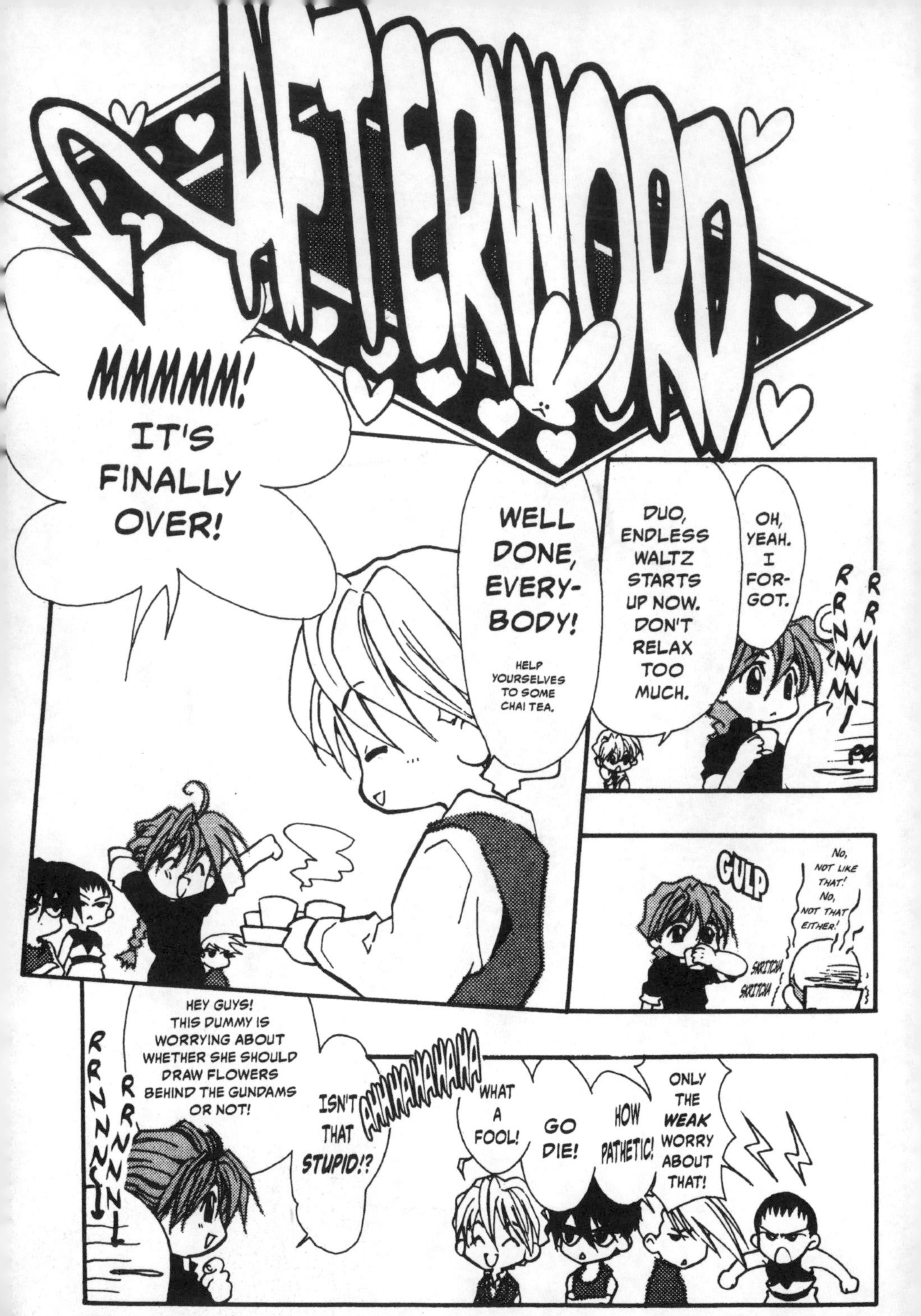
AFTERWORD
MMMMM! IT'S FINALLY OVER!
WELL DONE, EVERY-BODY!
HELP YOURSELVES TO SOME CHAI TEA.
DUO, ENDLESS WALTZ STARTS UP NOW. DON'T RELAX TOO MUCH.
OH, YEAH. I FOR-GOT.
RRNNNN!
GULP
No, NOT LIKE THAT! No, NOT THAT EITHER!
SKRITCHA SKRITCHA
HEY GUYS! THIS DUMMY IS WORRYING ABOUT WHETHER SHE SHOULD DRAW FLOWERS BEHIND THE GUNDAMS OR NOT!
ISN'T THAT STUPID!?
AHHAHAHAHAHA
WHAT A FOOL!
GO DIE!
HOW PATHETIC!
ONLY THE WEAK WORRY ABOUT THAT!

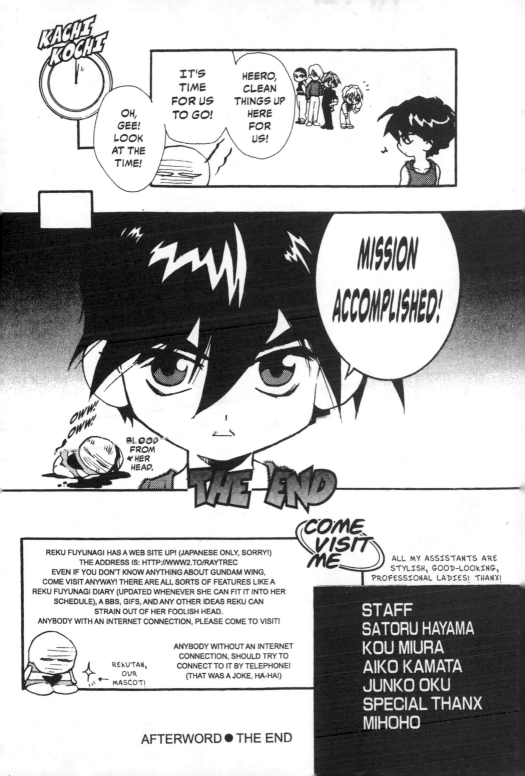

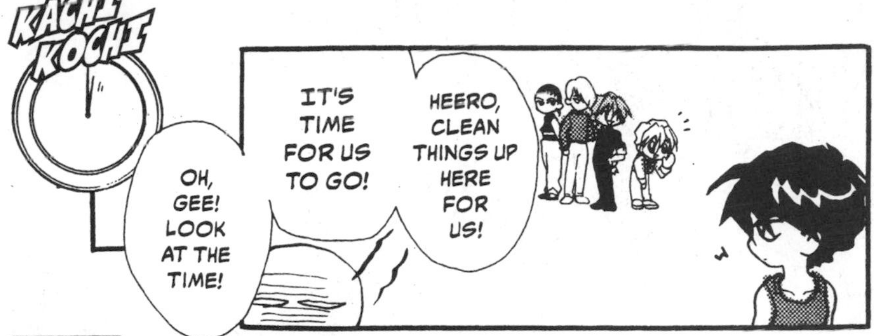
KACHI KOCHI
OH, GEE! LOOK AT THE TIME!
IT'S TIME FOR US TO GO!
HEERO, CLEAN THINGS UP HERE FOR US!

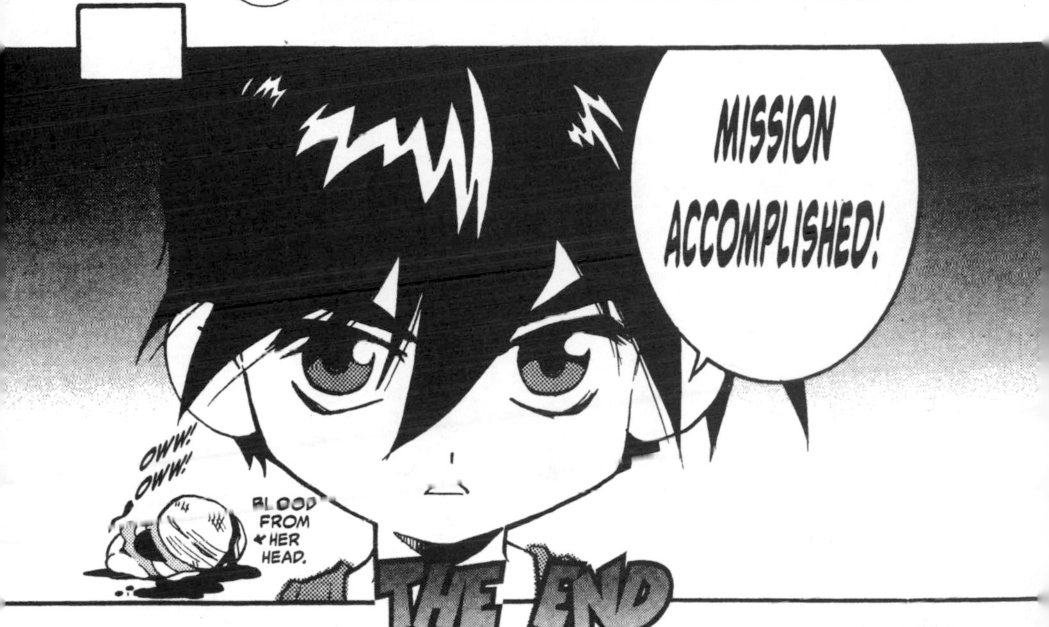
MISSION ACCOMPLISHED!
OWW! OWW!
BLOOD FROM HER HEAD.
THE END

COME VISIT ME

REKU FUYUNAGI HAS A WEB SITE UP! (JAPANESE ONLY, SORRY!)
THE ADDRESS IS: HTTP://WWW2.TO/RAYTREC
EVEN IF YOU DON'T KNOW ANYTHING ABOUT GUNDAM WING, COME VISIT ANYWAY! THERE ARE ALL SORTS OF FEATURES LIKE A REKU FUYUNAGI DIARY (UPDATED WHENEVER SHE CAN FIT IT INTO HER SCHEDULE), A BBS, GIFS, AND ANY OTHER IDEAS REKU CAN STRAIN OUT OF HER FOOLISH HEAD.
ANYBODY WITH AN INTERNET CONNECTION, PLEASE COME TO VISIT!

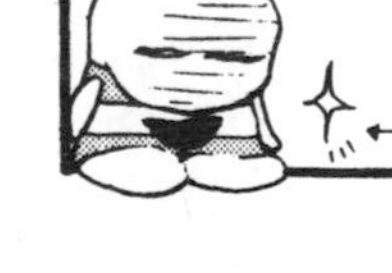

REKUTAN, OUR MASCOT!

ANYBODY WITHOUT AN INTERNET CONNECTION, SHOULD TRY TO CONNECT TO IT BY TELEPHONE! (THAT WAS A JOKE, HA-HA!)

ALL MY ASSISTANTS ARE STYLISH, GOOD-LOOKING, PROFESSIONAL LADIES! THANX!

STAFF
SATORU HAYAMA
KOU MIURA
AIKO KAMATA
JUNKO OKU
SPECIAL THANX
MIHOHO

AFTERWORD ● THE END

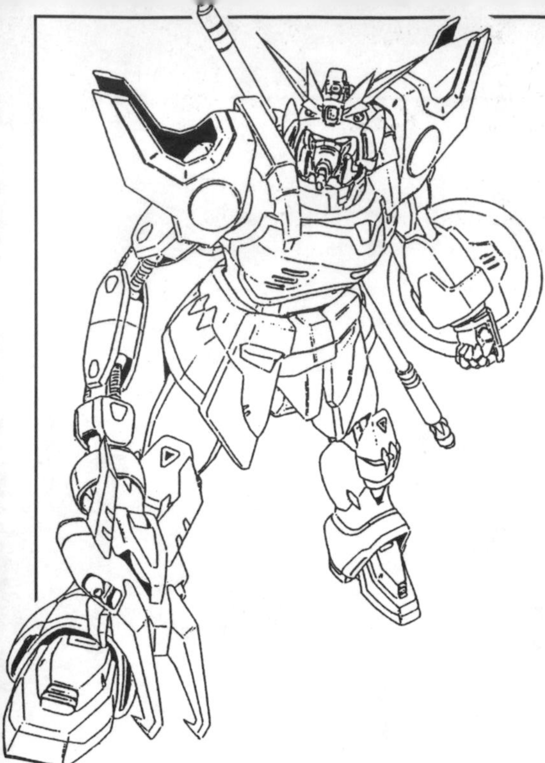
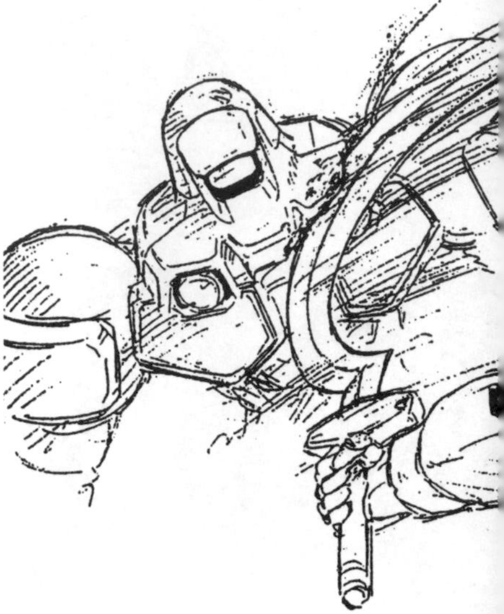
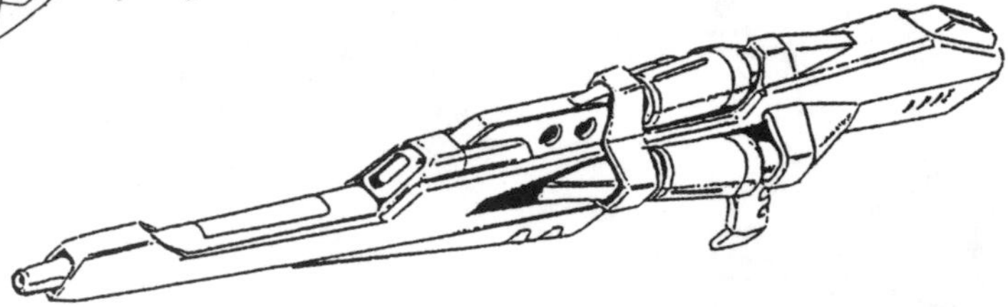
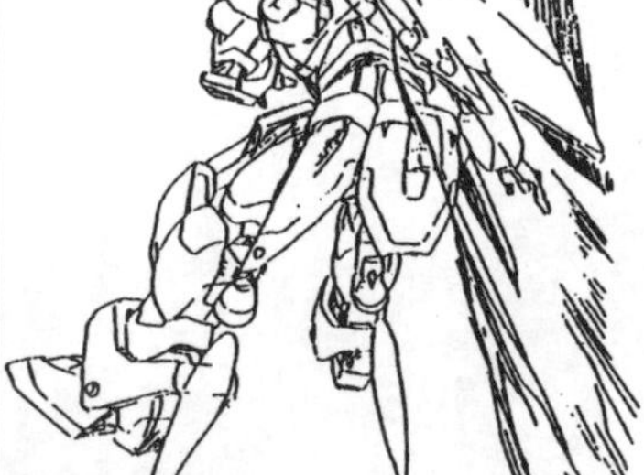
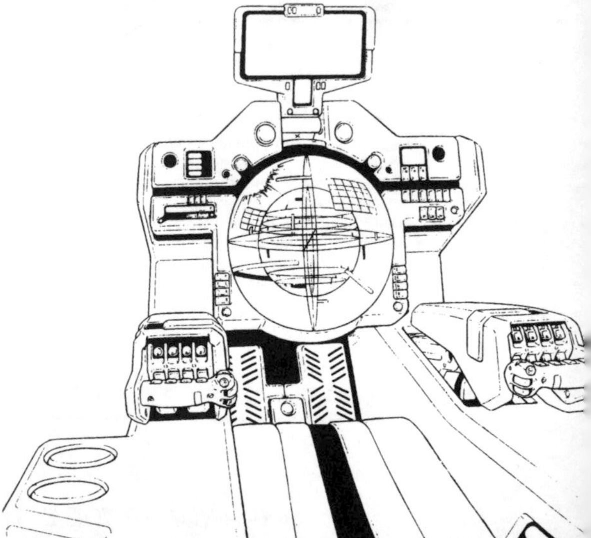

MECHA GALLERY

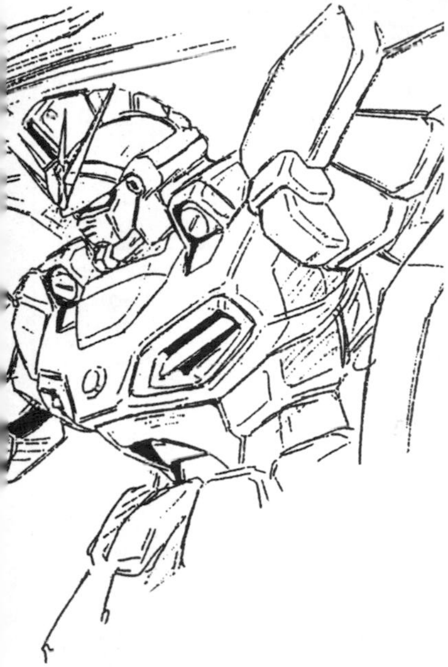

ONE OF THE MOST POPULAR ELEMENTS OF MOBILE SUIT GUNDAM WING IS CERTAINLY ITS MANY MOBILE SUITS. IT IS INTERESTING TO NOTE THAT IN DESIGNING THE MOBILE SUITS FOR THE FIVE MAIN PILOTS — HEERO, DUO, TROWA, QUATRE, AND WUFEI — THE PILOTS' CHARACTERS BECAME A LARGE FACTOR IN THE FINAL LOOK AND AND THE VARIOUS FUNCTIONS OF THEIR MECHA.

LET'S TAKE A LOOK AT A FEW OF THESE FACTORS....

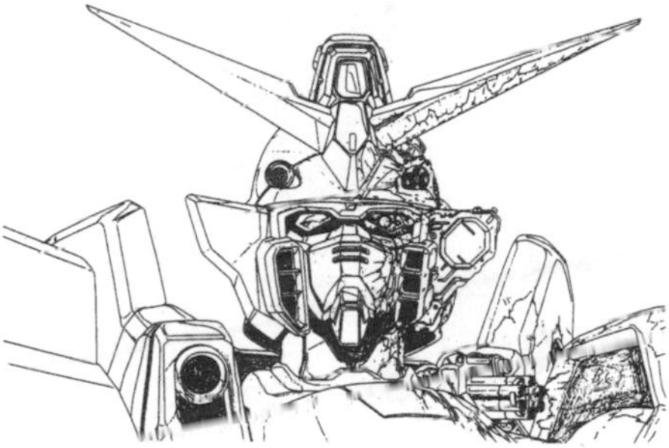

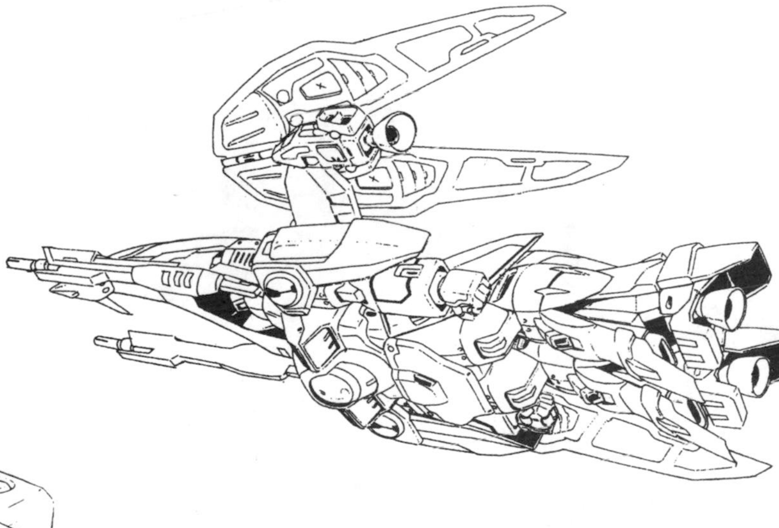

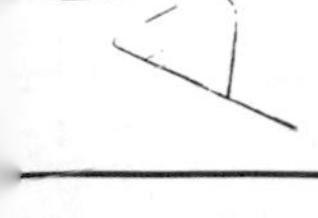

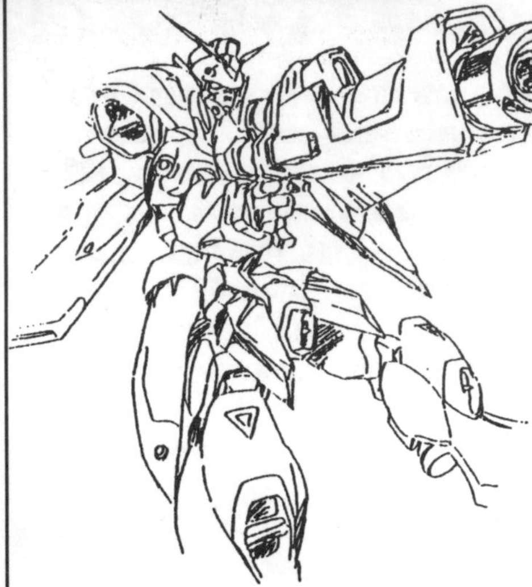

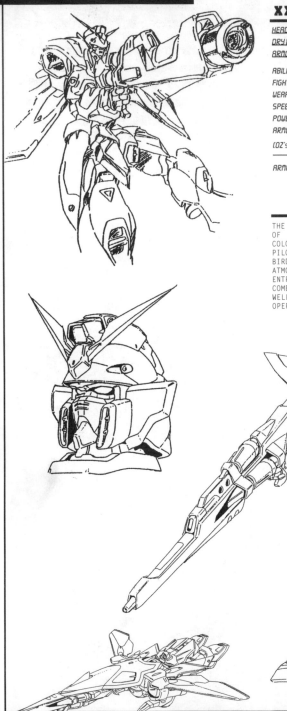

XXXG-01W WING GUNDAM

HEAD HEIGHT: 16.3 METERS

DRY WEIGHT: 7.1 TONS

ARMOR MATERIALS: GUNDANIUM ALLOY

ABILITY LEVELS:

FIGHTING ABILITY: LEVEL 130

WEAPONS ABILITY: LEVEL 140

SPEED ABILITY: LEVEL 150

POWER ABILITY: LEVEL 120

ARMORED ABILITY: LEVEL 130

(OZ'S MASS-PRODUCED MOBILE SUIT LEO IS RATED AT 100 IN EACH CATEGORY)

ARMAMENT: VULCAN X 2
MACHINE CANNON X 2
BUSTER RIFLE X 1
BEAM SABER X 2

THE WING GUNDAM WAS CREATED BY DOCTOR J, ONE OF THE SCIENTISTS INVOLVED IN THE SPACE COLONISTS' OPERATION METEOR PLAN, AND IT IS PILOTED BY HEERO YUY. BY TRANSFORMING INTO BIRD MODE, IT CAN NOT ONLY FLY IN EARTH'S ATMOSPHERE, BUT ALSO SURVIVE ATMOSPHERIC RE-ENTRY. EXCELLING IN BOTH FIREPOWER AND MELEE COMBAT ABILITY, THE WING GUNDAM IS THE MOST WELL-BALANCED OF THE FIVE GUNDAMS CREATED FOR OPERATION METEOR.

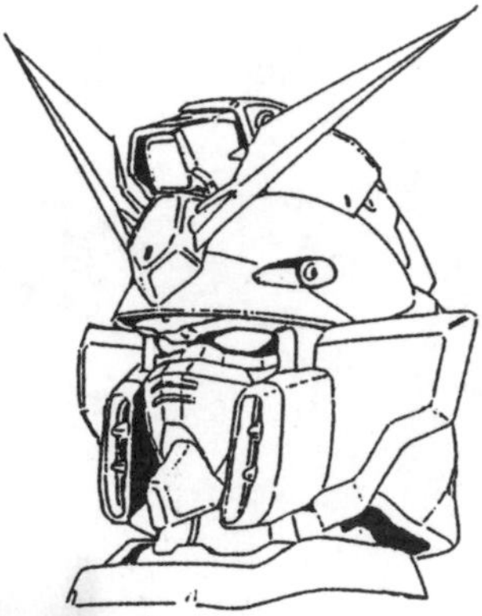

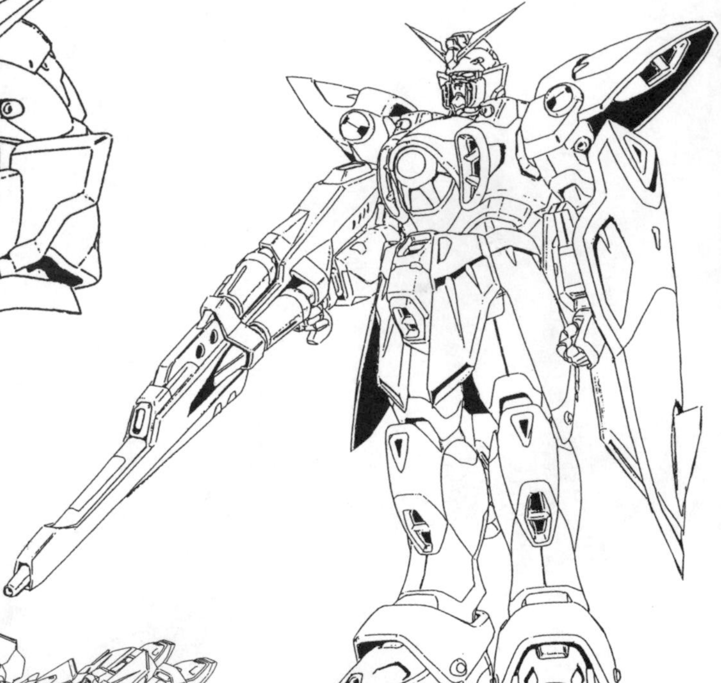

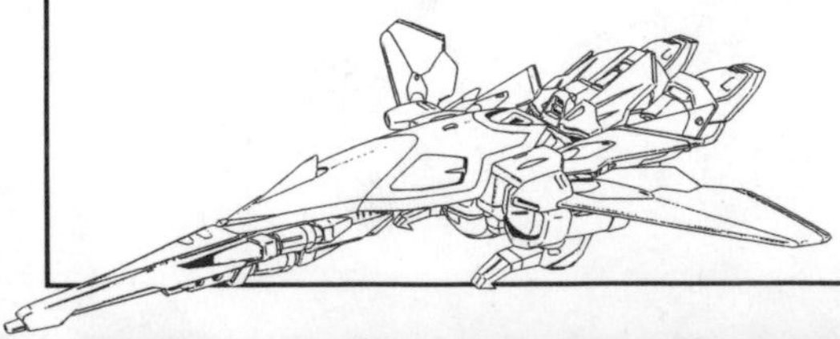

XXXG-00W0 WING GUNDAM ZERO

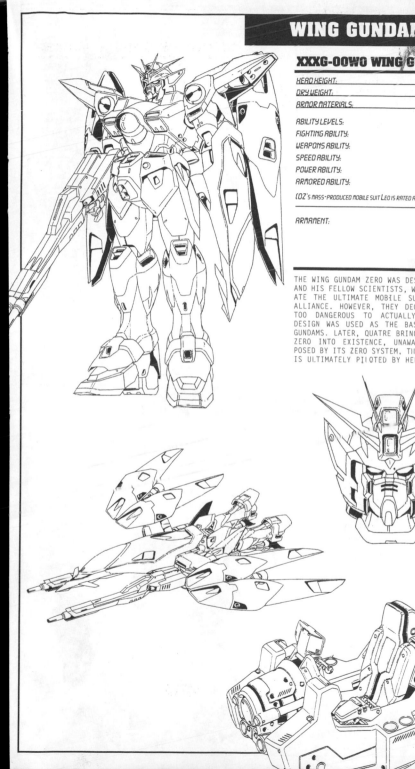

HEAD HEIGHT:	16.7 METERS
DRY WEIGHT:	8.0 TONS
ARMOR MATERIALS:	GUNDANIUM ALLOY

ABILITY LEVELS:

FIGHTING ABILITY:	LEVEL 150
WEAPONS ABILITY:	LEVEL 150
SPEED ABILITY:	LEVEL 160
POWER ABILITY:	LEVEL 140
ARMORED ABILITY:	LEVEL 140

(OZ's MASS-PRODUCED MOBILE SUIT LEO IS RATED AT 100 IN EACH CATEGORY)

ARMAMENT:	TWIN BUSTER RIFLE X 1
	BEAM SABER X 2
	MACHINE CANNON X 2
	WING VULCAN X 2

THE WING GUNDAM ZERO WAS DESIGNED BY DOCTOR J AND HIS FELLOW SCIENTISTS, WHO SET OUT TO CREATE THE ULTIMATE MOBILE SUIT TO BATTLE THE ALLIANCE. HOWEVER, THEY DECIDED THAT IT WAS TOO DANGEROUS TO ACTUALLY BUILD, AND THE DESIGN WAS USED AS THE BASIS FOR THE OTHER GUNDAMS. LATER, QUATRE BRINGS THE WING GUNDAM ZERO INTO EXISTENCE, UNAWARE OF THE DANGER POSED BY ITS ZERO SYSTEM. THE WING GUNDAM ZERO IS ULTIMATELY PILOTED BY HEERO YUY.

GUNDAM DEATHSCYTHE

XXXG-01D GUNDAM DEATHSCYTHE

HEAD HEIGHT:	16.3 METERS
DRY WEIGHT:	7.2 TONS
ARMOR MATERIALS:	GUNDANIUM ALLOY

ABILITY LEVELS:

FIGHTING ABILITY:	LEVEL 140
WEAPONS ABILITY:	LEVEL 120
SPEED ABILITY:	LEVEL 160
POWER ABILITY:	LEVEL 120
ARMORED ABILITY:	LEVEL 120

(OZ's MASS-PRODUCED MOBILE SUIT LEO IS RATED AT 100 IN EACH CATEGORY)

ARMAMENT:	VULCAN X 2
	MACHINE CANNON X 2
	BEAM SCYTHE X 1
	BUSTER SHIELD X 1
	HYPER JAMMER X 2

CREATED BY PROFESSOR G AND PILOTED BY DUO MAXWELL, THE GUNDAM DEATHSCYTHE IS EQUIPPED WITH A PAIR OF HYPER JAMMERS THAT NULLIFY ENEMY SENSORS. THANKS TO ITS HIGH SPEED, THE DEATHSCYTHE CAN QUICKLY CLOSE IN ON ITS TARGETS WHILE CONCEALED BY THE HYPER JAMMERS, THEN STRIKE THEM DOWN WITH A BEAM SCYTHE REMINISCENT OF THE GRIM REAPER'S BLADE.

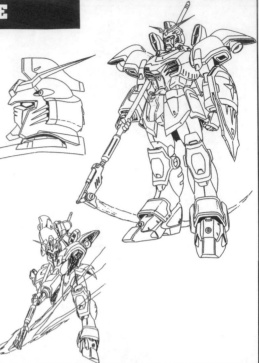

GUNDAM DEATHSCYTHE HELL

XXXG-01D2 GUNDAM DEATHSCYTHE H

HEAD HEIGHT:	16.3 METERS
DRY WEIGHT:	7.4 TONS
ARMOR MATERIALS:	GUNDANIUM ALLOY

ABILITY LEVELS:

FIGHTING ABILITY:	LEVEL 150
WEAPONS ABILITY:	LEVEL 120
SPEED ABILITY:	LEVEL 170
POWER ABILITY:	LEVEL 120
ARMORED ABILITY:	LEVEL 140

(OZ's MASS-PRODUCED MOBILE SUIT LEO IS RATED AT 100 IN EACH CATEGORY)

ARMAMENT:	VULCAN X 2
	BUSTER SHIELD X 1
	HYPER JAMMER X 2
	TWIN BEAM SCYTHE X 1

WHEN DOCTOR J AND THE OTHER SCIENTISTS WERE CAPTURED AND FORCED TO BUILD THE VAYEATE AND MERCURIUS, THEY USED OZ'S RESOURCES TO CREATE A SUCCESSOR TO THE GUNDAM DEATHSCYTHE. WHILE THE DEATHSCYTHE HELL'S WEAPONS AND MOBILITY ARE IMPROVED, ITS MOST IMPORTANT FEATURE IS ITS "ACTIVE CLOAK," WHICH NOT ONLY PROVIDES BETTER ARMOR PROTECTION BUT ALSO INCREASES THE EFFECTIVENESS OF ITS HYPER JAMMERS.

GUNDAM HEAVYARMS

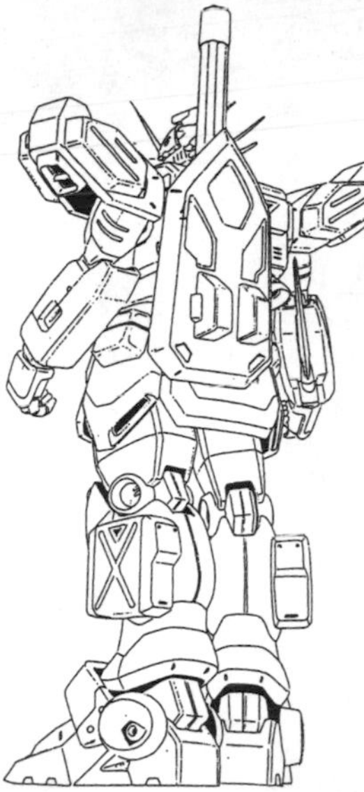

XXXG-01H GUNDAM HEAVYARMS

HEAD HEIGHT:	16.7 METERS
DRY WEIGHT:	7.7 TONS
ARMOR MATERIALS:	GUNDANIUM ALLOY

ABILITY LEVELS:

FIGHTING ABILITY:	LEVEL 110
WEAPONS ABILITY:	LEVEL 160
SPEED ABILITY:	LEVEL 110
POWER ABILITY:	LEVEL 140
ARMORED ABILITY:	LEVEL 140

(OZ's mass-produced mobile suit Leo is rated at 100 in each category)

ARMAMENT:

VULCAN X 2
MACHINE CANNON X 2
BEAM GATLING X 1
HOMING MISSILE X 6
MICRO MISSILE X 24
ARMY KNIFE X 1
GATLING X 2

CREATED BY DOKTOR S AND PILOTED BY TROWA BARTON, THE GUNDAM HEAVYARMS'S ENTIRE BODY IS PACKED WITH MISSILES AND MACHINE GUNS, GIVING IT UNRIVALED FIREPOWER. HOWEVER, ONCE ALL ITS AMMUNITION IS EXHAUSTED, THE HEAVYARMS IS LEFT WITH NO WEAPONS BUT THE SMALL ARMY KNIFE MOUNTED ON ITS RIGHT FOREARM; THIS IS THE ONE WEAK SPOT OF THIS FORMIDABLE MOBILE SUIT.

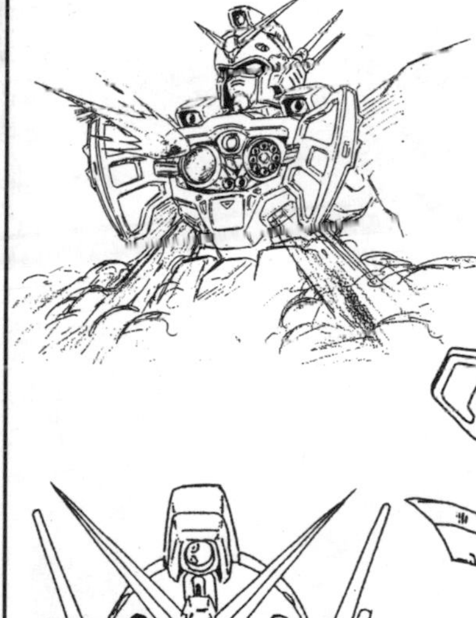

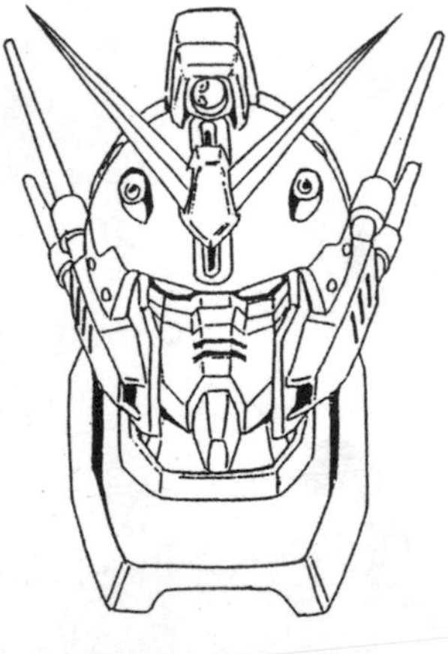

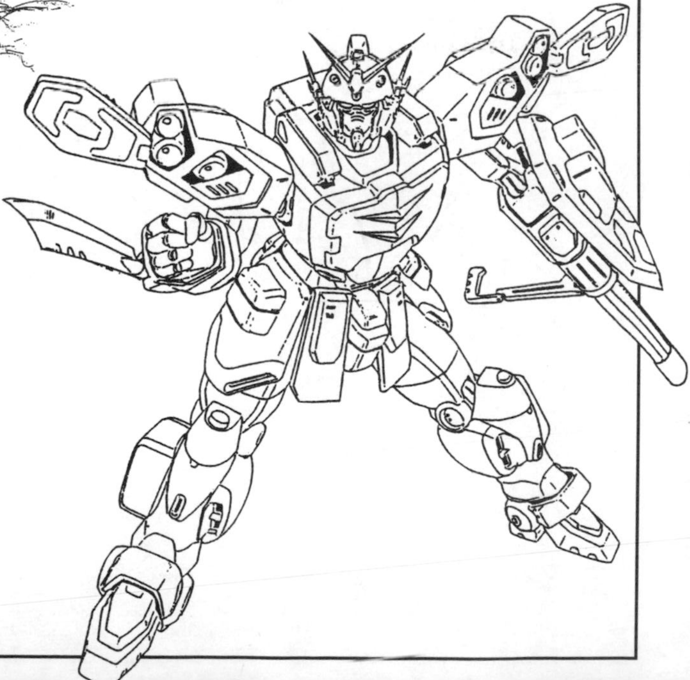

GUNDAM SANDROCK

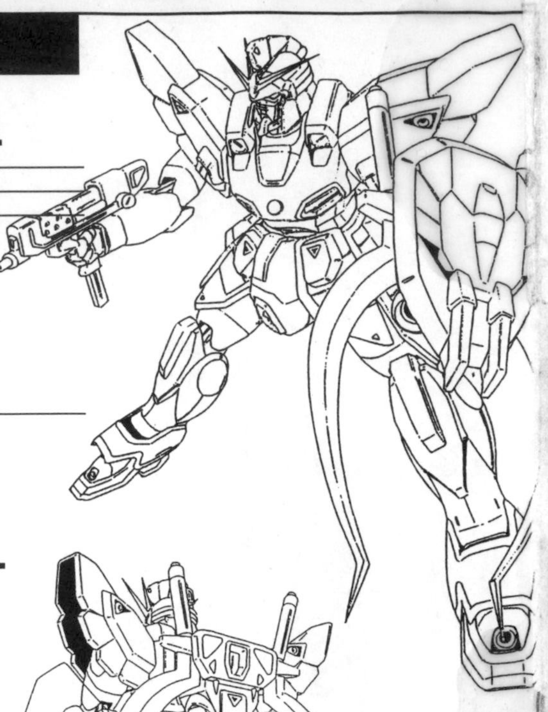

XXXG-01SR GUNDAM SANDROCK

HEAD HEIGHT:	16.5 METERS
DRY WEIGHT:	7.5 TONS
ARMOR MATERIALS:	GUNDANIUM ALLOY

ABILITY LEVELS:

FIGHTING ABILITY:	LEVEL 120
WEAPONS ABILITY:	LEVEL 120
SPEED ABILITY:	LEVEL 110
POWER ABILITY:	LEVEL 150
ARMORED ABILITY:	LEVEL 160

(OZ's mass-produced mobile suit Leo is rated at 100 in each category)

ARMAMENT:

VULCAN X 2
HOMING MISSILE X 6
HEAT SHOTEL X 2
SHIELD FLASH X 2
CROSS CRUSHER X 1

CREATED BY INSTRUCTOR H AND PILOTED BY QUATRE RABERBA WINNER, THE HEAVILY ARMORED GUNDAM SANDROCK IS DESIGNED FOR MAXIMUM POWER AND PROTECTION. ITS MAIN WEAPONS ARE THE MASSIVE CURVED SWORDS KNOWN AS "HEAT SHOTELS." AS THE SANDROCK'S NAME INDICATES, IT'S ESPECIALLY WELL-SUITED FOR FIGHTING IN DESERT REGIONS.

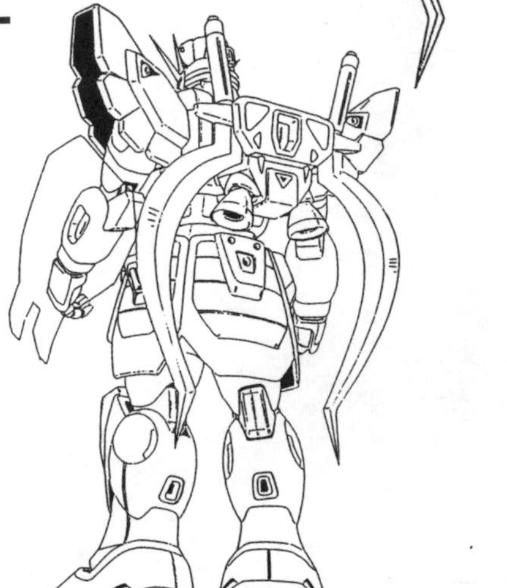

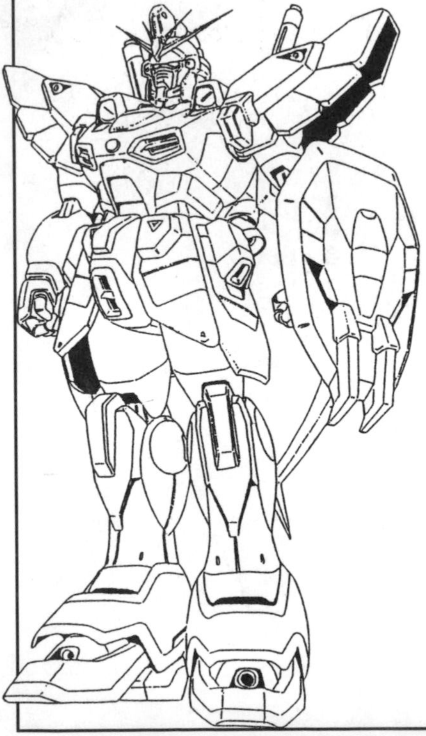

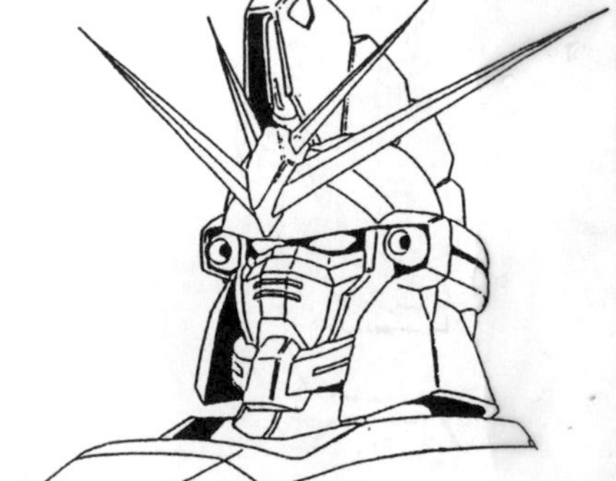

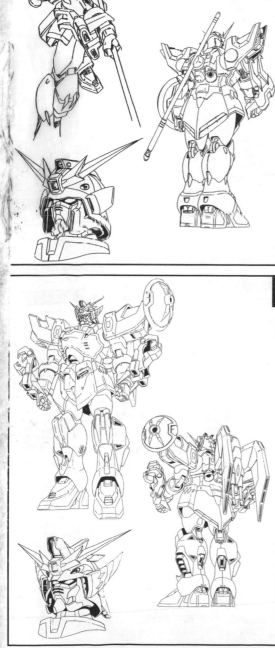

SHENLONG GUNDAM

XXXG-01S SHENLONG GUNDAM

HEAD HEIGHT:	16.4 METERS
DRY WEIGHT:	7.4 TONS
ARMOR MATERIALS:	GUNDANIUM ALLOY

ABILITY LEVELS:

FIGHTING ABILITY:	LEVEL 160
WEAPONS ABILITY:	LEVEL 110
SPEED ABILITY:	LEVEL 130
POWER ABILITY:	LEVEL 140
ARMORED ABILITY:	LEVEL 120

(OZ'S MASS-PRODUCED MOBILE SUIT LEO IS RATED AT 100 IN EACH CATEGORY)

ARMAMENT:	VULCAN X 2
	BEAM GLAIVE X 1
	DRAGON FANG X 1
	FLAMETHROWER X 2

CREATED BY MASTER O AND PILOTED BY CHANG WUFEI, THE SHENLONG GUNDAM'S APPEARANCE REFLECTS THE TRADITIONS OF THE CHINESE WARRIOR CLAN FROM WHICH WUFEI IS DESCENDED. THIS FEARSOME MOBILE SUIT IS UNSURPASSED IN MELEE COMBAT. IN HIS QUEST FOR JUSTICE, WUFEI CONSIDERS THE SHENLONG — WHICH HE CALLS "NATAKU" — TO BE THE ONLY ALLY HE NEEDS.

ALTRON GUNDAM

XXXG-01S2 ALTRON GUNDAM

HEAD HEIGHT:	16.4 METERS
DRY WEIGHT:	7.5 TONS
ARMOR MATERIALS:	GUNDANIUM ALLOY

ABILITY LEVELS:

FIGHTING ABILITY:	LEVEL 150
WEAPONS ABILITY:	LEVEL 140
SPEED ABILITY:	LEVEL 130
POWER ABILITY:	LEVEL 140
ARMORED ABILITY:	LEVEL 120

(OZ'S MASS-PRODUCED MOBILE SUIT LEO IS RATED AT 100 IN EACH CATEGORY)

ARMAMENT:	TWIN BEAM TRIDENT X 1
	VULCAN X 2
	FLAMETHROWER X 4
	BEAM CANNON X 2
	DRAGON FANG X 2

THIS UPGRADE TO THE SHENLONG GUNDAM WAS CREATED ALONG WITH THE DEATHSCYTHE HELL. THE ALTRON'S MELEE CAPABILITIES ARE EVEN FURTHER ENHANCED, AND BOTH ITS ARMS ARE NOW FITTED WITH EXTENDABLE "DRAGON FANG" CLAWS. IT'S ALSO EQUIPPED WITH BACK-MOUNTED BEAM CANNONS, GIVING IT THE LONG-RANGE FIREPOWER IT PREVIOUSLY LACKED.

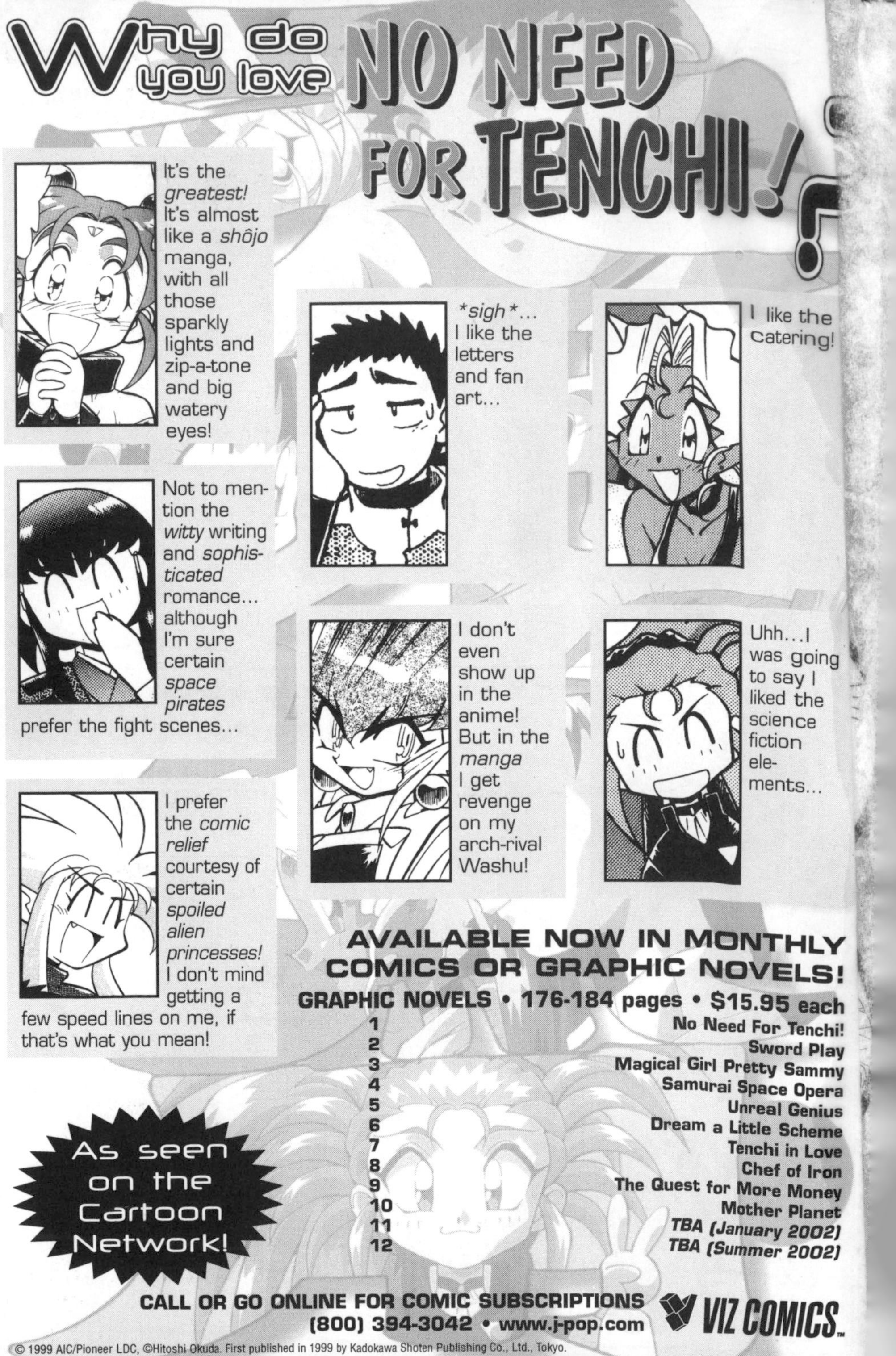
Why do you love NO NEED FOR TENCHI!?
It's the *greatest!* It's almost like a *shôjo* manga, with all those sparkly lights and zip-a-tone and big watery eyes!
sigh... I like the letters and fan art...
I like the catering!
Not to mention the *witty* writing and *sophisticated* romance... although I'm sure certain *space pirates* prefer the fight scenes...
I don't even show up in the anime! But in the *manga* I get revenge on my arch-rival Washu!
Uhh...I was going to say I liked the science fiction elements...
I prefer the *comic relief* courtesy of certain *spoiled alien princesses!* I don't mind getting a few speed lines on me, if that's what you mean!
As seen on the Cartoon Network!
AVAILABLE NOW IN MONTHLY COMICS OR GRAPHIC NOVELS!
GRAPHIC NOVELS • 176-184 pages • $15.95 each
1 No Need For Tenchi!
2 Sword Play
3 Magical Girl Pretty Sammy
4 Samurai Space Opera
5 Unreal Genius
6 Dream a Little Scheme
7 Tenchi in Love
8 Chef of Iron
9 The Quest for More Money
10 Mother Planet
11 *TBA (January 2002)*
12 *TBA (Summer 2002)*
CALL OR GO ONLINE FOR COMIC SUBSCRIPTIONS
(800) 394-3042 • www.j-pop.com
VIZ COMICS

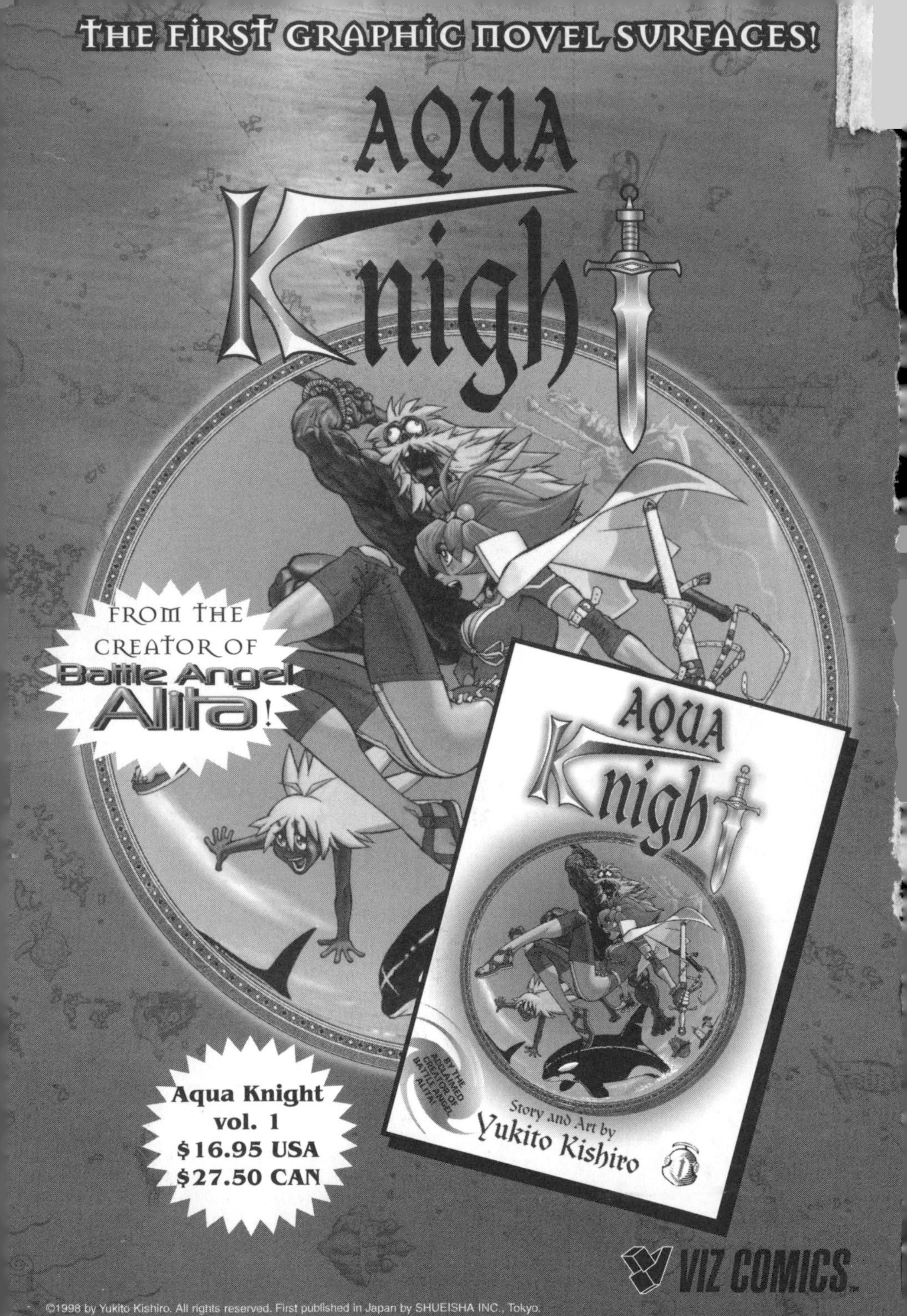
THE FIRST GRAPHIC NOVEL SURFACES!
AQUA Knight
FROM THE CREATOR OF Battle Angel Alita!
AQUA Knight
BY THE ACCLAIMED CREATOR OF BATTLE ANGEL ALITA!
Story and Art by Yukito Kishiro
1
Aqua Knight vol. 1 $16.95 USA $27.50 CAN
VIZ COMICS